The Analysis of Knowing

THE
ANALYSIS
OF KNOWING ─────────────

A Decade of Research

ROBERT K. SHOPE

Princeton University Press
Princeton, New Jersey

Copyright © 1983 by Princeton University Press
Published by Princeton University Press, 41 William Street,
Princeton, New Jersey 08540
In the United Kingdom: Princeton University Press, Guildford, Surrey

This book has been composed in Linotron Times Roman
Clothbound editions of Princeton University Press books
are printed on acid-free paper, and binding materials are
chosen for strength and durability.
Paperbacks, while satisfactory for personal collections,
are not usually suitable for library rebinding

Printed in the United States of America by Princeton
University Press, Princeton, New Jersey

To Judy, a joy to know,
and a fortunate counter to my example

Contents

Preface ———————————————————————————

The time is ripe for systematically reviewing the myriad recent contributions to the search for a satisfactory philosophical analysis of knowing. The present work considers the relations among the major perspectives that have emerged during approximately the last decade, and occasionally considers ways in which some of them might be strengthened. However, I am ultimately concerned to point out the difficulties faced by most of these analyses and to defend an analysis of knowing in terms of what I call justification-explaining chains. I concentrate throughout on that category of knowing which philosophers sometimes call "factual knowledge." This is, roughly, knowing that such-and-such is the case, in contrast, say, to knowing how to do something, or knowing a person. But at the end I have indicated a direction for future research when analyzing types of knowing that do not coincide with the important one which has most often preoccupied philosophers.

The discussion provides an introduction to the analysis of knowing for workers in related fields and for philosophers who have themselves not yet been entrapped within this particular thicket. Students of philosophy will find an opportunity to obtain an overview from which to extend their exploration of this central aspect of epistemology, as well as a sustained illustration of the role that is often played in contemporary philosophical debate by the technique of seeking counterexamples.

Acknowledgments _____

Initial impetus for this project came from an invitation by the *American Philosophical Quarterly* to contribute an article on recent work on the analysis of knowledge. But that manuscript eventually outgrew reasonable length limitations, and I wish to thank Gilbert Harman for having encouraged me to turn it into the present volume, and for having called it to the attention of the publisher.

My greatest debt is to Ernest Sosa, not only for having prompted the initial invitation from the above journal, but for his constant encouragement and helpful discussion of details of his views and those of Roderick Chisholm.

My colleagues in the Philosophy Department at the University of Massachusetts Boston, especially Howard Cohen, provided guidance concerning the appropriate arrangement of materials in Chapter 1, and Martin Andic saved me from overbold conjectures in that chapter concerning Plato. I am grateful to Roderick Firth for helping me to keep the beginning of Chapter 6 from becoming intractably complex.

Finally, I acknowledge the assistance of the National Endowment for the Humanities in pursuing this research.

The Analysis of Knowing

1.

The Significance of the Gettier Problem for an Analysis of Knowing

A certain account of knowing has often seemed to represent simple common sense, and was, indeed, regarded as obviously correct by one of the greatest epistemologists, Immanuel Kant (see Section 2). Edmund Gettier has characterized any such 'standard analysis' of person S's knowing that p as having a form similar to the following analysis:

(A$_1$) S knows that p if and only if
     (i) p is true,
     (ii) S believes that p, and
     (iii) S is justified in believing that p.
         (Gettier 1963, p. 121)[1]

Such an analysis treats conditions (i), (ii), and (iii) as individually necessary and jointly sufficient for S's knowing that p. Philosophers commonly call them the truth condition, the belief condition, and the justification condition.

The viability of this type of analysis of knowledge was not a serious issue until 1963, when Gettier presented two counterexamples to it. The reaction to his attack spawned a variety of additional 'Gettier-

---

[1] This formulation displays the common practice of using a schematic letter, such as "p," sometimes as a substitute for a phrase referring to or naming a proposition or statement, and sometimes as a substitute for a phrase expressing a proposition or statement. In view of variations in the typographical practices within the literature to be surveyed, I shall allow myself similar liberty. For convenience, I shall sometimes make such changes in a philosopher's own wording of his or her analysis, and even alter the choice of schematic letters.

type' counterexamples. I shall argue in Section 4 that an initial way to characterize all these examples is as follows:

(G)   In a Gettier-type example concerning S and p
    (1) the truth condition holds regarding p;
    (2) the belief condition holds regarding p;
    (3) the justification condition holds regarding p;
    (4) some proposition, q, is false;
    (5) either the justification condition holds regarding q, or at least S would be justified in believing q;
    (6) S does not know that p.[2]

One such counterexample, which is particularly well-known and less complex to describe than Gettier's own examples (see Section 4) was presented by Keith Lehrer and has led to many variations that we shall need to consider later:

(E 1)   *Mr. Nogot (Original Version)*: A pupil in S's office, Mr. Nogot, has given S evidence e that justifies S in believing 'Mr. Nogot, who is in the office, owns a Ford,'[3] from which S deduces p: 'Someone in the office owns a Ford.' But, unsuspected by S, Mr. Nogot has been shamming and p is only true because another person in the office, Mr. Havit, owns a Ford.

This example has form G, where one false proposition to fill the place of q is the proposition that Mr. Nogot owns a Ford.

[2] This form refrains from indicating any particular dependency among the six conditions. In particular, it does not suggest that whenever (4) and (5) are satisfied (6) is also satisfied. For that would mean we never know anything, since we are always justified in holding some false beliefs.

As it stands, G provides only some necessary conditions for a Gettier-type example and must eventually be modified. But it is suggestive enough at the start of our survey.

[3] For details of e, see Lehrer 1965, pp. 169-170. They include facts such as Mr. Nogot's having been reliable in his past dealings with S, having shown S a certificate saying that he owns a Ford, and driving one in front of S. I shall sometimes compress my description of examples, and the reader is referred to their sources for further details.

Gettier's attack on standard analyses has had special force and notoriety, especially during the last decade. For there has been general agreement, first, that such counterexamples cannot be dismissed and secondly, that epistemologists have typically used techniques to grapple with them which have produced unintended side effects, such as opening their accounts to still other counterexamples, many of which we shall need to survey. Thus, a study of the Gettier problem will lead to increased sensitivity to various types of examples that are important for the critical appraisal of any analysis of knowing.

1. THE FORM OF STANDARD ANALYSES OF KNOWING

The force of Gettier's argument has sometimes not been appreciated because the argument and the type of analysis that it attacks have not been described at a sufficient level of generality. As a result, the significance of the Gettier problem for the history of epistemology has been obscured, even though it has become customary to refer to the analyses in question as standard, or traditional, or classical analyses of knowing.

Gettier himself did not state the form of the analyses he wished to dispute, but merely alluded to it by means of several illustrations. For example, he said that any such analysis can be stated "in a form similar to" A_1. One might initially construe this as an illustration of an analysis of the form:

(F_1) S knows p if and only if
                    (1) p [or: p is true]
                    (2) $_sB_p$, and
                    (3) E_sB_p,

where "$_xB_y$" indicates that x has the propositional attitude of believing y and "E_xB_y" indicates that a particular epistemic status is assigned to x's propositional attitude of believing y.

But there are a number of reasons why we should not depict the form of all the analyses in question in this manner. First, one illustration that Gettier provides lacks this form, namely, the analysis found in Roderick Chisholm's *Perceiving*:

(A₂) S knows p if and only if
   (i) p is true,
   (ii) S accepts p, and
   (iii) S has adequate evidence for p.
   (Chisholm 1957, p. 16)

The significant difference[4] between A_1 and A_2 concerns condition (iii) in A_2. Chisholm defines it as follows: it would be unreasonable for S to accept *non-p* (p. 5). It is noteworthy that this *definiens* considers something that *would* be unreasonable without saying that it actually obtains. Chisholm explicitly acknowledges this when defining, in turn, the *definiens*:

> Let us say, then:
> "It would be *unreasonable* for S to accept h" means that *non-h* is more worthy of S's belief than h.
> If S *does* accept h, we may say, of course, that it is unreasonable of him to do so. (p. 5)

Clause (iii) in A_2 now comes to mean that p is more worthy of S's belief than *non-p* and that S does not accept *non-p*. We see that Chisholm's condition (iii) does not entail condition (ii). Therefore, analysis A_2 does not have the form diagrammed in F_1. In analyses of the latter form, the third condition entails the second.

Another limitation of F_1 is apparent upon considering Chisholm's desire to treat epistemic terminology, for example, the phrase "worthy of belief," analogously to ethical terms. Clause (3) of F_1 indicates appraisal of an instance of a type of propositional attitude, in this case, believing. Chisholm does compare appraisal of propositional attitudes to the appraisal involved in deciding which actions are right

---

[4] The difference between the wording of (ii) in A_1 and A_2 is insignificant insofar as Chisholm only wishes to guard against certain ambiguities concerning the term "believes" by speaking instead of acceptance; he acknowledges that in one sense the term "believes" does convey what he intends by "accepts" (p. 17).

or wrong, or what actions are praiseworthy or blameworthy (p. 7). However, we may sometimes say of a person who performs a wrong action that the *person* is nonetheless not blameworthy, in view of some excuse or mitigating factor. Thus, it is unclear whether Chisholm intends clause (iii) of A_2 to involve appraisal only of a propositional attitude, or also of person S. If Chisholm intends the latter, then F_1 is inappropriately limited by clause (3), which indicates appraisal only of the propositional attitude.

Appraisal of the person holding a propositional attitude is clearly intended in another illustration offered by Gettier of the analyses he rejects. The illustration is drawn from A. J. Ayer's *The Problem of Knowledge*:

(A_3) S knows p if and only if
     (i) p is true,
     (ii) S is sure that p is true, and
     (iii) S has the right to be sure that p is true.
           (Ayer 1956, p. 34)

Ayer quite clearly wishes to apply evaluative terms to persons. He says that clause (iii) is included because in attributing knowledge we are concerned with whether a person is "entitled to be sure," with whether "to concede to him the right to be sure"; we are concerned "to settle, as it were, the candidate's marks" (pp. 31, 33, 34). He grants that there may be "criteria for deciding when one has the right to be sure" and allows that they apply to propositional attitudes when he comments that "it is not hard to find examples of true and fully confident beliefs which in some ways fail to meet the standards required for knowledge" (pp. 34, 31). But satisfaction of standards for assigning marks is not to be confused with receiving the mark, just as "it is a mistake to try to incorporate our actual standards of goodness into a definition of good" (p. 35). A similar point might be proposed concerning Chisholm's reference to being worthy of belief, namely, that it is a status which a proposition has in virtue of various properties of S's situation, but should not be conflated with the presence of those properties.

Ayer's intention might be served by describing the form of his analysis as follows:

(F_2) S knows p if and only if
  (1) p [or: p is true],
  (2) $_sB_{c,p}$, and
  (3) $_sE_sB_{c,p}$,

where "$_xB_{y,z}$" indicates that x has a belief of strength y in z, and "$_wE_xB_{y,z}$" indicates that w has a certain epistemic status relative to x's having that particular propositional attitude.

One difficulty with this suggestion, however, is that it is not a form shared by Chisholm's analysis. Clause (2) of F_2 may be understood broadly enough so as to include as a special case clause (ii) of A_2. But clause (3) of F_2 will run counter to Chisholm's intent regarding (iii) in A_3, provided that his intent is, indeed, to appraise only a particular propositional attitude.

A more significant difficulty is that F_2 would lead us to restrict Gettier's attack to an unnecessarily narrow range of analyses. For there are some analyses against which the attack is effective that do not speak of the same type of propositional attitude in their second and third conditions. For example, Israel Scheffler suggests the following *analysans*: (i) p, (ii) S believes p, and (iii) S has the right to be sure that p (Scheffler 1965, p. 65). Scheffler says that this permits us to regard some timid students as knowing yet failing to claim their right to be sure. For example, the student may give an answer with considerable diffidence, and need to have his or her security and self-assurance bolstered (pp. 65-66). Again, some philosophers present definitions of knowledge whose second conditions mention propositional attitudes about evidence for p or reasons for p's being true, rather than merely a propositional attitude about p.

Moreover, analyses which remain subject to Gettier's criticisms sometimes maintain that for some instances of p one's believing p must be causally related to some other beliefs, such as S's belief in the evidence for p, or such as S's belief that the evidence supports p. Yet F_2 does not allow for this. Finally, Keith Lehrer has recently argued that the second condition in a proper analysis of knowing should speak of a type of acceptance that cannot be called believing in any ordinary sense (Lehrer 1979; 1981).

These considerations prompt me to describe the second condition in standard analyses of knowing as either asserting that S is presently in a psychological state of believing p, and as possibly also asserting in regard to each psychological state in a given set that it is or has been a psychological state of S. The concept of a psychological state is broad enough to include being in a propositional attitude, to include varying degrees of strength in propositional attitudes, and to include causal connections between various instances of belief or acceptance and phenomena involved in processes of inference.

A clue to a sufficiently broad characterization of the third condition in standard analyses is provided by Ayer's remarks that the right to be sure "may be earned in various ways" and that "normally we do not say that people know things unless they have followed one of the accredited routes to knowledge" (Ayer 1956, pp. 25, 33). This suggests that S must not have significantly violated procedures guiding rational inquiry. Inclusion of the qualifying term, "normally," allows that sometimes knowledge may be gained independently of these procedures. Ayer's examples of such a possibility are knowledge involving telepathy and the pronouncements of a seer. He adds a requirement that even in such cases *something* is a basis for granting S the right to be sure, for example, S's repeated successful forecasts in a given domain (p. 33). However, it will give our discussion greater generality to remain noncommittal at this point as to whether something else of this sort is required.[5] We shall merely interpret the form of the third condition in a standard analysis as applying an epistemic term to S or to one of S's psychological states partly in light of the assumption that S has not significantly gone counter to relevant procedures guiding inquiry.

It will be more useful to remain vague about the exact way in which S must not go counter to such procedures in view of the fact

[5] For further discussion of such examples, see Chapters 6 and 7.

that a person may arrive at a conclusion by two routes, one of which yields knowledge whether p but the other of which does not because it involves deviations from appropriate procedures of inquiry. If the person presumes only that at least one of these lines of investigation is sufficiently in order, then some philosophers may be prepared to grant the person knowledge. So it might restrict the range of the analyses which Gettier attacks too severely if we were to agree with Catherine Lowy that the justification condition indicates of S that "no more can reasonably be expected of him with respect to finding out whether that proposition is true" (Lowy 1978, p. 106). It is somewhat less misleading to say that S has discharged his responsibility as a truth-seeker "sufficiently thoroughly for him to be justified in believing as he does" (p. 107), except for the unfortunate implication that the justification condition entails S's believing p.

Since our attempt to characterize standard analyses is not itself meant to be an analysis of knowing, but only a way of pointing to a range of analyses against which Gettier's objections are directed, we may permit ourselves a degree of vagueness in depicting the nature of the justification condition. Any analyses which thereby become borderline cases of standard analyses may be individually assessed in order to see whether they escape Gettier's attack. Thus, we shall be able to grasp the general significance of Gettier's challenge if we describe the form of the analyses against which it is directed as follows:

(F₅) S's knowing p (at time t) is analyzed by three necessary and sufficient conditions, such that

    the first condition simply states p or states that p is true;

    the second condition either states that (at t) S believes p, or states that (at t) S accepts p, and may also state concerning each psychological state in a given set that it is or has been a state of S;[6] and

---

[6] I shall not bother to require that these psychological states be characterized without reference to knowing, since Gettier's argument would still apply to any such circular analyses.

the third condition applies an epistemic term or terms, E_1, . . . , E_n ($n \geq 1$) to S or to an actual or possible psychological state of S (where, if there are relevant procedures of rational inquiry concerning the question whether p,[7] then at least some of E_1, . . . , E_n are applied at least partly in virtue of its being true that S is not in outright violation of those procedures).[8]

The usefulness of characterizing standard analyses of knowing in such a fashion is confirmed by some of Chisholm's remarks in *Perceiving*. He says that ''whenever a man has adequate evidence for some proposition or hypothesis, he is in a state which constitutes a *mark of evidence* for that proposition or hypothesis,'' and that ''we hope . . . that our marks of *evidence* will also be marks of *truth*'' (Chisholm 1957, pp. 34, 38). The relevance of our characterization is further supported by Chisholm's clarification of his views on knowledge in his later works. In the first edition of *Theory of Knowledge* he speaks of what rational people would do who were motivated to seek truth and to avoid error (Chisholm 1966, pp. 21-22). In the second edition he stresses that ''every person is subject to a purely intellectual requirement—that of trying his best to bring it about that, for every proposition h that he considers, he accepts h if and only if h is true'' (Chisholm 1977, p. 14). Chisholm adds that the basic epistemic terms which he applies to a person concern whether the person's ''intellectual requirement, his responsibility as an intellectual being, is better fulfilled'' by adopting one propositional attitude than another (p. 14).

Even though the epistemic terminology involved in the third condition of a given analysis is not always the expression, ''is justified,''

[7] Or concerning other questions that may be formed out of the sentence, ''p,'' with minor grammatical modification.

[8] Keith Lehrer points out that if we wish to guarantee that the analysis lists logically independent conditions, we can replace each of the three conditions with a material conditional whose antecedent is the clause, 'S knows p,' and whose consequent is the condition in question (Lehrer 1974, pp. 21-23).

or "is justified in," I shall follow the customary practice of speaking
of this condition as the justification condition.

2. HISTORICAL COMMENTS REGARDING ATTENTION TO STANDARD ANALYSES

Gettier suggests (Gettier 1963, p. 121), without further explanation,
that Plato considered a standard analysis of knowing in the *Theatetus*
and that he may have accepted one such analysis in the *Meno*. There
is much disagreement, which I shall not survey, concerning the nature
of Plato's epistemology. However, let us consider one way of regarding these dialogues that will prove useful for our discussion.

Socrates tells Meno that true opinions are comparable to statues
of Daedalus, which run away until they are tied down. He says that
true opinions

> run away from a man's mind; so they are not worth much until
> you tether them by working out the reason. That process, my dear
> Meno, is recollection, as we agreed earlier. Once they are tied
> down they become knowledge, and are stable. That is why knowl-
> edge is something more valuable than right opinion. What distin-
> guishes one from the other is the tether. (97e-98a)[9]

Gettier, and others who have referred to this passage, apparently
take Socrates to be saying that every case of knowing involves one's
having true opinion plus one's having "tethered" it. But the passage
only indicates a sufficient condition for knowing, namely, beginning
with true opinion and then going through a certain process. So it is
not clear that Socrates is advancing a standard analysis of knowing.

Moreover, the remark that true opinions *become* knowledge may
need to be understood in relation to earlier remarks in the dialogue.
Meno had agreed that the *action* of acquiring gold and silver will
not "be" virtue unless accompanied by justice or temperance or
piety, or some other "part of virtue." Socrates then described Meno

[9] As translated in Plato 1961.

as having said that every act "becomes" virtue when combined with
a part of virtue (79b-c). Yet Socrates and Meno had already distinguished actions both from virtue itself and from a virtue which the
actions manifest. So when Plato has Socrates say in the above passage
that true opinion "becomes" knowledge, he may be inviting readers
to think of knowledge as nonetheless something other than true opinion and to think of having true opinion as one manifestation of
knowledge, as one illustration of what a person who knows may be
like. He may wish us to consider whether knowledge might be something else, e.g., the reasons that are worked out during recollection,
or perhaps something involved in the process of working them out.
If the latter process includes contemplation of the Forms, then a
further portion of it may involve working down from such contemplation by means of a derivation to the content of the earlier true
opinions. But we are not required to regard knowing as including
the latter part of the process, or as itself occurring at any other level
than that of the Forms. This leaves room for the possibility that at
least on some occasions knowing might occur without prompting
from various true opinions. Thus, tethering true opinions would be
sufficient for knowing, although not necessary for it.[10]

This interpretation of Plato would have several advantages. It
would make the passage in the *Meno* consistent with the doctrine of
the *Republic* that processes do not deserve to be called knowing
unless they at least partly involve contemplation of the Forms. Moreover, it would save the doctrine of recollection in the *Meno* from
becoming incoherent when Socrates says that gaining knowledge is
explicable in terms of our soul's having previously "seen all things
both here and in the other world" (81c). For if we need recollection
to explain every case of knowing then an infinite regress occurs.
Knowing in the earlier state of earthly existence will itself have to
be explained by recollection in relation to a still earlier state of
knowing, and so forth. The regress stops, however, if knowing

---

[10] Analogously, a vision of Daedalus could occur without the viewer's being led
to make a statue of him, and the ground can exist independently of whether a tether
is fastened to it.

involves occurrences at the level of contemplating the Forms, and can at least sometimes involve contemplation of the Forms independently of having an opinion that has been recalled. Finally, the interpretation I have been considering is in accord with Socrates' having said near the beginning of the *Meno* that he would be content if Meno were to provide a definition of virtue similar to a definition of shape as "the only thing which always accompanies color" (75b-c).[11] Contemplating the Forms would be, according to the *Republic*, the only thing that always accompanies working out for oneself the reasons for a true opinion of the geometrical sort discussed at the end of the *Meno*.

Young Theatetus does attempt to say what knowledge is when he recalls hearing someone having asserted that "true judgment with an account is knowledge, and the kind without an account falls outside the sphere of knowledge" (201c-d).[12] Socrates responds by considering three ways in which one might possess an account: (1) expressing one's judgment in words; (2) being able to enumerate the elements of an object; (3) being able to state some mark by which something differs from all else. Socrates rejects suggestion (1) because any true judgment can be put into words. He rejects (2) because a child might not yet know a name to the extent of knowing its syllables, even though the child does list the letters in the correct order.

It is instructive to consider in some detail certain of Socrates' reasons for rejecting (3). He takes as his example knowledge about

---

[11] Although Socrates tells Meno at the start that he prefers a definition of virtue which characterizes virtue, rather than characterizing something which accompanies virtue, Plato believes that the rational achievement of such a definition would require Meno to arrive at a vision of the Forms. Meno prefers to be told by others what virtue is, and prefers, prior to settling what virtue is, to inquire whether it can be taught. So "giving in" to Meno ironically leads Socrates to characterize properties of virtue and knowledge without articulating their essences, and thus merely results in his obliquely pointing to virtue and knowledge. Even though the *Meno* does not attempt to provide necessary conditions for knowing, it does call our attention to the possibility of analyzing knowledge without saying what it is. We shall consider in Section 7 whether some contemporary analyses of knowing might take this shape.

[12] As translated in Plato 1973.

Theatetus, and explores the following interpretations of what it is to add an account to true judgment about Theatetus: (A) adding a correct judgment of something that distinguishes Theatetus from all else; (B) getting to know something that distinguishes Theatetus from all else. Socrates criticizes (A) because the mere fact that the judgment it mentions is about Theatetus must already require the thinker to possess a way of cognitively responding to Theatetus differently than to other things (e.g., by being led by a memory trace of Theatetus to recall him upon encountering him, and, in being reminded, to judge about him). So if previous ways of distinguishing Theatetus are not good enough for knowledge, it is puzzling why merely supplying an additional way of distinguishing him would yield an instance of knowledge.

Socrates reacts to (B) by saying that it creates an "amusing" definition. For it leads to a downright "silly" result, thanks to the fact that "when it tells us to add an account, it's telling us to get to know, rather than judge, the differentness" (209d-e). Socrates concludes that (B) thereby makes the definition circular. For earlier discussion has shown that to get to know is to get hold of knowledge.[13]

One who is sympathetic to standard analyses of knowing might react to this portion of the dialogue by admitting that interpretation (A) is indeed deficient in failing to include an epistemic term in the third condition of knowing. But when Plato compensates for this by adding an epistemic term in interpretation (B), he mentions only one

---

[13] It is not surprising that the *Theatetus* does not go on to consider the possibility that having an account is what the *Meno* calls working out the reasons for true opinion. For our consideration of the *Meno* showed that the account it offers deals with what always accompanies knowledge. That type of account of anything is something which Socrates purports to refute in criticizing (3). Theatetus agrees that (3) merely requires a "differentiation of anything, by which it differs from everything else" and that "as long as you grasp something common [which might be a nonessential property, e.g., being what always accompanies such-and-such], your account will be about those things to which the common quality belongs" (208d). Since the *Meno* account of knowledge is one of this very type and therefore not able to provide *knowledge* of what knowledge is, it has effectively been refuted by the criticism of (3) in the *Theatetus* and need not be treated separately.

of several alternatives. Instead of adding the very epistemic term being defined, one might try speaking instead of justification, or of a right to be sure, or of adequate evidence.

I suspect that Plato is actually close to agreeing with the latter point, and may mean for the reader to notice that Socrates plays a trick upon Theatetus in order to get him to draw more deeply upon their previous discussion. The trick is similar to one that Socrates plays at the end of the *Euthyphro*, when he says that Euthyphro's final definition of piety has the absurd result of returning the discussion to a previously rejected definition. The supposed absurd result is that piety is what is loved by the gods. Euthyphro intends this as a description of what, given his final definition, is merely an accidental property of piety. But Socrates tricks him into thinking that it is an attempt to describe the essence of piety, and reminds him that such an attempt had been rejected earlier in their discussion. The fact that Euthyphro allows himself to be tricked demonstrates to the reader that Euthyphro has still not mastered Socrates' repeated distinction between seeking essential and seeking accidental properties.

Plato may intend the reader to notice that Theatetus, too, is at least momentarily tricked by Socrates when he accepts the wording of (B). For earlier in the dialogue, Socrates distinguished knowledge from an activity of getting or holding knowledge, allowing that at times one possesses knowledge (e.g., in retaining a memory) roughly in the way that an item may be owned, even though one is not at that time getting the knowledge. Indeed, an effort to deal with the distinction between activities and items they concern, and to think carefully about both, is relevant at many earlier points in the dialogue. But the wording of (B) conflates the activity of adding an extra item to the *definition* of knowledge (an item which might, for all that has been demonstrated, mention the activity of getting to know) with the activity of actually turning a state of true judgment into one of knowledge. That is, it conflates the former with the activity of getting to *know*. The item grasped in the latter activity is knowledge, and thus Socrates has made it look as if the only alternative to (A) is to add knowledge as the third factor in the definition. To catch the trick, Theatetus would need to be keener in recognizing different activities and would need to remember the earlier distinctions between items and activities. Reaching that point might eventually lead him to consider whether a definition of what it is to have an account would mention getting to know, where the latter is a distinct epistemic concept from the concept of knowledge—thereby saving the definition of knowledge from patent circularity. Perhaps this understanding of the *Theatetus* is what led Gettier to view it as advancing a standard analysis of knowledge.

However, there is a point which bears on recent appraisals of standard analyses that may be extracted from this interpretation of the *Theatetus*. If Theatetus had thoroughly refreshed his memory, he would have realized that the earlier discussion had explained the activity of getting to know by mention of knowledge. For knowledge was compared to a bird that one obtains when one grasps it, and that one may possess if one retains it, as one keeps a bird in an aviary. In subsequent recollection, one again gets to know this item, like a bird that one plucks again from the aviary (197ff.). Thus, the definition of knowledge that depends upon (B) would, after all, be circular.[14] The related issue for contemporary versions of a standard analysis of knowing is the possibility of a lurking circularity in the epistemic language that is employed in its justification condition, that is, the possibility that these epistemic expressions require definition in terms of knowing. (We shall return to this possibility in Section 5.)

Richard Aaron has pointed out the following explanation of knowing, found in Kant's *Critique of Pure Reason*:

> The holding of a thing to be true, or the subjective validity of the judgment, in its relation to conviction (which is at the same time objectively valid), has the following three degrees: *opining, be-*

---

[14] Similarly, Euthyphro might have been led to realize that at the end of his discussion he was moving toward a characterization of piety as moral righteousness taking account of one's relations to the gods. But this is seen to be circular if we say, as Euthyphro is likely to, that in order to characterize something as a god we need to mention its preferences. For Euthyphro has already admitted that the gods love piety because it is piety.

lieving, and *knowing. Opining* is such holding of a judgment as is consciously insufficient, not only objectively, but also subjectively. If our holding of the judgment be only subjectively sufficient, and is at the same time taken as being objectively insufficient, we have what is termed *believing.* Lastly, when the holding of a thing to be true is sufficient both subjectively and objectively, it is *knowledge.* The subjective sufficiency is termed *conviction* (for myself), the objective sufficiency is termed *certainty* (for everyone). There is no call for me to spend further time on the explanation of such easily understood terms. (A822, B850)[15]

This definition incorporates a belief condition when it requires that one's holding the judgment to be true involves subjective sufficiency. It includes a justification condition because it requires objective sufficiency, which is defined shortly before this passage: the grounds of a judgment are said to be objectively sufficient when the judgment is "valid for everyone, provided only he is in possession of reason" (A820, B848),[16] and the validity is said to concern whether the judgment has the "same effect on the reason of others" (A821, B849).

Aaron maintains that Kant omits a truth condition from the above explanation of knowledge (Aaron 1971, p. 8). We shall consider Aaron's reasons for urging the omission of such a condition in Section 7. However, he has misconstrued Kant because he has overlooked the stipulation that one's propositional attitude be "at the same time objectively valid." Kant generally uses "objectively valid" to indicate that something is related to an object.[17] He accepts the "nom-

---

[15] As translated in Kant 1963.

[16] Also see the following passage: "an objective ground (that is, one that can be comprehended *a priori,* antecedently to all empirical laws of the imagination) . . ." (A122).

[17] Cf. A93, B126; B137; B141-142; A165-166, B205-206; A241; A246; A253. Kant sometimes interchanges the phrases, "objective validity," and "objective reality" (cf. A156, B195), indicating that the latter concerns a relation to objects: "to have objective reality, that is, to relate to an object" (A155, B194). At other places, Kant interchanges the phrases, "objective reality," and "objective meaning," speaking of the latter as involving "relation to an object" (A197, B242; cf. B148; B150-151).

inal definition of truth, that it is the agreement of knowledge with its object," i.e., the knowledge must "agree with the object to which it is related" (A58, B82-83).[18] Since Kant recurs to such a definition just before the above explanation of knowledge,[19] he intends the requirement of objective validity in that passage to involve the actual truth of one's judgment. This interpretation is confirmed by his having spoken elsewhere of the "objective validity (truth) of empirical knowledge" (A125).[20] So Kant does represent a major figure who proposes a standard analysis of knowing.[21]

3. SOME QUESTIONABLE ATTACKS ON STANDARD ANALYSES

Although it took Gettier's paper to generate much of the complex research of the last decade, hindsight has led commentators to suggest that there are examples in earlier work which would have served to raise an objection to standard analyses of knowing.

Israel Scheffler suggests that the following example from Russell would have served such a purpose:

(E 2)   *The Stopped Clock*: *S* has a true belief, *p*, as to the time of day, but only because he is looking at a clock that he thinks

---

[18] Cf. A191, B236.

[19] Cf. A820, B848.

[20] Compare his remark that the objective validity of sensible knowledge does not apply to noumena, at A254-255, B310. (Also see A306, B363; A308-309, B365-366.)

[21] Provided, of course, that we do not choose to disregard all passages in the first *Critique* which clash with a wholly subjective idealist reading.

It should be noted that Kant is prepared to speak of some knowledge as false when its form is in accordance with logical requirements but its content involves error; he adds that logical laws are not sufficient to determine "the material (objective) truth of knowledge" (A58-60, B83-85). However, rather than persist in speaking of two types of truth in knowledge, Kant seems to have preferred by the end of the *Critique* to speak of "opining" as sometimes involving both some true entailments, which constitute knowledge, and some false entailments, which do not: "I must never presume to *opine*, without *knowing at least something* by means of which the judgment, in itself merely problematic, secures connection with truth, a connection which, although not complete, is yet more than arbitrary fiction" (original emphasis; A822, B851; compare A239, B298).

is going. In fact, it happens to be stopped. (Russell 1948, p. 154)

Russell only presents (E 2) in order to show that there can be true belief without knowledge. But Scheffler suggests that if we modify the example so that S "has good grounds to suppose that the clock *is* going" then S will have "a true belief as to the time, which is, moreover, *justified* . . ." (Scheffler 1965, p. 112). Yet S still will not know that the time is what the clock says. In that case, the modification of (E 2) is a counterexample to standard analysis A_1.

But it is not at all clear that this is a counterexample. For some philosophers would say that S violates a relevant procedure of rational inquiry by employing a measuring instrument that is not working, and so S does not actually satisfy the intent of the third condition of a standard analysis, as characterized by F_5. This is true even if S is justified in believing that the clock is working. That justification does not carry over to S's belief as to the time simply because the clock is a measuring instrument which is not properly set up to take the measurements which S presumes that it is taking.

Thus, some philosophers would not treat Scheffler's modification of (E 2) as a counterexample to a standard analysis. We can reasonably expect people to employ measuring instruments in working order when they use them to find out what is true about the phenomena that they measure. This is not to deny that people may sometimes have perfectly good excuses for not living up to this responsibility and for not realizing that the instruments are not working.

After agreeing with Scheffler about the significance of Russell's example, Roderick Chisholm suggests that several earlier examples described by Meinong would have served to refute a standard analysis of knowing. Chisholm describes one such example as follows:

(E 3) *Auditory Hallucination*: An Aeolian harp stands in a garden nearby (in order to frighten birds when the wind makes it whistle). S has often heard it sound, but by now is hard of hearing and has acquired a tendency to auditory hallucination. Because of such an hallucination, S now acquires what happens to be a true belief in p: 'The harp is sounding.' (Chisholm 1977, p. 104)

But some philosophers would refuse to admit that this is a counterexample. For procedures of rational inquiry require that one not trust mere hallucinations and significantly weakened sensory capacities in order to arrive at judgments about one's surroundings. This is not to deny that it may sometimes be difficult to realize that one is not fulfilling this responsibility. Indeed, colorblind people who have no opportunity to discover their limitation may be excused for certain color judgments, but that is not to say that they are justified in the relevant sense when making those judgments.[22]

4. GETTIER-TYPE EXAMPLES

By noticing certain details in (E 3) and in the modification of (E 2), we can see why Scheffler and Chisholm relate them to Gettier's approach. It will also help us to understand why the rough characterization of Gettier-type examples, G, given at the beginning, provides a sufficiently abstract description of such examples to apply not only to the particular illustrations that Gettier presented in his paper, but also to the many additional cases constructed by philosophers in imitation of his technique.

In (E 3) and in the modification of (E 2), S purportedly is justified in having true belief in some proposition, p. But in each example, at least one other proposition figures that is false. In Scheffler's example it is the false proposition, q_1: 'The clock is going.' Scheffler regards it as an important detail that S is justified in believing q_1 and does not realize that it is false. Apparently, this satisfaction of the

---

[22] A similar comment holds regarding another example from Meinong, which Chisholm describes as "involving a man who is disturbed by a ringing in his ears at a time when, as luck would have it, someone happens to be ringing the doorbell" (Chisholm 1977, p. 104n). Many would regard the man as less than fully justified in judging a certain range of sounds in his environment while having a ringing in his ears.

justification condition concerning q_1 is needed, in Scheffler's opinion, in order for the justification condition to be satisfied concerning p.

Chisholm may regard (E 3) in a similar fashion. In that example the false proposition is q_2: 'S is not having an auditory hallucination,' that is, S is hearing some sounds in S's environment. Only if the justification condition is satisfied in relation to this proposition will justification arise for belief in p, a belief whose provenance, or at least whose justification, draws upon S's frequent past perceptions of sounds coming from the nearby garden.

If, as I have previously suggested, these examples do fail to run counter to a standard analysis of knowing, it is because in the circumstances they describe, satisfaction of the justification condition regarding q_1, or q_2 is not enough for satisfaction of the justification condition regarding p. Gettier's paper sets out to present examples where there is unlikely to be dispute over whether the justification condition is satisfied regarding p, once it is granted that it is satisfied regarding another (false) proposition, q. The details of his own counterexamples accomplish this because the particular way in which p and q are connected is so unexceptionable that we clearly may treat the justification condition as satisfied regarding p.

However, if we are to see why philosophers have spoken of Gettier-type examples, we must characterize the form of any such example quite abstractly, as in G, without mentioning the particular way in which Gettier's own two examples connect p and q. However, G indicates what may be called the surface structure of a Gettier-type example. Once we have sifted through the various attempts surveyed in later chapters that philosophers have made to deal with such examples, we shall be in a position at the end to characterize the fundamental structure of Gettier-type examples and to find a way of allowing for them in an analysis of knowing.

Gettier's description of his own examples shows them to be of form G. It is sufficient for our purposes to illustrate this by describing just one of his examples:

(E 4)   *Brown in Barcelona*: Smith has strong evidence for a proposition which he does not realize is false, namely, f: 'Jones
owns a Ford.' He selects a place name, "Barcelona," at
random and constructs proposition p: 'Either Jones owns a
Ford or Brown is in Barcelona.' Not having any idea of
Brown's actual whereabouts, Smith accepts p on the basis
of f. As it happens, Brown is coincidentally in Barcelona,
and so p is true. (Gettier 1963, pp. 122-123)

In describing the example, Gettier merely tells us what Smith's
evidence for f "might be," mentioning evidence similar to that
involved in example (E 1), but allowing us to add to it whatever is
enough to make the strong evidence so strong that the justification
condition is satisfied regarding f. This spares us the concerns that
arise regarding example (E 3) if we wonder whether S's having
ignored previous hints that he has become hard of hearing or has
developed a tendency to auditory hallucinations might prevent the
justification condition from being satisfied regarding q_2.

Satisfaction of the justification condition regarding f is then connected with satisfaction of the justification condition regarding p,
thanks to Smith's "taking a step which is *truth preserving*" to
adopt terminology suggested by Lowy (Lowy 1978, p. 107).

Of course, Smith is subject to a requirement of consistency, and
if Smith had already disbelieved p with some degree of justification
before acquiring evidence for f, then we might not say that upon
Smith's receipt of the evidence for f he was justified in believing f.
This possibility may initially appear incoherent if one mistakenly
takes "is justified in believing f" to imply "believes f." But we
cannot make such an assumption about the concept of justification
involved in the Gettier examples. For it is meant to be analogous to
Chisholm's use of "has adequate evidence for f," which we acknowledged not to entail "believes f." Nonetheless, in a Gettier-
type example, such justified disbelief will be absent in order to ensure
satisfaction of condition (5) of G.

Gettier's description of example (E 4) has led some philosophers to interpret it as saying that Smith actually believes the false proposition that Jones owns a Ford.[23] For Gettier describes Smith as accepting p "on the basis of" that false proposition. A similar belief in a false proposition might seem to be involved in Lehrer's example (E 1). For when commenting on the example, Lehrer says that S's believing p is "based on" q. This might be taken to imply that S's believing p has a connection with a state of S's believing q.[24] But Lehrer soon modified the example in order to avoid such an implication:

(E 5) *Mr. Nogot (Non-Discursive Version)*: A pupil in S's office, Mr. Nogot, has given S evidence e (as in example [E 1]), from which S directly infers p: 'Someone in the office owns a Ford.' But unsuspected by S, it is Havit who owns a Ford and Nogot does not. (Lehrer 1970b, p. 125)

An additional variation which does not involve such direct inference but still avoids false beliefs on S's part is described in Lehrer's book *Knowledge*:

(E 6) *The Clever Reasoner*: A pupil in S's class, Mr. Nogot, has given S evidence e' (analogous to e in [E 1]), which is sufficient to justify S's believing q: 'Mr. Nogot owns a Ferrari,' but S lacks evidence bearing on r: 'Mr. Havit owns a Ferrari.' The teacher is not interested in who the Ferrari owners in his class may be but only in whether it is true that p: 'Someone in the class owns a Ferrari.' The teacher reasons that although the evidence supports q there is at least the possibility that someone else in the class owns one, and,

[23] Cf. Armstrong 1973, p. 152; M. Clark 1963, p. 46; Johnson 1980, p. 120; Meyers and Stern 1973, p. 147; Sosa 1964, p. 1.

[24] Lehrer required that S be able to provide a "plausible line of reasoning to show how one could reach the conclusion he believes from the evidence that he has," e.g., inasmuch as S is completely justified on the basis of his evidence in believing 'Mr. Nogot, who is in the office, owns a Ford,' he "might deduce from this" that p (Lehrer 1965, p. 169).

hence, that it is safer to accept the more general statement, p, than to accept q. Accordingly, S accepts p. Mr. Nogot again has been shamming, but r and p are true. (Lehrer 1974, pp. 20-21)

Brian Skyrms proposed another well-known example that does not involve either actual belief in false propositions or their employment in inference, calling it a "causal" counterexample to the standard analysis of knowing:

(E 7)   *The Pyromaniac*: Striking a match, S infers that it will light directly from S's knowledge that it is a dry match of a brand ("Sure-Fire" matches) that has often and always lit for S when dry and struck. However, unsuspected by S this one cannot be lit by friction because of impurities and is going to light only because of a burst of rare Q-radiation. (Skyrms 1967, p. 383)

Although Skyrms does not regard this as a Gettier-type example, we can see that it has form G, thanks to Marshall Swain's observation that S is justified in believing various false propositions, e.g., q: "This match is like previously struck Sure-Fire matches in all respects relevant to ignition" (Swain 1976, p. 427).[25]

Some philosophers may wish to question whether the direct inferences from evidence to p in the above examples is enough for S to be justified in believing p. In that case, the following Gettier-type example may be more persuasive:

(E 8)   *Mr. Nogot (Feldman's Version)*: This case is similar to (E 1), except that S does not arrive at belief in p by relying on considerations about q, but instead by relying on belief in a true existential generalization from his evidence, of the form: 'There is someone in S's office who has given S evidence e.' (Feldman 1974, p. 69)

---

[25] (E 67), described in Chapter 5, is a variant of this example that requires a more complex statement for the false q. (See Shope 1979c, p. 403.)

Thus, there are Gettier-type examples which do not include false beliefs on S's part nor false premises in S's reasoning to S's conclusion, and the Gettier problem cannot be solved simply by ruling out such false beliefs or premises.

5. The Gettier Problem Is Genuine

Gettier's argument is that Gettier-type examples run counter to, and thus refute, all versions of a standard analysis of knowing. Thus, the Gettier problem is the problem of finding a modification of or replacement for a standard analysis that is not subject to counterexamples of form G, or, more precisely, of the form that we shall eventually develop to specify the fundamental structure of such counterexamples.

Of course, the Gettier problem is not a genuine problem if examples of such a form never do actually run counter to a standard analysis. Robert Almeder has attempted to show that these examples fail to refute such an analysis because they err in holding that "satisfaction of the evidence [i.e., justification] condition does not entail satisfaction of the truth condition . . ." (Almeder 1974, p. 367; cf. 1976, p. 163). (The independence of these conditions is indicated by the inclusion of (4) and (5) in our characterization, G, of the surface structure of Gettier-type examples.) Almeder maintains that (a) 'S is justified in believing h' entails h; even though he admits that (b) the evidence S possesses may not itself entail h (Almeder 1973, pp. 243-244; 1974, p. 367).[26]

George Pappas and Marshall Swain object that in common speech we sometimes say that people have inductively "good evidence" which "constitutes a justification" even when what they believe is false (Pappas and Swain 1978, p. 13). But this only proves that (c) 'S's evidence is a justification for (believing) h' does not entail 'S's evidence entails h.' As Douglas Odegard points out, (c) is compatible

---

[26] William Hoffman's criticism overlooks (b) (Hoffman 1975).

with statement (d): '(*S*'s believing) *h* is justified by evidence *e*' entails
e and also entails *h* (Odegard 1976, p. 565).

Pappas and Swain also ask what could explain the difference
between Gettier's cases and ones where the intermediate step in
reasoning is true and *S*'s believing it is indeed justified. They maintain
that the mere fact that the step is true could not explain the difference
(Pappas and Swain 1978, p. 13).

Some philosophers would reply that the difference is explained
by the fact that in the latter cases *S* *knows* the intermediate step to
be true. In other words, they would claim that the concept in the
standard analysis of *S*'s being justified is intelligible only in terms
of a prior understanding of the concept of *S*'s knowing, rather than
the reverse. In that case, the standard analysis fails to provide an
enlightening philosophical analysis. The latter view has, in fact, been
explicitly adopted by Richard Aaron and James Cargile (Aaron 1971;
Cargile 1971). However, these philosophers provide no strong positive support for such a view, and Almeder eventually explained that
he only wished to stress the following principle:

(AP)   In cases where there is no way of directly seeing that *h* is
        true, and we must rest our judgments on evidence, then '*S*
        is justified in believing *h*' entails *h*. (Almeder 1976, pp. 164-
        165)

But this way of construing the connection between justification
and knowledge is unnecessarily strong for Almeder's purposes. Philosophers such as Chisholm and Ayer, who view the epistemic terms
in the justification condition as having a normative force, regard *S*'s
being justified in believing (having the right to believe) as supervenient upon various justification-making (right-conferring) characteristics, such as *S*'s possession of evidence. Suppose that S_1 wishes
to determine whether *S*'s believing *h* has or would have the supervenient normative status. This may require S_1 to consider whether
evidence is possessed by *S* that can also be used by S_1 in relation to
the question whether *h* is true. But this does not force us to say that
the remark in which S_1 applies the normative expression to *S*'s be-

lieving h entails that the justification-making (right-conferring) characteristics in question are present which do or would give rise to the supervenient normative status. Nonetheless, it does explain why it is correct for Almeder to regard the following comment as absurd: "Your belief is justified, but is it true?" (Almeder 1974, p. 368). For S_1 seriously to question another person S in an actual situation in this fashion is absurd to the extent that S_1 is both taking account of and then setting aside evidence which S_1 takes to be relevant in deciding whether the belief is true. But that admission is quite compatible with treating the question as, in G. E. Moore's terminology, an open question, that is, as a question that is not settled in the sense that justification entails truth.[27]

Even if Almeder's principle AP is rephrased so that truth is merely said to be a justification-making characteristic, it remains subject to two objections raised by Odegard. First, Odegard offers as a counterexample to the principle a case where my discernible feelings, observations, and memories confer justification on my belief that I have a (public) body, but do not entail the latter proposition (Odegard 1976, pp. 565-566). Secondly, Odegard says that there is an epistemic scale along which beliefs fall, extending from justified beliefs, near the high end, to beliefs merely more reasonable than not, near the low end. Since beliefs may be false yet still have the lower status, it is gratuitous to insist on truth for some higher status (pp. 566-567).

But Almeder might treat Odegard's counterexample as moot by resisting his gradualistic account of the status of beliefs. Almeder might point out the following analogy: Various lands that presently lie outside a town's boundaries may form a sequence whose members are more and more suitably situated for belonging to the town (e.g., because of the water resources they would make publicly available, because of their proximity to present boundaries). But we cannot say without qualification that any one is suitably situated so as to belong to the town until it is actually incorporated, and incorporation into

[27] For a related point, see Odegard 1976, p. 564.

the town is not simply a matter of an increased degree of its former status. Analogously, Almeder might urge that for a proposition or a belief to be justified in the manner required for knowledge is not simply a matter of degree.

However, reflection on our earlier account of the content of the justification condition provides a way of strengthening Odegard's objections. We saw that the condition relates to S's role as an inquirer in relation to epistemic goals. Thomas Morawetz has remarked that in Gettier-type cases, "S is not culpably ignorant; that is part of what we mean by saying that his belief is justified" (Morawetz 1975, p. 10; cf. Ravitch 1976, pp. 347-349). Lowy more guardedly allows that there may be a significant distinction between "S's belief in h is justified" and "S is justified in believing h." As we noted earlier, she says that the latter phrase concerns whether or not in collecting and assembling his evidence, S has discharged his responsibility as a truth-seeker sufficiently thoroughly. Somewhat differently, Ernest Sosa suggests that when S shows "epistemic irresponsibility," for example, by neglectful data collection, S need not fail to be rationally justified in believing, but may instead fail to be "in a position to know" (Sosa 1974a, pp. 116-117).[28] Sosa seems to be concerned in part with a distinction between the degree of support that S's evidence provides for h and the effort S reflectively makes in gathering and taking account of the evidence. We might cover both factors by the phrases, "S has justified belief in h," and "S is justified in believing h," if we understand those phrases to mean that S's having that belief rather than holding some alternative propositional attitude regarding h manifests S's rationality more fully in relation to certain goals the speaker has in mind. When the context concerns an analysis of knowledge, the relevant goals are epistemic ones (see Chapter 7). Almeder cannot deny that in this sense a belief may be justified without being true. For proceeding in the most rational way presently

---

[28] Additional ways of failing to be in a position to know may involve having faulty cognitive or perceptual equipment, or may involve various social aspects of knowing. See Chapter 3.

available to one does not guarantee achieving one's goals, e.g., the epistemic goal of accepting true propositions.

Moreover, acceptance of Almeder's principle would at most force us to modify our description of Gettier-type cases by dropping clause (5) from G. Examples such as Feldman's version of the case of Mr. Nogot would again satisfy the amended formula. Almeder tries to show that the example violates principle AP by saying that, according to Feldman, "the evidence cited is logically consistent with the falsity of p [i.e., the falsity of the proposition, 'Somebody in the office owns a Ford']. And *this means* that if p had been false, S would still have been (completely) justified in believing that p" (emphasis added; Almeder 1975, p. 59). But the conclusion is a non sequitur, and Almeder is ignoring his own distinction between positions (a) and (b). The false proposition in both Feldman's and Lehrer's versions of the example which most philosophers would regard S as being justified in believing is, of course, 'Mr. Nogot owns a Ford.' But in Feldman's version the application of Almeder's principle to such a q would not directly prevent S from being justified in believing p. For S's inference to p proceeds independently of q and independently of any statement that it is justifiable to believe q.

Irving Thalberg attacks only the earliest Gettier-type examples, such as (E 1) and (E 4) (Thalberg 1974). He draws a useful distinction between asking whether one is justified by evidence in believing p and asking whether believing p increases one's prospects of believing a proposition that is true. Taking the former to be what is at issue regarding a standard analysis of knowing,[29] Thalberg expresses a doubt "that evidence concerning only Nogot's Ford ownership could support belief in a proposition which can be true when others own one" (pp. 351-352).

However, it frequently happens that we do have good evidence for an existential generalization and yet there are cases that would make the generalization true even if the specific cases of which we

---

[29] For a related distinction between having justified belief and having a "well-taken" belief, see Meyers and Stern 1973, pp. 156ff.

are already aware did not.[30] We should thus presume that a more careful expression of Thalberg's view is to be found in the following passage:

> With regard to disjunction and existential generalization . . . your evidence will vindicate these maneuvers only when it is not conclusive about one individual or proposition, and it bears on other individuals of the same description or on further propositions. (pp. 353-354)[31]

I have three objections to the above requirement. First, it is too weak for Thalberg's purposes in relation to disjunctions, and fails to block a move to the proposition, "Either Mr. Nogot owns a Ford or Mr. Also-Nogot owns a Ford or Brown is in Barcelona," in an example similar to (E 4) in which one's evidence does support the false proposition, 'Mr. Nogot owns a Ford or Mr. Also-Nogot owns a Ford,' but where the evidence is not conclusive as to which of those two men own one.

Secondly, the requirement incorrectly rules out common existential generalizations where there is conclusive evidence for the case at hand. Thus, it implies that, although I have conclusive evidence that Judy is my wife, I do not thereby have evidential justification for the proposition that Judy is a wife, or for the proposition that there is someone who is my wife.[32]

Thirdly, the following conversation is clearly not an abuse of language:

DEFENSE ATTORNEY: What evidence can the prosecution produce that either of the defendents in this conspiracy trial, Mr. Gettier

---

[30] Ralph Slaght has raised this objection against Thalberg (Slaght 1977, p. 17). Slaght also provides a useful discussion of some of Thalberg's other arguments, including ones that appeal to considerations concerning probability (pp. 13-19).

[31] In order to avoid triviality, I assume that by "further propositions" Thalberg means further disjuncts or further descriptions of an individual of the type mentioned in the existential generalization. For the evidence will always *bear* on the conjunction of itself with any other proposition logically consistent with it.

[32] Thalberg's requirement would, of course, block generalization of S's evidence in Feldman's version of the Nogot example (E 8).

or Mr. Lehrer, were involved in actually handling the document marked, "exhibit #1"?

PROSECUTING ATTORNEY: I shall prove beyond a doubt, your Honor, that Mr. Gettier got the document from the safe and inspected its contents. It is crucial for our case that, although he did not handle the document, Mr. Lehrer learnt of its contents from Gettier after the latter had returned it to the safe.

Here, the prosecutor admits that he intends to provide evidence which bears on only one disjunct. Surely, it is not plausible to say that he construes the defense attorney as having asked for evidence about two separate propositions rather than evidence for their disjunction. Indeed, for the purpose of eventually securing a conviction, perhaps all that matters is whether the disjunction is true but not which disjunct is true.

In another passage, Thalberg offers a somewhat different approach to these issues. He says that the teacher "lacks *evidential* justification for expecting" the disjunction, 'Either Jones owns a Ford or Brown is in Barcelona,' "to be true in the way it comes true" (original emphasis; p. 353; cf. p. 354). Apparently, Thalberg wishes to emphasize not merely that the disjunction might come true in a way which is independent of Jones's owning a Ford, but that it actually does come true in such a fashion. This interjects a metaphysical consideration, by proposing that the following requirement must be satisfied in order for S to have evidential justification for believing p: There is a way, w, in which p comes true and S has evidential justification for believing that the way p comes true is w.

However, I may have evidence that someone will win a lottery and evidence that either Tom or Dick or . . . or Harry will win it, but lack any evidence of how that will come true, for example, lack any evidence of the fact that it will come true by Dick's winning and by his ticket's being drawn.

Suppose that we insert a corresponding restriction into Thalberg's requirement, so that it does not attempt to cover cases where S has evidence for a disjunction but lacks evidence as to which disjunct is true. Even then, the requirement is too strong in relation to existential generalization. For knowledge of a lawful connection between the occurrence of an A and changes in a B may, once we know that a particular A has occurred, allow us to have evidential justification for believing that a change in some B will take place, even though we lack any evidence as to what makes it true that such a change will occur. We may be open to the possibility that the occurrence of an A is not the cause of the corresponding change in a B and that these phenomena are collateral effects of a common, presently unknown cause. Moreover, we may even lack any evidence as to which B will be involved in the change.[33]

Thus, we can find in neither Almeder's nor Thalberg's attacks any cogent grounds for refusing to regard the Gettier problem as genuine.

6. A RELATED PROBLEM CONCERNING THE SOCIAL ASPECTS OF KNOWING

An additional reason for regarding the standard conditions as insufficient for knowing concerns situations where the relation of S to other inquirers may deny S knowledge without affecting S's being justified in believing what he does. An example that has been frequently discussed is the following:

(E 9)   *The Newspaper*: S believes a bylined report in a generally reliable newspaper that a famous civil-rights leader has been assassinated. The report was written by a reporter who was an eyewitness. Unknown to S, those surrounding S do not know what to think because they have additional information consisting in later news reports to the contrary. Yet those later reports were due solely to an unsuspected conspiracy

---

[33] It seems to me gibberish to say of this example that the way in which the proposition, 'A change in some B will occur,' comes true is simply by the occurrence of a change in some B. If it is not gibberish then we can make a similar move concerning Gettier-type examples and have them satisfy Thalberg's requirement.

of other eyewitnesses aimed at avoiding a racial explosion. (Harman 1968, p. 172)[34]

Most replacements for the standard analysis of knowing that I shall survey attempt to deal with the above counterexample to a standard analysis by means of the same techniques they use to meet Gettier-type objections. But this leads to difficulties for the new analyses. We shall see in the final chapter that the Gettier problem relates to a different aspect of the justificational structure related to knowing than does the problem of properly acknowledging the social aspects of knowing. Accordingly, different solutions are required for the two problems.

7. ANALYSIS AND THE ART OF COUNTEREXAMPLES

Some philosophers have responded to Gettier by speculating that knowing may be unanalyzable. Others, who have made efforts to amend or to replace a standard analysis of knowing, usually relate the *analysandum*, '*S* knows *p*,' to its *analysans* by means of the connective, ''if and only if.'' But those authors seldom explain either the manner in which they are using this connective or their view of analysis.

Some epistemologists do say that their *analysans* specifies the content of the concept of knowledge, or specifies the meaning of sentences having the form indicated in the *analysandum*. But lack of clarity in talking about concepts, and widespread contemporary suspicion of the analytic/synthetic distinction have led most authors to avoid committing themselves to such views of analysis. Of course, we might try to make talk about meaning more respectable by relating

---

[34] Harman has credited (Harman 1968, p. 173) an early discussion by Ernest Sosa (Sosa 1964) with introducing the issue of social aspects of knowing.

Douglas Odegard argues that (E 9) does not refute a standard analysis of knowing, on the grounds that ''if my evidence fails to justify a knowledge claim when augmented, then it also fails to justify it before being augmented'' (Odegard 1978, p. 124). But Odegard's requirement for knowledge is too strong—see n. 34 to Chapter 2.

it to a theory of semantics and by embedding the analysis of '*S* knows *p*' in a theoretical context. But such an approach touches on basic issues of semantic theory and a major project of this type has generally not been attempted in the works that we shall discuss.

In light of this fact, Keith Lehrer suggests that we should distinguish analyzing the meaning of such sentences from the task of analyzing knowledge. The latter task, according to Lehrer, employs the connective, "if and only if," to indicate that the *analysans* specifies necessary and sufficient conditions for a person to have knowledge (Lehrer 1974, pp. 5-9).

Certain philosophers would be inclined to express this point by saying that the *analysans* attempts to indicate truth conditions for sentences of the form specified in the *analysandum*. The analysis might thereby help to clarify our talk about knowing, since, as W. V. Quine puts it, "a reasonable way of explaining an expression is by saying what conditions make its various contexts true" (Quine 1970, p. 40; cf. pp. 91-92). But a puzzle arises because some philosophers construe a set of truth conditions for a given sentence, s_1, to be provided by any sentence, s_2, that is materially equivalent to s_1 (that is, true in actual cases where s_1 is true, and false in actual cases where s_1 is false). This seems to open the door to an overly broad view of analysis, according to which an analysis of knowing may not have the useful side effect of explaining expressions involving "know" or its cognates. For example, suppose that an extreme form of skepticism is true which holds that sentences of the form '*S* knows *p*' are always false. According to the interpretation of truth conditions that we are considering, a correct analysis of knowing would be provided by writing as the *analysans* any false statement whatsoever. (Of course, *per hypothesis*, we would not *know* that the resulting analysis is correct.) Again, even if such skepticism is false, an *analysans* might merely list something that is the *effect* of *S*'s knowing *p*. (Recall our discussion of the *Meno*.)

One might be tempted to reply by suggesting that we should view analysis in much the way we view ostensive definition. The latter involves (i) getting a person into *some* relation to an item to which the term being defined applies, even if one does so only by alerting the person to an effect of that item, and (ii) succeeding in getting the person to understand the term being defined. Similarly, one might try to view any material equivalence of the above type as becoming an analysis of knowing provided that it happens to have the power, for whatever reason, of helping one understand expression of the form '*S* knows *p*.'

Yet if an *analysans* specifies effects of knowing, the analysis may appear merely to be a speculation about the *significance* of knowing. Alternatively, if the *analysans* speaks of causes of knowing, then the analysis would appear to be speculation within the part of psychology called learning theory.

Lehrer offers a way of avoiding the latter implication when he contrasts describing how we come to have knowledge with describing what knowledge is. He compares this to the contrast between a physicist's specifying how something comes to have a given mass versus specifying conditions that are necessary and sufficient for an object to have the given mass.

Although this will rule out an *analysans* that merely describes a process leading up to the time at which *S* knows *p*, or that merely describes what comes after *S*'s knowing *p*, it does not rule out the possibilities that (1) the *analysans* describes an accidental correlation between knowledge and something that happens always to obtain simultaneously with knowing, or (2) the *analysans* describes something simultaneously causally connected with knowledge. That is, one might view Lehrer as focusing on "what it is like" to have knowledge, rather than focusing on the question of what knowledge is (just as Meno initially led Socrates to focus on what a person is like who has knowledge).

But if the question, "What is knowledge?" is tantamount to the question: "What does the state of affairs *S*'s-knowing-p consist in or with what is it identical?" and if providing truth conditions for knowing amounts to answering the latter question, then it is just as well to regard the answer to such a question as lying beyond the concern of an analysis of knowing. For such a question raises metaphysical and logical issues about identity and states of affairs that are seldom broached in works purporting to provide an analysis of knowing.

Lehrer's response to possibility (1) is not to rule it out for analyses, but simply to regard any such analysis as uninteresting, just as it is an uninteresting analysis to say that "a necessary and sufficient condition for the application of the expression 'S knows that p' is precisely the condition of S knowing that p" (Lehrer 1974, p. 6). Philosophers seek an analysis of anything for some objective (p. 4). What a theory of knowledge does, according to Lehrer, is to pursue various objectives partly by means of an analysis of knowing that is interesting in relation to those objectives.

Few of the philosophers to be surveyed in future chapters state their objectives for a theory of knowledge. But they do at least appear to have the aim of expressing an analysis that is true. So we might take it as obvious that any purported counterexamples to such an analysis must indeed be discussed.

However, expressing ourselves in this fashion conceals a difficulty which may be exposed by taking note of one of the objectives that Lehrer sets for his theory of knowledge. He says that he wishes to promote the development of epistemology "to the point where the theory of knowledge should be poured out into a special science . . ." (p. 7). Thus, an analysis of knowing will not be interesting to Lehrer unless it is itself consistent with the rest of his theory of knowledge, and unless there is no "experiment of fact or thought . . . that is a logical possibility and is consistent with the other postulates of the theory" which would falsify the resulting equivalence, "in short, there must be no counterexample" (p. 8). Lehrer's wording of the latter requirement helps to expose the fact that immunity to counterexamples can take two forms: (a) no actual examples, past, present, or future run counter to the analysis; (b) the analysis sustains counterfactual conditionals connecting the *analysans* and *analysandum*.

Alternative (a) treats the connective, "if and only if," in the analysis as indicating material equivalence. Lehrer adopts alternative (b), however, which treats the connective as expressing a stronger type of equivalence, compatible with the nomological connection contemplated in (2), above. A reason for Lehrer's taking this path may be that he accepts the usual view of science as seeking generalizations that sustain counterfactuals. Indeed, even a philosopher who fails to share Lehrer's objective of eventually pouring the theory of knowledge from the pot of unsolved intellectual problems into science might still regard a metaphysical account of knowing as aiming at generalizations that sustain counterfactuals, and thus might also prefer option (b).

Philosophers who adopt alternative (a), however, may balk at considering the various counterexamples that we have already mentioned to the standard analyses of knowing. For the examples mentioned are fanciful, fictitious cases that do not bear on whether the *analysans* and *analysandum* are materially equivalent. For example, it is doubtful that Gettier knows an *actual* Smith who is silly enough to go through the process described in Gettier's example (E 4).

Perhaps some of the counterexamples which our discussion concerns were indeed constructed on the assumption of alternative (b), so that their authors considered themselves free to test an analysis by means of counterfactual antecedents in conditionals linking *analysans* and *analysandum*. But when one seeks to discern the *form* of one of these counterexamples, it often becomes highly plausible to suppose that at least one actual case has that form, even if it differs in some details from the given counterexample. This surely may be said of the form G of Gettier-type counterexamples to a standard analysis of knowing (cf. Skyrms 1967, p. 378). The reader may judge in what follows whether the same may be said of other counterexamples to various analyses that we consider.

A deeper problem about the role of counterexamples arises, however, when one considers the fact that some philosophers urge us to construct analyses or definitions where the *analysans* or *definiens* provides, in Nelson Goodman's words, one among a number of possible ''maps'' of the domain which the *analysans* or *definiendum* concerns. The structure of the latter domain may be illuminated by the structure of the map, but some sentences about the domain may not have the same truth values as their translations. Goodman remarks that "a definition must be such that every sentence *we care about* that can be translated into the system shall have the same truth value as its translation" (emphasis added; Goodman 1977, p. 9).

This approach to an analysis of knowing might seem to allow for an easy dismissal of counterexamples as "don't cares." But, of course, this is comparable to the ease of accepting the laurels after the race. The hard work comes in clearly indicating the purposes of one's "map" and in establishing that the structure it succeeds in delineating regarding the domain at hand is interesting in relation to those purposes. Moreover, one may allow that the disparate purposes of other inquirers may reasonably lead them to treat certain counterexamples which one has dismissed as nonetheless constituting important details of the original domain that a map ought not to distort or to neglect (Goodman 1978; C. I. Lewis 1946, p. 30).

We can at least say that because a very large number of interrelated examples have been discussed in the literature, and because these have been related to a large number of hypotheses concerning knowledge, a study of them will serve to sensitize one to the landscape one is attempting to map, if one chooses to pursue analysis or definition in Goodman's fashion.

The analogy of mapping raises the possibility of a process of sensitizing in the opposite direction as well. A map that works well may lead one to look more carefully at details which one initially thought it failed to capture, and this may change one's opinion of the original domain. Thus, the judgment that a given example constitutes a counterexample to a given analysis of knowledge must be admitted to be a fallible judgment.

This is true even regarding the analysis of knowledge sought by Lehrer. One might decide to reverse one's view of some class of putative counterexamples in light of the systematic power that a given analysis has in dealing adequately with other classes of examples which remain problematic for alternative analyses. However, philosophers have not yet resolved the issue of how to decide when such a move is appropriate. Perhaps it is Lehrer's view that only an integration of theory of knowledge with science will settle such issues. For it would subject the revision of one's description of examples to whatever processes are used in scientific investigation in order to let the success of generalizations and theory revise descriptions of particular instances.

There is reason to suppose that Lehrer's approach to knowledge is even more complex, and may actually relate to yet another view of analysis. Some philosophers regard an analysis as an attempt to develop a terminology better than ordinary language for the pursuit of one's philosophical objectives. In this case, the *analysans* in an analysis of knowing would aim at providing an understanding of expressions of the form "*S* knows *p*" that does not agree with an understanding of the role of such expressions in ordinary language. Philosophers have spoken of providing an *explication* of expressions in such a context, usually with the aim of eliminating some vagueness, or unclarity, or inconsistency concerning the use of the expressions in ordinary language (Hanna 1968). But Lehrer seems to carry this idea to the point of eliminating the outright falsity of ordinary statements applying "know":

> Thus, our theory of knowledge is a theory of knowledge without certainty. We agree with the skeptic that if a man claims to know for certain, he does not know whereof he speaks. However, when we claim to know, we make no claim to certainty. We conjecture that to speak in this way is a departure from the most customary use of the word 'know.' Commonly, when men say they know, they mean they know for certain, and they assume there is no chance of being in error. (Lehrer 1974, p. 239)

Of course, Lehrer may merely be saying that he is appealing to a *less* customary, but still ordinary, use of "know." Nonetheless, he does go on to say that the purpose of his theory is to "explicate" the uncertain epistemic adventure of man (p. 241). Thus, it is possible that he agrees with the skeptic in regarding all ordinary statements of the form '*S* knows *p*' as false, even ones about counterfactual situations.[35] But this creates a puzzle regarding Lehrer's attention to Gettier-type examples, since conditions (3) and (5) of G would now never be satisfied. The degree of justification that they require would never obtain.

Perhaps the direction in which to seek a solution to this puzzle is to regard Lehrer as attempting to understand expressions of the form "*S* knows *p*" in a manner that (a) is not far from an understanding of their present role in our language, (b) creates an application of the expressions that corresponds in large measure to the manner in which rational people presently apply those expressions when they neglect to notice whatever aspect of their speech it is that accounts for the universal inapplicability of the expressions, and (c) yields a connection with the application of other epistemic terminology that is interestingly similar to ways the expressions were previously thought to be connected in meaning or in reference.

Consideration (c) may be what Lehrer has in mind when he responds to the skeptic by saying that Lehrer's *own* justification con-

---

[35] Clarence Lewis maintained that only an explication of the everyday usage of '*S* knows *p*' can be given because the ordinary sense of that expression relates to incompatible demands resulting "from the natural but inadmissible tendency to impose requirements appropriate to one type of knowledge upon all" (C. I. Lewis 1946, p. 29). One of these requirements is that *S*'s belief that *p* have a 'warrant' or 'sufficient ground' or 'justifying ground or reason' or something that 'constitutes justification of the belief,' and another requirement is that knowledge must be 'certain' or have 'theoretical certainty' (pp. 27-28). Empirical knowledge fails to satisfy the latter requirement, but 'immediate apprehensions of sense confined to just the directly given content and as it is given' do not satisfy the former requirement (p. 28). Yet it seems that Lewis admitted that such apprehensions are justified since he went on to call them 'self-justifying' even though "it is at least doubtful whether such apprehensions have a ground or reason" (p. 28). Lewis explained that he was prepared to explicate '*S* knows *p*' differently for different types of knowledge (in the everyday sense), although he preferred not to speak of knowledge of the immediate apprehensions of sense because they do not meet the further requirements of permitting a contrast with some corresponding kind of possible error, or of pointing to or signifying something beyond the experience (p. 30). Regarding empirical knowledge, Lewis adopted an explication which counts as a standard analysis of knowing, and which treats the justification condition as requiring that *S*'s believing is justified (at least to a particular degree) by grounds or reasons. But Lewis imposed no restrictions on those grounds or reasons which would avoid Gettier-type counterexamples.

dition does apply despite the risk of error we run, so that there are things we "know" (p. 240). Consideration (b) mentions an achievement akin to a situation in science where a new theory offers explanations of many phenomena to which a previous theory applied misleading labels. The combination of all three considerations indicates why we should avoid as much as possible the recurrence, after the new understandings of explicated terms are adopted, of counterexamples that depend on a Gettier-type connection between purported knowledge and psychological or epistemic factors. That is, we need to ascertain that the old counterexamples did not hinge upon a structural difficulty remaining in the new framework, thanks to the fact that the new one is modeled to some extent upon the old.[36]

---

[36] As an example, consider the explication attempted by Oliver Johnson (1980). Johnson believes that "ordinary usage leaves us with an incoherent conception of knowledge" just because ordinary usage is, indeed, captured by a standard analysis or definition of the sort we have been considering (p. 125). The incoherency supposedly arises because the account fails to meet one of the criteria of an "adequate" definition, or, at least, of a definition that is not a "bad" one: "we must be able to apply the definition of that term to an object in order to determine whether it satisfies the definition and so falls under the term" (p. 118). Johnson maintains that this creates a difficulty for the conception covered by a standard definition because such a definition allows that the "good reasons" which pertain to the justification condition are such that "a belief may be false in spite of the reasons"; thus, if we give either those reasons or reasons of the same type in support of S's belief, e.g., when attempting to apply the standard definition, then "we have not determined that it satisfies the truth condition of knowledge" (pp. 124-125). But this is only a difficulty if we follow Johnson in regarding "determined" as having a very strong sense. Suppose that we offer reasons through which we have determined, for example, that h: 'Belief b satisfies the truth condition in a definition of "S knows p." ' According to Johnson, we must be able to say of belief b that "given the reasons we have provided in its support, it is true. We can do this, however, only if, given these reasons, the belief cannot be false" (p. 124). But this arbitrarily reintroduces the generally discredited quest for infallibility into philosophy at the heart of a search for definitions or analyses. (See Johnson's talk of 'deciding' or 'showing' that h as a matter of 'guaranteeing' or 'establishing' or 'certifying' that the belief is true [pp. 118, 119, 120, 124]).

In an earlier discussion (Johnson 1971), Johnson instead traced the concern with certainty to the supposed origins of the concept of knowing in a situation where one of our long-cherished beliefs is upset, possibly with disastrous practical consequences, so that we resolve to avoid such experiences in the future. However, this alone only says that we resolve to avoid possession of false beliefs in the future. Moreover, to seek guidance and skills in pursuit of a goal is not ipso facto to expect an unfailing method to be involved.

The very fact that I have been led to speak so vaguely at this point, however, attests to insufficient clarity and agreement in contemporary views concerning the nature of philosophical analysis. Nonetheless, the present section may have conveyed some reasons why philosophers who are of different persuasions concerning analysis will need to attend to the role of counterexamples in the remainder of our discussion. Moreover, I shall attempt in the final chapter to provide a way of applying expressions of the form "*S* knows *p*" that should be of interest to all those philosophers and that succeeds in avoiding every counterexample surveyed concerning the social aspects of knowing or Gettier-type situations.

Because I intend to arrive at that ultimate goal, and because I wish to avoid unmanageable complexity, I shall not attempt to explain the full power of each analysis considered along the way, nor to specify which counterexamples it manages to avoid that defeated previously considered analyses. I shall instead emphasize the difficulties that each analysis faces, especially any additional counterexamples which may be constructed in order to refute it.

Before embarking on this survey, however, we may note that the preceding discussion helps to avoid an unnecessarily narrow view

---

Because Johnson regards our ordinary conception of knowing as defective, he suggests that we explicate it by reinterpreting the justification condition so that "*S*'s believing *p* is justified" is taken to mean that *S*, in Johnson's words, "can justify it to be true" or "can justify that his belief that *p* is true" (pp. 116, 117). In that case, "satisfaction of the justification condition *does* entail satisfaction of the truth condition. . . . for the proposition 'Smith can justify that *p*, but *not-p*' states a contradiction" (p. 117). These remarks appear to contain linguistically deviant usages of "justify," which term should either be replaced by the term "demonstrate," or, perhaps, be regarded as technical vocabulary defined in the following passage: "we can justify certain of our beliefs as true, i.e., the [good] reasons we can give in their support entail their truth . . ." (p. 124). Thus, if we echo *S*'s reasons when we determine that the justification condition is satisfied, we ipso facto determine that the truth condition is satisfied.

Johnson mistakenly thinks that this explication of "*S* knows *p*" avoids counterexamples close to Gettier-type cases. He says that *S* lacks the requisite ability in those cases to demonstrate that *p*, inasmuch as *S* will appeal to false premises in providing arguments which entail that *p* (p. 120). But Johnson has overlooked the structure of examples where *S* would make no such appeal, and which run counter to his analysis, such as (E 5), (E 6), or (E 8).

of what it is for an *analysans* to list "necessary and sufficient conditions" for knowing. Richard Aaron objects that to describe the *analysans* in such a fashion "inevitably" leads proponents of a standard analysis to "think their theory provides means of checking whether *A* knows that *p* when he is sure that *p*" (Aaron 1971, pp. 25, 23). According to Aaron, this is to construe each condition, e.g., the truth condition, as a "criterion" whereby we may "test" a claim to knowledge (p. 23). A criterion, he adds, would be an "objective" rather than "subjective" justification for attributing knowledge (p. 22). Thus, the truth condition is a criterion for knowing only if we can form our judgment about whether *S* knows *p* thanks to our having direct access to the fact that *p* which bypasses any reliance on our possession of evidence or our own psychological state of being sure. Aaron applauds Kant for supposedly realizing that there is no such independent access and therefore not listing a truth condition in his analysis of knowledge.

In fact, Aaron makes an even stronger claim, namely, that sufficient conditions provide justifications and tests which "finally settle" an issue, which "guarantee" a correct view of it, and in that sense "establish" and provide a "proof" of the view (pp. 16-17, 24-25). He says that if we appeal to a variety of subjunctive conditions, such as evidence acceptable to *S* and to others, "the skeptic's question remains. . . . May they not all be in error?"

But our previous considerations indicate that the project of developing an analysis of knowing may have objectives other than providing an answer to the skeptic. Indeed, a better perspective on skepticism might be obtained by setting aside its concerns while working on an analysis of knowing. Skepticism can thereafter be addressed when considering what an otherwise plausible analysis of knowing requires in order for me either to know or to be justified in believing that *S* knows *p*. One might at that point be prepared to let the chips fall where they may concerning knowledge or reasonable opinion about the truth of knowledge ascriptions.

2.

Additions to Standard Analyses I: Subjunctive Conditionals

1. DEFEASIBILITY ANALYSES

Certain modifications of a standard analysis of knowing involve what are commonly called "defeasibility conditions," but there is no agreement about the definition of that technical label.

1.1 *What Is a Defeasibility Condition?*

For example, Steven Levy speaks of a defeasibility condition in an analysis of knowledge as "a requirement to the effect that for S to know that p there must be no other evidence against p strong enough to undermine S's belief that p, should this evidence come to S's attention" (Levy 1977, p. 115). However, speaking of undermining belief seems to concern the psychological change consisting in weakening or ending belief, whereas the analyses Levy means to discuss are instead concerned with changes in the justification of belief, as the characterization offered by Pappas and Swain indicates: "the evidence e must be sufficiently complete that no further additions to e would result in a loss of justification and hence a loss of knowledge . . ." (Pappas and Swain 1978, p. 27).

The latter way of characterizing defeasibility allows that justification may be undermined by evidence which is relevant to p even though it is not evidence against p, as in the following example:

(E 10) *Tom Grabit's Actual Twin*: S believes that his acquaintance, Tom Grabit, stole a book from the library since S saw Tom do it. But, unsuspected by S, Tom has an identical twin brother who was in the library near the time of the theft. (Klein 1971, p. 474)

Indeed, there are circumstances where something would undermine justification if it were added to one's evidence, even though it is not itself relevant evidence. For example, the fact that S is redgreen colorblind might undermine S's justification for believing a certain tie to be red, yet the fact is not in any usual sense relevant to the question of whether the tie is red (Shope 1979d; Sosa 1974a). So the following definition of defeasibility appears to be more useful:

(D) A defeasibility condition requires that there is no other true statement, d, such that if d were believed by S, or supposed by S to be true, or evident to S,[1] then S would not be justified in believing p.[2]

However, this definition allows the possibility that if S were to believe d, then S would cease to have some of the evidence S actually has for p. The result is that the corresponding analysis of knowing is unsatisfactory. (See the discussion of [iv$_2$] and [iv$_3$] below.)

Some authors have dealt with this by proposing a different definition of defeasibility:

(D′) A defeasibility condition requires that there is no other true statement, d, such that the conjunction of S's present evidence for p with d would fail to make S justified in believing p. (Lehrer and Paxson 1969, p. 230)

As we shall see, it soon became apparent that some candidates for d which satisfy D′ do not prevent S from knowing p, namely, those which have been called a "defective defeating statement," describing "misleading evidence." Accordingly, further qualifications have been added to definitions of defeasibility, e.g., that d not

---

[1] Levy says, "known to S," but that would permit a defeasibility analysis to be circular (Levy 1977, p. 117).

[2] Assuming S were to delete the negation of d from S's prior evidence, should it have been included (Hilpinen 1971, p. 31).

be in certain ways "defective" (Annis 1973, p. 202). These qualifications have varied from author to author, leaving it unclear what shared sense is left for the technical label, "defeasibility condition." I suggest that any such condition satisfies the following definition:

(D″) A defeasibility condition in an analysis of knowing is one that is not entailed by satisfaction of the justification condition, and that requires a particular truth value for some subjunctive conditional(s) about the justification of p, or the justification of S's believing or accepting p, in hypothetical circumstances.

In examples where the conditional(s) have a truth value opposite to that required yet the justification condition is satisfied, we may technically speak of S's actual justification as "defeated." That is, it fails to be enough, when added to the satisfaction of the truth condition and the belief condition, to let S know p.[3]

1.2 Almeder's Rejection of Defeasibility Conditions

Robert Almeder offers the following example in order to argue that all analyses of knowing which include defeasibility conditions in the sense of D or D′ are too strong and rule out some cases of genuine knowledge:

(E 11) *The Humanly Unknowable Defeater*: God decrees that no human being will ever know a particular truth that would, if added to S's justification for believing p, prevent S from being justified in believing p. Yet S's actual justification is good enough for him to know p. (Almeder 1973, pp. 241-242)

According to Almeder, we cannot object to S's actual justification

---

[3] Some philosophers interchange the expressions, "defeasible justification" and "defeated justification." But this clashes with their also tracing the terminology in question back to Roderick Chisholm's discussion of normative issues. Chisholm treats a moral requirement as defeasible when there are *possible* situations in which it would be defeated as a determinant of the right thing to do, and contrasts this with saying that the requirement *is* defeated in one's actual situation (Chisholm 1964).

by saying, "But that's not enough," unless we are willing to state specifically what would be enough (p. 242).

However, Almeder may have confused the fact that in this imaginary case the truth of the defeater is unknowable with the statement that the content of the defeater is unknowable. Odegard has objected that people could "conditionally" deny S knowledge on the supposition that an essential premise is false (Odegard 1976, p. 564).

Perhaps Almeder's point is that God has chosen to conceal even the content of the defeater from men, so that the defeater is a proposition other than a negation of an essential premise in S's reasoning. But we can still allow the *possibility* that the possession of some (unspecified) information which S lacks is crucial to S's knowing p. If this is an erroneous intuition, Almeder needs to show why it is, especially since one easy way God could be imagined to fulfil his decree is merely by ending all human inquiry by means of a nearby supernova whenever we are just about to conceive the defeater.

1.3 *Lehrer's Psychologistic Condition*

Because philosophers who present defeasibility analyses employ subjunctive conditionals, many of them have committed some version of the conditional fallacy (Shope 1978). For example, consider the fourth condition of knowledge proposed by Keith Lehrer in an early defeasibility analysis:

(iv$_1$) for any false statement, f, if S were to suppose, for the sake of argument, that f is false, then S would still be able to completely justify his believing p. (Lehrer 1970b, p. 127)

Lehrer has committed the second version of the conditional fallacy. He has overlooked examples of knowledge in which satisfaction of the antecedent in his conditional would render the consequent false. Suppose that f is a false proposition which S does not believe to be false, and that the following proposition, p, is known by S to be true: 'S is not supposing, for the sake of argument, that f is false.' If S *were* to suppose, for the sake of argument, that f is false then S would be conscious of supposing this, and would not be completely justified in believing p. In this example, Lehrer's conditional is not true, yet S does actually know p.

Lehrer might respond that his fourth condition is meant for inferential knowledge, not for basic knowledge of one's own psychological states. However, we can then simply let p_1 be anything S knows inferentially only because S knows p. Satisfaction of the antecedent of the conditional would keep S from being completely justified in believing p_1 by keeping S from being completely justified in believing p.[4]

This counterexample is more effective than several questionable or controversial cases that have been proposed against Lehrer's analysis. Gilbert Harman has urged that when S knows p on the basis of evidence e, there will always be a false statement satisfying Lehrer's *analysans*. Statement f will have the form: '$p\&k$,' where k is a true proposition irrelevant to p but antecedently highly improbable, given what S already knows (Harman 1973, p. 152). However, Odegard has replied that because the improbability of k is conditional upon S's total information, after S supposes that f is false the evidence for p will combine with the supposition in question to form evidence for k (Odegard 1978, p. 127).[5]

Another example that has been said to run counter to Lehrer's analysis is the following:

(E 12) *Demented Mrs. Grabit*: This example is similar to (E 10) except that the twin is merely a product of the demented imagination of Tom's mother, who has vowed v: 'Tom's identical twin was at the library at the time of the theft and Tom was thousands of miles away.' (Lehrer and Paxson 1969, p. 228)

---

[4] The same example runs counter to the analyses of Doris Olin and B. L. Blose (Olin 1970, p. 134; Blose 1977, p. 207). Another problem facing their analyses is Levy's point that a defeater of a defeater can be misleading and so on into a regress which, if referred to in an analysis of knowledge, would drive us toward a requirement of total evidence and thereby toward skepticism (Levy 1977).

[5] Harman has an additional objection to Lehrer that depends upon attributing to him a principle which Lehrer, in response, disavowed. For discussion see Slaght 1977, pp. 21-23.

Peter Klein objected to Lehrer's analysis by pointing out that in the above example, adding the following statement, not-f, to S's evidence or suppositions may very well prevent S from remaining justified in believing that Tom stole the book: 'v and statements made by mothers in such situations are generally reliable' (Klein 1971, p. 480). However, Klein later admitted that even when not-f is added, S might justifiably persist in believing Tom stole the book, since S knows that it is possible that Mrs. Grabit is trying to save Tom from punishment (Klein 1976, p. 805). Although the latter knowledge does not discredit Mrs. Grabit's testimony, it might counterbalance its effect. Risto Hilpinen has gone further in arguing that not-f actually "is not entirely true; it includes an incorrect estimate of the reliability of the testimony" of Mrs. Grabit (Hilpinen 1971, p. 32). After all, in this situation, the testimony is given by a deranged person.[6]

Some philosophers regard Skyrms's example (E 7) as running counter to Lehrer's analysis. But Ralph Slaght has offered reason to suppose that the example fails to refute Lehrer (Slaght 1977, pp. 23-24).[7] Nor is Ernest Sosa's modification of the case a clear counterexample to Lehrer:

(E 13)   *The Numb Pyromaniac*: This is similar to (E 7), except that S justifiably believes f: 'S will see and smell the ignition of the match.' However, f is false because of a totally unexpected sensory numbness that will accompany the ignition. (Sosa 1970, pp. 62-63)

Slaght questions the force of this example when he expresses doubt that S's conjoining not-f with S's present evidence for p: 'The match will ignite' need prevent S from being completely justified in believing p (Slaght 1977, p. 98). This suspicion may be bolstered by noting that S is not prohibited by Lehrer's *analysans* from also sup-

---

[6] The same objection affects a version of (E 12) which includes the 'social aspect' that Mrs. Grabit presents her testimony in a public hearing. For further discussion, see n. 10 and Shope 1979d.

[7] Slaght also argues that Skyrms's barometer example is no genuine counterexample (pp. 23-24).

posing that it is possible for him to be struck by such numbness, so that the new evidence would thereby be counterbalanced.

Just as Lehrer's analysis is flexible enough to permit this reply, it is unfortunately flexible enough to suffer from a defect noted by David Coder. The psychologistic reference to S's ability to justify leaves open the possibility that in some cases of genuine knowledge, the habits and 'sets' of S would make him incapable when confronted with new information of coming up with a justification rather than changing his belief in p. Lehrer's *analysans* would then fail to be satisfied (Coder 1974, p. 116).[8]

1.4 *Nonpsychologistic Conditions*

1.41 KLEIN AND GINET

Defeasibility analyses advanced by Klein and by Carl Ginet avoid this psychologistic component. Klein's fourth condition of S's knowing p at time t is quite close to definition (D) of defeasibility:

(iv$_2$)   there is no true proposition, r, such that if r became evident to S at t, p would no longer be evident to S. (Klein 1971, p. 475)[9]

Ginet proposes the following condition:

(iv$_3$)   there is no truth, r, such that, were S to be justified in believing r and to retain all his properties that are compatible with his having justification for believing r, then S would be very far from justified in being confident that p. (Ginet 1975, p. 80)

The latter proposal offers an alternative way of dealing with the case of the demented Mrs. Grabit. One might say that for S to assume the existence of her testimony would not make S very far from justified in being confident that Tom stole the book.

However, both Klein and Ginet have committed the second version

---

[8] Lehrer's analysis thus commits the *ceteris paribus* fallacy (Shope 1978, p. 405).
[9] Lehrer made a rather similar proposal, which is subject to the same objections a Klein's analysis (Lehrer 1965).

of the conditional fallacy. Suppose that S knows p: 'S is not justified in believing r.' But suppose, in addition, that r is true. If S were to satisfy the antecedents of (iv$_2$) or (iv$_3$), that would make their consequents false in any case where satisfaction of the antecedents would make S justified in being confident that he was justified in believing r.

1.42 PAXSON AND LEHRER

Paxson and Lehrer were moved to deal with the case of the deranged Mrs. Grabit by adding the following condition to the standard analysis of knowing:

(iv$_4$) if e is the evidence that completely justifies S in believing p, then there is no proposition, r, such that (1) r is true, (2) the conjunction of e and r does not completely justify S in believing p, (3) S is completely justified in believing that r is false, and (4) if c is a logical consequence of r such that the conjunction of c and e does not completely justify S in believing p, then S is completely justified in believing that c is false. (Lehrer and Paxson 1969, p. 231)

In the case of the deranged Mrs. Grabit, S does not satisfy clause (3), when r is a description of Mrs. Grabit's having vowed v, so her testimony cannot figure in any conjunction defeating S's justification.

Klein has shown that inclusion of clause (3) makes such an analysis of knowledge too weak to rule out S's knowing in (E 10) the case of Tom Grabit's actual twin. For in that case, (3) is not satisfied because S is not justified in believing not-r_1: 'Tom has no identical twin who was in the library' (Klein 1976, p. 808).[10]

A modification of (3) might avoid this objection. In (E 10), conjoining r_1 with e would undercut S's justification by resulting in S's being justified in accepting another defeater, r_2: 'S could not distinguish Tom's participation in the theft from that of other nearby people who had an opportunity to steal the book.' We might accordingly add a conjunct to (3) to the effect that if the conjunction of r and e

---

[10] Lehrer's condition (iv$_1$) is at least able to deal with this example.

would fail to completely justify S in believing p only because it would completely justify S in believing some true proposition, r', then S is presently completely justified in believing r' to be false. For in (E 10) S may be presumed to be completely justified in believing r_2 to be false.

However, whether or not we modify the Paxson and Lehrer analysis as suggested, it remains open to an objection by Bredo Johnsen. He argues that the analysis is too strong because it rules out knowledge in the following example:

(E 14)   *Shrink-and-Grabit*: This is similar to the case of the demented Mrs. Grabit (E 12), except that S's colleague, Dr. Shrink, whose information about students is known by S to be generally reliable, says to S that he has been concerned about Tom's conduct in view of the fact that Tom's mother died recently. Unknown to Shrink and to S, Dr. Shrink has mistaken Tom's stepmother for his mother. (Johnsen 1974, p. 275)

Johnsen says that S does know that Tom stole the book, even though he is completely justified in believing it to be false that Tom's mother has just given the testimony she did (since dead women tell no tales).[11]

1.43 LEHRER'S ANALYSIS IN *Knowledge*

Before discussing Johnsen's own defeasibility analysis, let us consider how Lehrer's more recent account in *Knowledge* fares in the face of the Shrink-and-Grabit example.

---

[11] Johnsen's example may overcome Klein's and Hilpinen's reluctance to admit that clause (2) of (iv₄) is satisfied in Grabit-type cases, provided that we add the following details: (a) Mrs. Grabit has only said v to a friend in order to save face and not because she is demented, and (b) S knows that Mrs. Grabit (while alive) is not the sort to assert v falsely in a serious situation.

Ernest Sosa objects that clause (4) is never satisfied in examples of knowledge (Sosa 1970, p. 61). Ralph Slaght argues at length that (iv₄) is unable to cope with the case of Mr. Nogot (Slaght 1977, pp. 78-86). But Slaght also admits that both Sosa's objection and his own rest on a controversial intuition about justification (p. 86).

As an improved definition of defeasibility, Lehrer suggests the following:

(iv₅) S would be completely justified in believing p in the verific alternative to the corrected doxastic system of S. (Lehrer 1974, p. 225)

The technical terms used in this condition may themselves be explained as follows:

The *doxastic* system of a person, S, is a set of statements of the form, S believes that p, S believes that q, and so forth, which describes what S believes.[12] The *corrected* doxastic system of S is that subset of the doxastic system resulting when every statement is deleted which describes S as believing something he would cease to believe as an impartial and disinterested truth-seeker [what Lehrer calls a "veracious man"] (pp. 189-190).[13]

Let D be the corrected doxastic system of S. Every statement in D is of the form: S believes p. Form a set V from D by retaining all such statements of D in V when it is true that p, and when it is false that p substitute in V the statement that S believes the denial of p. We shall call V the verific alternative to D (p. 224).

S is completely justified [(a) within the actual doxastic system of S, (b) within the verific alternative to the corrected doxastic system of S] in believing p if and only if, [(a)] within the corrected doxastic system of S [(b) within the verific alternative to the corrected doxastic system of S], p is believed to have a better chance of being true than the denial of p or any other statement that competes with p . . . on the condition that the other statements of . . . [the respective system] are true. (pp. 198, 233)[14]

---

[12] In this analysis, Lehrer interprets "believes" in such a way that "a man who believes that p must be convinced that p and ready to affirm that p in the appropriate circumstances . . ." (p. 209).

[13] Lehrer also imposes a consistency condition on corrected doxastic systems (pp. 202-204).

[14] Slaght explains the need for the first two bracketed additions to Lehrer's own definition of complete justification, although Slaght's wording is slightly different

We must first take up a difficulty concerning the definition of S's being completely justified in believing something. All that happens when an actual doxastic system is turned into a corrected one is that some beliefs are dropped. Since no beliefs are added, and since those beliefs in the corrected system which concern chances are estimates of the chances conditional upon other statements in the corrected system, those beliefs about chances will be in the corrected system only if they were already in the actual doxastic system. But it is quite rare that such beliefs will already have been in the actual system. For S himself will hardly ever know which of his actual beliefs would be dropped in forming the corrected doxastic system.

Perhaps Lehrer would reply by allowing some new beliefs to be formed in the corrected doxastic system, including the beliefs in questions concerning chances. For he does allow certain additions in order to deal with the objection that, on his definition, a man will be completely justified in believing that God exists, provided that the man believes that God exists, believes that this statement has a better chance of being true than its denial, and believes nothing else. Lehrer answers that "a veracious man . . . would not arbitrarily restrict his beliefs in this way. Hence, for the man in question the beliefs of his doxastic system would not be beliefs of his *corrected doxastic system*" (pp. 208-209).

But this permissiveness destroys the usefulness of Lehrer's analysis of knowledge. For it might be true that if a man were veracious then he would find new, cogent lines of argument from his present evidence to a belief he presently holds on quite worthless grounds. Yet we do not wish to say he presently knows that which he believes.

A way out may be offered by Lehrer's appeal to an objective propensity theory of chance. He says that the statement, 'p has a better chance of being true than q on the condition of the truth of other statements in the corrected doxastic system,' is itself true or false depending on the way the world actually is (pp. 232-234). So

(Slaght 1977, pp. 122-123). Slaght also provides an exegesis of Lehrer's complex conception of competition among propositions (cf. pp. 112-117).

the following modification of Lehrer's definition of justification avoids both the difficulty I have pointed out, and the objection concerning belief in God:

> S is completely justified within the actual doxastic system (within the verific alternative to the corrected doxastic system) of S in believing p if and only if p has a better chance of being true than the denial of p or any other statement that competes with p on the condition that the statements within the corrected doxastic system (within the verific alternative to the corrected doxastic system) of S are true.

The resulting analysis of knowledge deals adequately with the case of the demented Mrs. Grabit, since S lacks beliefs concerning Mrs. Grabit's testimony, and no such beliefs will be mentioned in the corrected doxastic system or its verific alternative.[15]

In the Shrink-and-Grabit example, S has a belief, thanks to Dr. Shrink's remarks, that Tom's mother did not say the things in question. This belief is still attributed to S in the corrected doxastic system, inasmuch as Dr. Shrink is correctly believed to be a generally reliable source of information about students. But S's corrected doxastic system also contains the statement that S believes that Tom's mother did not say those things as demented ravings. Thus, in the verific alternative to S's corrected doxastic system, the latter statement gets changed to the statement: 'S does believe that Mrs. Grabit said those things as demented ravings.' Accordingly, S's justification for believing Tom stole the book is not undercut.

The very strength of Lehrer's account in dealing with the above example, however, renders it incapable of standing against a variant of (E 9), Harman's newspaper example. Lehrer shows that his analysis is adequate to deal with the original version of that example, because a false belief is crucially involved. For "part of what justifies the man in believing that the civil-rights leader has been assassinated

---

[15] The modification would deal with one of Mark Pastin's reasons for regarding Lehrer's analysis as too strong (Pastin 1977, p. 436).

is his belief that the newspaper story is generally considered to be a reliable source of information'' (p. 223). Lehrer then notes that the verific alternative to the man's corrected doxastic system will include beliefs in the true counterparts to these false statements, and he will be said to believe that other people generally do not believe the report in the newspaper to be reliable. According to Lehrer, this is sufficient to make the person fail to be completely justified in believing the story in that hypothetical situation, which, on Lehrer's analysis, denies the man knowledge in the actual situation.

Lehrer points out that if the analysis were to require too many new true beliefs in the verific alternative, e.g., ones concerning the conspiracy of other eyewitnesses, we would then incorrectly be led to treat the person as knowing of the assasination. Thus, in order to obtain results matching our intuitions, descriptions of S's beliefs in the verific alternative are by definition limited to the original true beliefs described in S's corrected doxastic system plus the reversal of the false beliefs contained in that system (p. 225).[16]

This admission, however, alerts us to the fact that the newspaper example can be altered in a fashion similar to that in which Johnsen altered the Tom Grabit example, and it will then run counter to Lehrer's analysis of knowledge:

(E 15)   *Pol-and-Grabit*: This is similar to the newspaper example, except that S recalls the fact that his friend, Mr. Pol, who S knows to be generally reliable about recent political events concerning civil rights, previously told S that the wife of

---

[16] In the newspaper example, the following evidence, q_1, is misleading: 'The newspaper story is not generally considered by those surrounding S to be a reliable source of information as to whether the assassination occurred.' David Annis suggests that a proposition, q, is evidence which fails to defeat S's justification for believing p on the basis of e if and only if "there is a true statement r which explains why q is misleading evidence with respect to S, e, and p such that the conjunction of e, q and r justifies S in believing p but r alone does not justify S in believing p" (Annis 1973, p. 201). But this would incorrectly grant S knowledge in the newspaper example, in view of the following truth, r_1: 'The other news reports known of by those surrounding S are due mainly to an attempt to avoid a racial incident.' For further criticism, see Olin 1970.

the civil-rights leader has died. Unknown to Pol and to S, Mr. Pol has confused the man's wife with his mother. While reading the newspaper story of the assassination, S reflects, "Well, at least his wife was not around to witness this sorry turn of events." In fact, she was one of the eyewitnesses who joined in the cover-up. Moreover, upon reading the story, S presumes that some effort may have been made to cover up the assassination, perhaps extending to the issuance of denials to news sources not present at the event.

Here, S is completely justified in believing that the (supposedly) dead wife was not involved in such a cover-up. Nonetheless, in S's verific alternative, his false beliefs about the wife get reversed, and he then believes in the occurrence of the conspiracy. Once that belief is added, Lehrer seems prepared to admit that S remains completely justified in his belief that the assassination occurred. However, I think that our intuitions about (E 15) are no different from those concerning Harman's original example.

A number of counterexamples of this type have been presented against Lehrer's analysis (Binkley 1977; Carter 1977; M. Clark 1977; Pastin 1977; Sosa 1976). However, Randolph Carter has remarked that some of them may need modification in case Lehrer's analysis requires that the beliefs added in the verific alternative upon which the justification of belief in p would rest must themselves be completely justified (Carter 1977, p. 333).

It is not difficult to satisfy such a requirement. It is met by the following examples, which also serve to demonstrate that Lehrer has committed both versions of the conditional fallacy:

(1) Let q be some proposition believed by S but something that S would refrain from believing if S were a veracious man. Since S actually believes q, we may assume that in the usual fashion S believes that he believes this, i.e., believes p: 'S believes q.' Indeed, S knows p, in view of his awareness of his own conscious beliefs. But Lehrer's analysis denies this knowledge. For if the antecedent of the conditional in the definition of complete justification were to obtain in the verific alternative, then S would not believe q, and the

statement that S believes q would be kept from the system. There would then be no way of showing p to be more probable than its denial or than its competitors relative to other members of the verific alternative. (This example does not even depend upon added beliefs in the verific alternative; the example has also occurred to Richard Feldman [Feldman 1979].)

(2) Suppose that S would persist, even as a veracious person, in falsely believing r: 'There is nothing with property ϕ near the periphery of S's visual field,' and would persist in believing p: 'S believes r.' Lehrer's analysis incorrectly denies that S presently knows p. For in the verific alternative, p is false and the alternative contains instead of p the statement p_1: 'S believes not-r.' Moreover, S would then be completely justified in believing not-r. But there seems to be no reason to say that in the verific alternative p would be more probable than its competitor p_1.

We may note that to include the requirement mentioned by Carter would be to prevent Lehrer's account from being able to deal with another example:

(E 16)   *The Unseen Sheep*: Mistaking a dog for a sheep, S justifiably believes from the way things look to him that p: 'There is a sheep in the field.' But p is true only because of the presence of an unseen, unsuspected sheep. (Chisholm 1977, p. 105)

Lehrer points out that in this example statement t: 'S believes w' will be included in the verific alternative, where w is the statement: 'The object S takes to be a sheep is not a sheep.' For S has an actual false belief that what he takes to be a sheep is one. So in the verific alternative, ''the belief that what he takes to be a sheep is not a sheep undermines his justification for his belief that he sees a sheep'' (Lehrer 1974, pp. 224-225).[17] But the objective chances are poor that a statement such as w is true in the perceptual situations where

---

[17] Thus, Randolph Carter errs in suggesting that we might save Lehrer's analysis merely by deleting false beliefs when forming a verific alternative instead of requiring their reversal (Carter 1977, pp. 334-335). Compare the case of Papa Grabit as a vicarious kleptomaniac (Blose 1977, p. 206). (See also n. 35 below.)

a person actually believes that what he takes to be a sheep is one, and has other beliefs similar to S's actual ones. So Carter's requirement for S's failing to know p is not met.

Before turning from Lehrer's account in *Knowledge*, let us consider its relation to his own case of the clever reasoner (E 6). Lehrer employs this example as a Gettier-type objection to the following fourth condition for knowledge:

(iv$_6$) S's justification for believing p does not crucially depend on S's having false beliefs.[18]

However, David Annis charges that Lehrer is in the ironic position of being unable to deal with this example by means of the analysis given in *Knowledge* (Annis 1976).

Perhaps Lehrer thought that he could respond to this case as he did to the objection concerning belief in God, namely, by saying that a veracious man would not restrict his beliefs as the clever reasoner does. For a veracious man seeks not only to avoid believing falsehoods but also to believe truths. But we have seen above that this general strategy is not satisfactory.

1.44 JOHNSEN

Johnsen's treatment of defeasibility has the virtue of withstanding all of the preceding counterexamples. He suggests that knowledge will be absent when "not even the most gerrymandered selection of the available evidence for p will avoid the commitment" to the justified status of S's believing some false proposition "except at the cost of commitment to p's truth" (Johnsen 1974, p. 278). Accordingly, Johnsen introduces the expression, "p-justifier," for any conjunction that is made up from a portion of S's evidence and that completely justifies S in believing p. Johnsen then offers the following defeasibility condition:

(iv$_7$)   if e is evidence that completely justifies S in believing p, then there is no proposition, q, such that (1) q is true, (2) the

---

[18] For extended discussion, see Shope 1979c and Chapter 3.

conjunction of e and q does not completely justify S in believing p, and (3) every p-justifier completely justifies S in believing q false. (pp. 278-279)[19]

In the Shrink-and-Grabit example (E 14), as in the case of the demented Mrs. Grabit (E 12), the evidence for p can be narrowed or "gerrymandered" without justifying any speculations about Mrs. Grabit's testimony, and condition (iv$_7$) is satisfied. Similarly, in the case of the numb pyromaniac (E 13) gerrymandering of S's evidence avoids justifying any expectations about S's perception of the ignition, and S's knowledge is preserved.

In contrast, the Pol-and-Grabit case (E 15) remains similar to the original newspaper example insofar as false beliefs about people who surround S or about other news reports cannot be excluded from the set of completely justified beliefs that S has when S is also completely justified in believing the newspaper story, no matter how one restricts the evidential base that justifies the latter belief. So on Johnsen's analysis, S's justification is indeed defeated in both examples.[20] Similarly, in the case of Tom Grabit's actual twin (E 10), q is the false statement that S could tell the difference between Tom's participation and that of other nearby possible culprits. Finally, in the case of the clever reasoner (E 6), as in other previous cases concerning Mr. Nogot, the false statement is that Mr. Nogot owns the individual car in question.

It is important to notice, however, that Johnsen's characterization of defeasibility does not require the false statement to be either part of S's evidence for p or to be directly justified by that evidence. Thus, there will be some cases where I know p but my learning that I am in error in expecting q to be false on the basis of p would undermine my justification for believing p. So Johnsen's condition for knowledge is too strong, as the following example demonstrates:

---

[19] Terence Ackerman offers a similar analysis and defends it against an objection by Ernest Sosa (Ackerman 1974).

[20] My criticism is not affected by the fact that Johnsen goes on to complicate the statement of clause (3) in order to avoid a technical objection.

(E 17) *Relator-and-Nogot*: Mr. Relator, a teacher who S knows to be generally reliable as a source of information about events at school, reports to S the information which led Mr. Relator justifiably to believe not-q_1: 'Mr. Nogot owns a Ford.' For example, Mr. Relator reports p_1: 'Mr. Nogot, one of my students, drove a Ford in front of me, solemnly affirmed that he owned it, showed me papers to that effect, and has been generally reliable in past dealings with me.' Accordingly, S knows p_1. Moreover, both Mr. Relator and S are completely justified in believing not-q_1, neither of them having any reason to suppose it is false. But it is false.

If q_1 were added to S's evidence for p_1 then S might very well no longer be justified in accepting p_1. Alternative possible explanations of the teacher's report might occur to S which require suspension of judgment as to the truth of p_1. For example, Mr. Relator might have misremembered some of the details, or might have rubbed his eyes just as Mr. Nogot gave a wink to indicate that he was only joking, or the teacher might have been inattentive or tired when glancing at the papers, which might actually have had the name of Mr. Nogot's father on them, and so forth. (Whether Mr. Relator, as opposed to S, need justifiably be subject to such doubts upon learning q_1 does not matter here.) Thus, Johnsen's analysis improperly denies that S knows p_1 in his actual situation, where S does not believe q_1.[21]

---

[21] For further criticism of Johnsen, see Olin 1970, pp. 130-132.

The Relator-Nogot example also runs counter to David Sanford's defense of the standard analysis of knowledge against Gettier-type examples (Sanford 1975). Sanford introduces the technical concept of an "intermediate conclusion": A statement q is a conclusion intermediate between e and p if and only if (1) e justifies p, (2) e justifies q, and (3) (e & not-q) justifies p to a significantly lesser degree than e justifies p (pp. 61-62). Sanford claims that Gettier-type examples violate the following epistemic principle: If one knows p on the basis of e then all the conclusions intermediate between e and p are true (p. 62). But in the Relator-Nogot example, the false proposition, 'Mr. Nogot owns a Ford,' will count as a conclusion intermediate between the description, p_1, of Mr. Nogot's reliability and behavior in front of Mr. Relator, and the evidence S has justifying S's belief in that description.

Another difficulty affecting Sanford's analysis appears when we consider his treatment of the following case:

1.45 VARIATIONS

This example could be dealt with by the following condition, which avoids defeasibility considerations altogether:[22]

(E 18)   *The Two Fords*: As in (E 1), except that Mr. Nogot was not deceiving S by his behavior and did own a Ford when he showed the certificate of ownership, etc., this morning. But, unknown to S, Nogot sold the car during the afternoon and between that time and this evening won another Ford in a raffle. This evening, S continues to believe p: 'Someone who was in the office owns a Ford.'

Sanford says that S fails to know p because of the following false intermediate conclusion:

(r)   Mr. Nogot said that he owned a Ford because he did own a Ford which he has owned continuously ever since, and the certificate which he showed is a certificate for a Ford which he has owned continuously since he showed the certificate. (p. 63)

It certainly cannot be said that S's evidence justifies r so strongly that S is completely justified in believing in Mr. Nogot's continuous ownership of the car. (In this connection, see the discussion of this example by J. H. Kress [Kress 1971, pp. 78-82].) But Sanford is speaking of justification to *some* degree (Sanford 1975, p. 61). S is justified to some degree in believing in the continuous ownership, since he knows that the typical person on a typical day does not sell his car, and perhaps we should count that as part of S's evidence in the evening that Nogot still owns a Ford.

But all we need to do in order to refute Sanford's analysis is to change the example so that it concerns Mr. Nogot's present ownership of a Hershey bar he showed S this morning and claimed that he owned. People's habits of consuming candy bars are so varied that S may surely be imagined to have no evidence for the proposition that Nogot has continuously owned the bar in question during the interim. Yet S's evidence this evening does justify to some degree the proposition, q': 'Mr. Nogot presently owns a Hershey bar.' For S may realize that people generally form habits about candy-buying and often buy the candy bars they like in quantities greater than one. But S does not know that Nogot owns a Hershey bar if the only reason it is true that he owns one is because of the single bar won in an afternoon raffle of which S is ignorant.

Of course, in this example S has general knowledge about the frequency of raffles and types of prizes at raffles which supports the false proposition, w: 'It is not true that Mr. Nogot has since this morning lost ownership of all Hershey bars he had and won some new ones in a raffle.' But neither S's evidence for w nor w itself are justified by S's evidence for q'.

[22] The condition is related to ones offered by Ernest Sosa (Sosa 1974b) and Roderick Chisholm (Chisholm 1973, p. 240; 1977, pp. 108-109). Chisholm does not discuss Johnsen's analysis, but does make a point akin to one I raised against Johnsen: Chisholm says that in a Gettier-type case, S knows his evidence e to be true, even

(iv₈)   there is some conjunction of propositions such that (1) the conjunction entails p, (2) for each conjunct, c, the set of basic propositions which makes S completely justified in believing c does not completely justify S in believing any false proposition, f, unless p also completely justifies S in believing f.[23]

But the resulting analysis may be too strong. For it entails that S fails to know in a situation Johnsen regards as involving genuine knowledge. Johnsen points out that when S knows some truth, p, and S's knowledge depends entirely upon what he has learned from a reliable source, such as a newspaper, then

> *every* p-justifier he has will include the proposition that the newspaper is reliable. But if so, then every p-justifier S has will justify S in believing [a proposition we may suppose to be false, namely,] f: the next (or nth) story I read in this newspaper will be accurate [or: if there is a next page and a story on it then its reports are accurate]. But clearly, p will in general be completely unrelated to f. . . . (Johnsen 1974, p. 281)

Let us call this case (E 19) *Additional Reports*. In it, proposition p itself, although known by S to be true, does not make S completely

---

though "whatever confers evidence upon e also confers evidence upon a false proposition," such as the false proposition that Mr. Nogot owns a Ford (Chisholm 1977, p. 108; see 1973, p. 238). Douglas Odegard objects to Chisholm's remark on the grounds that in such a case the evidence e' that confers evidence upon e involves evidence both that an informant or witness asserts what he does "and that he is reliable. If we discovered that the testimony is false, then the part of our universe [evidence?] which supports the witness's reliability would have to be changed . . . [and] e' cannot be a source of knowledge" because our discovery "would eliminate part of e' as evidence" (Odegard 1978, pp. 127-128). This overlooks the fact that a witness may have been reliable up to t but at t happens to become unreliable. Description of evidence e' refers to the period before t, even though it is evidence supporting the person's reliability at t, where t is, for example, the time that Mr. Nogot begins to tell S that he owns the Ford.

[23] When p itself is not a conjunction, we can conjoin it with any proposition that is basic for S or certain for S in order to obtain a conjunction that entails p. The point of this maneuver is to avoid having to speak of noncompound propositions as themselves (degenerate) conjunctions. For further discussion, see n. 8 to Chapter 4.

justified in believing f. So any basic propositions that make S completely justified in believing p also make S completely justified in believing a falsehood that p does not make S completely justified in believing.[24]

We shall eventually return to the issue of whether this is a genuine counterexample (see note 6 to Chapter 4). Assuming that it is genuine, it can be met by adding to (iv_8) a phrase similar to clause (2) of the Paxson and Lehrer analysis, and rewording the ending of (iv_8) so as to reintroduce defeasibility considerations:[25]

(iv_9) ... unless either (a) p also completely justifies S in believing f or (b) the conjunction of that set of basic propositions with not-f would completely justify S in believing p.

This emendation survives (E 19) because the combination of my basic evidence for the reliability of the newspaper with the fact that the next (or nth) story I shall read in it will be inaccurate (or with the fact that there is an inaccurate story on the next page) would not keep me from being completely justified in believing p. Moreover, an analysis of knowledge that includes (iv_9) remains adequate to deal with the case of Relator-and-Nogot (E 17). For in that case, p does make S completely justified in believing the false proposition, f_1:

---

[24] Ernest Sosa describes the following case:

(E 20)   *The Vain Wife*: S is a congenitally blind man and W his wife. S knows e: 'W is reliable, honest, and asserts a: "W is now looking into a mirror and W sees herself to be incredibly beautiful." ' S's basis for knowing e permits S to know p: 'Here is someone who is reliable, honest, and vain.' (Sosa 1970, pp. 65-66)

Sosa maintains that S's basis for knowing e also makes evident for S the falsehood, q: 'Here is someone who is reliable, honest, and incredibly beautiful.' But the data which the wife needs to make a reliable judgment about the first conjunct of a is significantly different from that which she needs to make one about the second conjunct. Sosa must show that this does not reduce the degree of justification of q for S himself below that of being evident, or completely justified. (Douglas Odegard's criticism of the example [Odegard 1978, p. 128] overlooks the mention in e of W's honesty and reliability.)

[25] Another possible response to the above example is mentioned in n. 3 to Chapter 4.

'Mr. Nogot owns a Ford,' and S's being completely justified in believing the conjunction of not-f_1 and S's evidence for p would keep S from being completely justified in believing p.

We shall eventually see that an analysis including (iv$_9$) is too weak. However, one aspect of (iv$_9$) may also make any such analysis too strong. For the wording of (iv$_9$) allows a possibility which may be roughly described as follows: the way in which each set of basic propositions makes S completely justified in believing the corresponding conjunct, c, is not through a path that involves f or involves S's being justified in believing f. Because of this, the way in which S is made completely justified in believing p is itself quite independent of f. Consequently, the analysis remains too strong.

It is not easy to find an example to illustrate this. One is tempted to turn to the history of science and to look for a body of evidence sufficient to make one completely justified in believing two hypotheses, p_1, and p_2, the former of which is true and the latter false. But the full statement of (iv$_9$) provides for gerrymandering the evidence. So p_2 may need to be an hypothesis of such fundamental status in S's world view that S's belief in its falsity would affect S's justification for believing p_1 mainly by making it rational for S to doubt her general orientation toward reality and her present grasp of even simple empirical truths.

Such considerations suggest the possibility of the following counterexample, which imagines a restricted form of eliminative materialism to be true.[26] Unrestricted eliminative materialism says that it is logically possible for science one day to show that human beings lack all mental states. I shall appeal to the more restricted possibility that only a large portion of what we now use as mentalistic concepts will be abandoned by future science, leaving us with a useful concept of belief but not with applicable concepts of desires, wishes, or sense experiences.[27] However, most human beings do not presently have (to put it in our contemporary vocabulary) an adequate conceptual

---

[26] For another example which shows the analysis to be too strong, see (E 36) in Chapter 3.

[27] For a defense of this portion of eliminative materialism see Shope 1979a.

scheme for describing the phenomena occurring within their bodies to which they mistakenly apply our supposedly ill-fated mentalistic concepts. So if those people were simply to cease to believe the propositions called into question by restricted eliminative materialism concerning their putatively mental phenomena, they might feel quite disoriented toward reality in general, having failed to understand what seems so obvious about their own natures. Consider:

(E 21)   *The Piece of Wax*: S is an ordinary person who knows p: 'A piece of wax is present,' upon (as we presently put it) seeing the wax. Nonetheless (granting the possibility envisaged by restricted eliminative materialism), the following proposition, q, is false: 'S is having sense experiences.' If S were to believe not-q, it would so shake S's belief that she is in touch with reality that S would not even be completely justified in believing particular truths about her material environment, such as p.

A restricted eliminative materialist may count S as knowing p even if q is false. For even though S uses the wrong vocabulary to speak of her inner states when formulating beliefs constituting part of her evidence for p, she is, according to the restricted eliminative materialist, still thinking about and referring to the inner states in question and thanks to that may still be said to know p and other truths forming 'observation statements' in scientific investigation.[28]

There is a way of evading this objection by altering (iv$_9$) in a fashion inspired by John Barker's analysis of knowing. Barker shows that many of the usual examples, including several discussed above, are compatible with an analysis containing the following condition:

(iv$_{10}$)   there is some way that any other true proposition besides p could come to be justifiably believed by S without destruction of S's original justification for believing p. (Barker 1976b, p. 303)

---

[28] See Rorty 1965; 1970 and compare Keith Donnellan's views concerning reference by means of definite descriptions (Donnellan 1966).

In spite of its appeal, we shall see below that condition (iv$_{10}$) is too strong. Nonetheless, it does point to a way in which we might amend clause (b) in (iv$_9$) by altering the latter condition so that it concludes as follows:

(iv$_{11}$)   . . . or (b') there is a way for S to become completely justified in believing the denial of f such that if S were to become completely justified in believing the denial of f in that way then the conjunction of the set of basic propositions with the denial of f would completely justify S in believing p.

This meets the example concerning the piece of wax because there is some way in which the person in that example could learn that q is false without having it undermine her justification for believing p. For she could learn the truth of q together with learning a true substitute theory and accompanying 'observational' vocabulary about the material states of humans that are presently mistaken for mental states, thereby being spared the hypothetical disorientation.

Nonetheless, both (iv$_{11}$) and (iv$_9$) turn out to be too weak, as may be seen by constructing one more variant of the Nogot example:

(E 22)   *Lucky Mr. Nogot*: This is similar to the original examples concerning Mr. Nogot, except that Mr. Nogot happens (unknown to himself and to S) to win a Ford in a lottery while he is deceiving S, and S believes p_1: 'Either Mr. Nogot owns a Ford or Mr. Nogot does not own any blue Ford that he drove in front of S.'

The basis that makes S completely justified in believing p_1 does so because it makes S completely justified in believing the first disjunct in p_1. Thus, it makes S completely justified in believing the false proposition, f_1: 'Mr. Nogot owns the Ford he drove in front of S.' So clause (a) in (iv$_{11}$) and (iv$_9$) fails to be satisfied, since p_1 does not completely justify S in believing f_1. But clauses (b) and (b') also fail to be satisfied. For, regardless of the way in which S becomes completely justified in believing the denial of f_1, the combination of that denial with S's previous basis for believing p_1 does completely justify S in believing the second disjunct in p_1 and thus in believing p_1. So defeasibility analyses resting on either (iv$_{11}$) or (iv$_9$) incorrectly treat S as knowing p_1.[29]

1.46 DEFEASIBILITY CONDITIONS CONCERNING ONE'S ACTUAL JUSTIFICATION

A number of defeasibility analyses, including Barker's, utilize conditionals that consider the effect that false propositions would have on the justification S *actually* has for believing p, rather than considering merely whether S would have *a* justification for believing p if the false proposition were added to his evidence (as in [E 22], where S would have a new route for justification of belief in p_1).

1.461 Swain

For example, Marshall Swain has shown that many Gettier-type examples can be avoided if we consider "what would happen if a man were to become justified in believing to be true *all* of those true propositions that he is in fact justified in believing to be false," and if we require that some part of S's actual justification would survive under such conditions and remain adequate to justify S's believing p without depending on S's acquiring any further information (Swain 1974, pp. 15, 22, 24-25).[30]

Not only is the Shrink-and-Grabit case (E 14) a counterexample to this analysis, but Swain has committed the conditional fallacy. Let f be a false statement that S is justified in believing true. Suppose S also knows p: 'S believes f.' When the antecedent of Swain's conditional is satisfied, S's belief in f gets *replaced* by a belief in

---

[29] Another example which (iv$_9$) would fail to rule out as constituting knowledge is a case described by Robert Audi, which is like the case of Judy's mole (E 52), mentioned below in Chapter 5, Section 2, but where S has also been given reasons to believe in the details of the strange accident involved which S should accept but stubbornly does not (Audi 1980, p. 91).

[30] This is an improvement on Swain's analysis in Swain 1972b, which was criticized in Paxson 1974. (See also Chapter 5, n. 32.)

the denial of f. Obviously, S would thereby lose his actual justification for believing p.[31]

1.462 Klein

In his recent defeasibility analysis, Peter Klein uses the term "defeater" to mean any true proposition whose conjunction with S's actual evidence for p would fail to justify S in believing p. Klein speaks of a defeater, d, as a "misleading defeater" if such a failure

---

[31] These are more satisfactory counterexamples than Hector-Neri Castañeda's case of the cross-wired rememberer (E 65), for reasons explained in n. 25 to Chapter 5, below.

Klein says that Swain's analysis incorrectly allows S to know in the case of Tom Grabit's actual twin (E 10). But Swain can reply that it is the following false statement, which S is justified in believing to be true, which defeats S's justification in that example: 'S was able to distinguish Tom's participation in the theft from that of other nearby people who had an opportunity to steal the book.' See Swain's response to criticism by R. B. Scott (Scott 1976; Swain 1976).

Perhaps we could save Swain's analysis from my counterexample if we could show that all introspection is retrospection and that one never knows anything about one's own simultaneous mental states. So, when S knows at t, 'S believes f,' the latter proposition should be rephrased, 'S believes f at t-Δt.' Then satisfaction of the antecedent of Swain's conditional would, indeed, not replace at t or at t-Δt any belief in f with belief in the denial of f.

Swain says that his conditional requires us to consider "how things might change for S if his body of evidence were purged of all false members, each of these being replaced by its denial" (Swain 1974, p. 22). This certainly sounds like replacing one belief with a contradictory belief. However, perhaps Swain means to suppose only an epistemic rather than doxastic change, so that in my example in the text S's belief in the false proposition would remain but its justified status alter. (Strictly speaking, Swain should, if that is his intention, not use in the antecedent of his conditional the phrase, "were to become justified in believing" but instead, "were to become such that S would be justified in believing.") It is worth noting that even under that interpretation Swain commits the conditional fallacy concerning my knowing p: 'I am (not) justified in believing q,' when q is some false (true) proposition which I do not suspect is false (true). For satisfying the antecedent of Swain's conditional would put me in a situation where p is false, and it is not clear that my justification for believing p could survive.

In order to avoid this result, Swain might maintain that I never know my simultaneous epistemic states and that the most I could know at t is p': 'I was justified in believing f at t-Δt.' Then satisfaction of Swain's antecedent at t would not alter any belief at t-Δt. However, that move raises the question how it could have *any* epistemically relevant effect on p' to add at t *any* justified beliefs which S lacked at t-Δt.

would occur only because d would justify S in believing some false proposition. Accordingly, in order for S to know p, Klein requires that every defeater of S's justification for believing p be a misleading defeater (Klein 1976, p. 809).

For example, in the case of the demented Mrs. Grabit (E 12), the proposition that Mrs. Grabit gave her testimony is at most a misleading defeater. For if it defeats, it does so only because it justifies S in believing the false proposition, v, that was articulated as the content of Mrs. Grabit's testimony. So in that example, S retains knowledge. (The same may be said regarding the piece of wax example [E 21].) Whereas, in the case of Tom Grabit's actual twin (E 10), there is a nonmisleading defeater, d_1: 'Tom has an identical twin brother who was in the library near the time of the theft.'

Klein argues (Klein 1980) that his analysis serves to clarify the concept of a restorable justification utilized by Barker in defeasibility condition (iv$_{10}$), thereby rendering Barker's analysis of knowing superfluous. According to Klein, the cases where S's original justification is merely defeated by d but nonetheless restorable are those cases where there is a proposition, r, which entails the denial of the proposition upon which d depends in order to defeat, i.e., are those cases where d is a nonmisleading defeater in Klein's sense (p. 84).

But Klein has overlooked the possibility that the proposition which destroys the old justification itself creates a new justification for S's old belief, as in the case of Lucky Mr. Nogot (E 22), which shows that Klein's analysis is too weak. Moreover, Klein's analysis is too strong because there can be defeaters in his sense that are not misleading yet do not prevent knowing, as in the following example:

(E 23)   *Klein-and-Grabit*: This example resembles the case of Tom Grabit's actual twin (E 10), except that while he is observing Tom's theft, S momentarily entertains proposition d_1 (see above) because S has just finished reading Klein's paper at the library, and S takes note of the fact that S does not believe d_1. That is, S knows p: 'S refrains from believing d_1.'

Here, d_1 is a defeater, for if it were added to the evidence (if any) that S has for believing p, that is, if S were also to believe d_1, then S would not be justified in believing p. Yet d_1 is not a misleading defeater. For it would not justify S in believing some false proposition to be true. So Klein's analysis incorrectly denies that S knows p.[32]

1.463 Barker

This example does not run counter to Barker's analysis of knowledge, based upon defeasibility condition (iv_{10}). Indeed, Barker shows that his analysis, which treats knowledge as "of its very nature indefinitely extendible," is able to handle a variety of examples (Barker 1976b, pp. 303ff.). For instance, the case of Tom Grabit's actual twin (E 10) fails to yield knowledge because S's original justification has to be rendered inadequate in itself upon S's acquisition of a justified belief in the presence of the twin.[33] Whereas, in the case of the demented Mrs. Grabit (E 12), S's coming to know of her testimony need not destroy the adequacy of S's previous justification, provided that S learns of it while simultaneously learning of her disturbed motivation for speaking. Again, we might grant that in the Klein-and-Grabit example (E 23) S's original justification for believing p would not be *destroyed* merely by S's coming to justifiably believe d_1 and thereby ceasing to believe p; although S's previous justification for believing p would thereby be *removed*. Finally, even without a precise definition of when an original justification is restored, it seems obvious that in the case of Lucky Mr. Nogot (E 22) S only acquires a new justification for belief.

However, Barker's claim that knowledge is indefinitely extendible is at best true of knowledge as Karl Popper prefers to view it, namely, as a set of propositions in socially constructed portions of a true

---

[32] Steven Levy's criticisms (Levy 1978) have been adequately rebutted by Klein (Klein 1979).

[33] Notwithstanding the fact that, as Barker indicates, even *more* information, such as that concerning the precise movements of the twin, could be used *in combination* with all the preceding information "in such a way as to 're-justify' the belief that Tom stole the book" (Barker 1976b, p. 305).

explanatory framework of propositions. It surely is not true of knowledge taken as a state of a knowing subject. For the following example shows that Barker's analysis is too strong because it commits the second version of the conditional fallacy:

(E 24)   *The Executed Mathematician*: S is a mathematician who, because he knows that he is about to be executed, also knows *p*: '*S* will never justifiably believe the correct answer to the question, "Is Goldbach's conjecture true?" '

There is no way in which the mathematician could come to believe *justifiably* the *correct* answer to that question (e.g., by having the proof flash through his mind as the poison pellets drop) without having his justification for believing *p* be destroyed even before his life.[34]

1.47 LEHRER'S CONDITION CONCERNING DOUBTFULNESS

It is fitting to conclude this portion of our survey of defeasibility theories by returning to the indefatigable defeasibilist, Keith Lehrer, whose most recent defeasibility condition is the following:

(iv$_{12}$)   there is no false proposition, *f*, such that if *f* were doubtful for *S* then *p* would not be evident for *S*,

where *f* is doubtful for *S* if and only if it would be more reasonable for *S* to decline *f* than to accept *f*, and declining *f* is defined as not accepting *f* but leaving open the question whether to accept the denial of *f* (Lehrer 1979).

Unfortunately, this is no more successful in avoiding the condi-

---

[34] This example suffices to refute the defeasibility conditions advanced by Risto Hilpinen (Hilpinen 1971, pp. 31-32) and Douglas Odegard (Odegard 1978, p. 123).

Robert Audi argues that Barker's analysis is too weak to rule out knowledge in some cases where *S*'s justified, true belief is "simply not justified in the right sort of way to qualify as knowledge" (Audi 1980, p. 79). He offers an example where *S* believes she will lose in a 1,000-ticket lottery. But one might question whether *S*'s belief in this example has the degree of justification Barker is demanding. A more relevant counterexample would be the type to be discussed in Chapter 3, where *S* is not, as Ernest Sosa puts it, in a position to know.

tional fallacy than any of Lehrer's other analyses. Let p be the proposition, 'S accepts f,' where f is false and S knows p. We can easily suppose that if it were more reasonable for S to decline f than to accept it, then S would realize this and not accept f, so that p would not be evident for S.[35]

Perhaps the failure of so many defeasibility analyses[36] provides good reason to suppose that the defeasibility approach to the analysis of knowledge is itself destined to be defeated beyond restoration.

---

[35] Perhaps Lehrer is attempting to deal with this difficulty when he adds that the subjunctive conditional "may be eliminated in terms of current possible worlds analyses of such conditionals provided that consideration of possible worlds is restricted to those in which f is doubtful for S in a way that is the least unfavorable to . . . [p] being evident for S" (p. 78). But Lehrer does not discuss objections to current possible worlds analyses, and leaves the sense of "unfavorable" unexplained. One wonders whether applying these considerations to my example will involve law-countervening speculations, since f is not itself evidence for or against p.

Since this manuscript was finished, an even more recent discussion by Lehrer has appeared in which he explains condition (iv$_{12}$) in possible worlds terminology as follows:

> For any f that is false, there is a world w minimally different from the actual world a so that 'f is doubtful for S' is true in w, there is no world w^* minimally different from a so that 'f is doubtful for S' is true in w^* such that it is more reasonable for S to accept p in w^* than in w, and S is completely justified in accepting p in w. (Lehrer 1981, p. 92)

But this does not rule out the counterexample I have described, which involves no obvious changes in S's cognitive dispositions other than the required alteration of S's believing f to a state of f's being doubtful for S. S's ordinary disposition to be aware of S's conscious cognitive states is retained.

In this work, Lehrer does note several shortcomings in the earlier analysis presented in *Knowledge*, including the one I pointed out by means of example (E 15) (cf. Lehrer 1981, pp. 83-84). He also argues that Carter's emendation, which proposed dropping all false beliefs in forming the verific alternative, is insufficient because doing so in some cases where S fails to know would unblock a line of justification for believing that S had lacked because of one of his actual false beliefs (cf. pp. 84-85).

[36] I shall not consider the complex defeasibility analysis advanced by Ernest Sosa in an early paper (Sosa 1964). A helpful exegesis is provided by Ralph Slaght (Slaght 1977, pp. 55-57). Slaght defends the analysis against Brian Skyrms's criticisms, but agrees with those provided by Lehrer and by Sosa himself, who later replaced the analysis with one considered in Chapter 3.

2. OTHER CONDITIONALS CONCERNING JUSTIFICATION AND BELIEF

2.1 *Harman on Knowing by Inference*

The discussion of knowledge provided by Gilbert Harman in *Thought* (Harman 1973) includes a subjunctive conditional concerning warrant. However, we must stop short of labeling Harman a defeasibility theorist in sense D″, for he attempts no *analysis* of knowing, and expresses a suspicion that the latter concept will be needed in order to clarify the concepts of warrant and justification, rather than the reverse (Harman 1976). However, since philosophers who do not share this suspicion might be tempted to adopt Harman's subjunctive conditional as part of their own analyses of knowing, it is important for us to make note of its limitations.

Harman arrives at his conditional in the course of attempting to deal with Gettier-type examples by means of the following principle: Reasoning that essentially involves false conclusions, intermediate or final, cannot give one knowledge (Harman 1973, p. 47). Thus, Harman would insist that in the case of the clever reasoner (E 6) *S* believes, perhaps unconsciously, some false statement involved in the way *S* arrives at his belief that someone in the class owns a Ford. Since it is highly implausible to say that the clever reasoner unconsciously believes the very statement he says that he refrains from believing, namely, *q*: 'Mr. Nogot owns a Ferrari,' Harman might say that the crucial false belief is instead of a type which Harman insists is included as a conjunct in the conclusion of every inductive inference, namely: 'There is no undermining evidence to this conclusion' (p. 154). Perhaps Harman would say that the falsity of *q* in this example is undermining evidence.[37]

However, Harman realizes that sometimes one succeeds in gaining knowledge even though one's inferences involve some false initial

---

[37] In an earlier paper, Harman required that "no further evidence exists that would, if known, cast doubt on one's conclusion" (Harman 1968, p. 173n). But that failed to allow for merely misleading defeaters.

premises or false intermediate conclusions used as bases for further steps in one's reasoning. In order to say that one's reasoning does not *essentially* involve these false propositions, Harman suggests as a necessary condition for a person, say, Mary, to come to know something by inference

> . . . not that the actual premises of the inference (everything Mary believes ahead of time) be known to be true but only that the inference remain warranted when the set of antecedent beliefs is limited to those Mary antecedently knows to be true and continues to know after the inference. (p. 170)

This appears to advance the following conditional as a necessary condition for S's coming to know p by inference i at t:

(HC) If (a) S were to have only those true beliefs S actually knows to be true prior to t and still knows to be true after S's actual inference i, and (b) S were to make a (substitute) inference to the conclusion(s) of inference i, then (c) S's (substitute) inference would be warranted.

The reference in (c) to warranted inference is, on Harman's account of inference,[38] quite close to saying that S would be justified in believing the conclusion(s) of the (substitute) inference. Thus, some defeasibility theorists might attempt to adapt Harman's conditional to their purposes by replacing talk about knowledge in (a) with talk of completely justified believing.

Michael Williams charges that Harman cannot deal properly with the following example:

(E 25) *Visual Fire*: Upon seeing a candle, S knows that it is there. But S arrives at this belief by relying upon the erroneous ancient view that we see objects by bombarding them with visual fire. So S arrives at his belief because of the inference:

---

[38] Harman says that inference is "a change that can be described simply by mentioning what beliefs are given up and what new beliefs are added" (p. 169). "Our 'premises' are all our antecedent beliefs; our 'conclusion' is our total resulting view" (p. 159).

Things look to S the way they do because S is bombarding a candle with visual fire. (Williams 1978, p. 260; cf. Nelson 1978, pp. 322-323)

According to Williams, Harman cannot say that no false propositions are "essentially involved" in S's reasoning, if that means that S's inference would be warranted were false propositions deleted. For deleting the proposition about visual fire would destroy the inference. Alternatively, if Harman says that S knows because some more satisfactory inference might have been made, the same could unfortunately be said of some Gettier-type examples (Williams 1978, pp. 260-261).

Between these two responses, however, lies a position adopted by Adam Morton when discussing a similar example in which an ancient mariner knows his latitude from computations based on observations of heavenly bodies, but thinks about the connections of the two in terms of ancient, false astronomical theories. Morton allows gerrymandering of the evidence and of S's responses to it down to "a less extensive process that consists of little more than the calculations behind the determination of position" (Morton 1977, p. 60). Morton remarks that in that respect, "the captain has gotten his result by a method that is reliable" (p. 57). Thus, gerrymandering in the previous example might yield: Things look the way they do to S because there is a candle in front of S.

Moreover, just as the captain's method is not reliable in circumstances where slips are made in calculations, or where observations of heavenly bodies are due in part to bizarre air disturbances, so the 'method' in the visual fire example might be unreliable when applied in a Gettierized perceptual situation. In such a situation, there is undermining evidence, namely, the fact that circumstances are not sufficient for reliable application of the method.

However, even if this defense of Harman could be satisfactorily fleshed-out, the following example shows that HC involves the conditional fallacy, as does the analogous condition in which (a) speaks of justified belief rather than knowledge:

(E 26)   *The Safari*: *S* is on a vacation safari and falsely believes *f*:
'*S* sees a dinosaur moving along the edge of a high plateau.'
S responds by coming falsely to believe *g*: 'Someone now
has a true belief concerning the present whereabouts of
dinosaurs now living on land.' Thanks to this, *S* knows *p*:
'*S* believes *g*.' (Shope 1978, p. 411)

Harman is committed to speaking of *p* as part of what *S* has
inferred.[39] But his conditional incorrectly prevents us from saying
that *S* knows *p*. For satisfaction of (a) in HC removes the false
'premise' *f* (or *g*), and the resulting substitute inference to 'conclusion' *p* is not warranted by *S*'s remaining true beliefs.

2.2 *Harman on Reasons Supporting Belief*

Harman also utilizes a conditional in order to clarify the relation
between *S*'s reasons for believing *p* and *S*'s knowing *p*. We shall
see in Chapter 5 that some of the difficulties facing Harman's account
on this point also arise for certain analyses of knowing which incorporate similar conditionals.

Harman wishes to deal with the fact that *S* may have reasons for
believing *p* which constitute reasons that give *S* knowledge that *p*,
even in cases where the reasons within some subset were acquired
after *S*'s initial inference that *p*. Whereas some of the philosophers
to be considered later attempt to describe the connections of reasons
with belief in *p* as special types of causal connections, Harman
intends to provide what he calls a "functional" rather than causal
account of these connections. Harman maintains that to explain why
someone believes something is like explaining why a nondeterministic automaton is in a particular state, where automata are sets of
states functionally related to one another and to input and output.

[39] Since Harman speaks of inference as a change, and since it may by psycholog-
ically implausible to suppose that *S* comes to believe *p'*: '*S* believes *f*,' later than *S*
comes to believe *f*, I have needed to add to the example *S*'s belief in *g* as a belief
which might more plausibly be supposed to occur after belief in *f* and allow us to
speak of *S* as making an inference to belief in *p*, even if the latter belief turns out to
be simultaneous with *S*'s belief in *g*.

To specify an automaton as nondeterministic is "to specify the possible states of the automaton, possible input, and possible output, and what output can follow any given state and input" without employing causal language in the specification (Harman 1970, pp. 848, 850).

So when Harman wishes to allow that someone may have several sets of reasons supporting a belief, he avoids construing this as a case of causal overdetermination or of multiple causation. Instead, he offers the following suggestion:

> Other things equal, if a person believes a conclusion for certain reasons and becomes doubtful about those reasons, he becomes doubtful about the conclusion. "Other things equal" is meant to rule out the possibility . . . in which one acquires new reasons as one comes to doubt the old. The phrase must also be used to rule out [the analogue of] overdetermination and the analogue of multiple causation. In case there are several sets of reasons for which someone believes something, he must become doubtful about all sets before becoming doubtful about his belief. The relevance of any of the sets is this: if he became doubtful of all the other sets, his belief would rest crucially on that set so that, if he should then become doubtful of it, he will become doubtful of his belief, other things equal. Any set of reasons supports someone's belief in a way that a subset of its legs may support a table. (pp. 847-848)

Thus, Harman may be proposing the following subjunctive conditional[40] as an account of what it is for several sets of reasons each independently to support S's believing p:

(C)   For any one of the sets, r, if (A) S were doubtful of the reasons in all the sets except r and were still to believe p, then (B) both (i) other things equal S would not doubt that belief and (ii) if S were doubtful of the reasons in set r then other things equal S would be doubtful of his belief in p.

---

[40] A slightly different conditional that Harman may be proposing is also considered in Shope 1978.

In specifying when other things are not equal Harman has allowed for the analogues of causal contexts involving overdetermination and multiple causation. But he has overlooked the analogue of another type of causal context, where absence of some of the actual causes of an event would have been accompanied by occurrence of a new factor that would have prevented the remaining actual causes from bringing about the event.[41] Just such an analogue occurs in the following example, which shows that Harman's understanding of condition C renders it too strong a condition for a set of reasons to support a belief:

(E 27)   *Loss of Intellectual Nerve*: S has several sets of reasons for believing p: 'There is no God.' He presents these in a lecture and goes home. However, the lecture was put together in haste and fatigue in order to fill in for an ill colleague, and S has never before carefully scrutinized the reasons for his habitual atheism. Nor does he regard philosophy of religion as at all his field. If, as S was about to present his reasons to the class, he had suddenly doubted all the sets of reasons but one, this would have led to a heightened sense of fallibility, and S would not have regarded the reasons in the remaining set as having any *force*. That set accordingly would not have supported S's atheism. (Shope 1978, pp. 408-409)

Because Harman has committed the second version of the conditional fallacy, he is required to deny that S actually has these sets of reasons for believing p. We shall see in Chapter 5 that analogous difficulties arise concerning Marshall Swain's characterization of causal relations between reasons and a belief based upon those reasons.

---

[41] For example, it may be that if the legs in one of the sets supporting an old table had begun to fall off, this would have led someone who was in the process of restoring the table to pick it up in order to turn it over for repairs, thereby canceling the support of the remaining legs. Yet in actuality, no legs collapsed and he did not pick up the table.

3.

Additions to Standard Analyses II: Limitations on the Presence of Falsehoods in Justification

There is no way of proving that every possible exploration along the paths considered in the previous chapter is doomed to reach a dead end. But the stumbling blocks that have been encountered call for serious investigation of another path. It is an alternative that rules out certain roles for false propositions in a full account of a justification of proposition p which is relevant to S's believing that proposition.

1. DREHER ON EVIDENCE

John Dreher has attempted to develop this approach to the Gettier problem by presuming that a standard analysis of knowing employs the phrase, "justified belief," to mean believing on good evidence, in a sense of "evidence" in which there can be no such thing as false evidence (Dreher 1974, pp. 435-436). Improving upon Dreher's wording, we can at least agree that there can be no such thing as a false proposition describing the evidence for something.

Thus, the false proposition, f_1: 'Mr. Nogot owns a Ford (Ferrari),' cannot be—or cannot describe—good evidence for proposition p_1: 'Someone in the office (class) owns a Ford (Ferrari).' Letting e_1 describe the evidence concerning Mr. Nogot's behavior (including his general past reliability), Dreher points out that the conjunction of e_1 and f_1 also cannot describe evidence for p_1, since that conjunction is false. Thus the only remaining candidate to describe evidence for p_1 is e_1. But, Dreher observes, if e_1 is good evidence for p_1 then e_1 is good evidence for p_1 *only* because e_1 is good evidence for f_1, and e_1 does not "directly" support p_1 in the way in which facts sometimes support disjunctions without supporting either disjunct (cf. p. 437). Dreher claims that the falsity of f_1 prevents e_1 from describing evidence for p_1, even though the teacher, who does not know that f_1 is false, may mistakenly think that e_1 describes good evidence for p_1. Dreher concludes that Gettier-type examples fail to be counterexamples to the traditional analysis of knowledge as justified, true belief. For in such examples, the person lacks good evidence for what he believes and is not in the relevant sense justified in believing it.

Such a conclusion is, I believe, too extreme, and many philosophers have thought it unexceptionable to regard e_1 as describing good evidence for p_1. Nonetheless, Dreher's approach contains a worthwhile insight when it attempts to rule out certain roles for falsehoods in relation to the justification of what S believes. However, it is not clear from Dreher's own remarks how to formulate a general requirement for a true proposition, e, to describe good evidence for another proposition, h, in order to be able to deal with all Gettier-type examples. Let us consider a number of possibilities:

(1) It would be too strong to require that there be no false proposition, f, such that e describes good evidence for h thanks to describing good evidence for f. Suppose that a scientist, who is looking at a measuring instrument that she knows to be a generally reliable source of information about a certain range of phenomena, realizes that e_1 is true: 'The instrument is showing reading R on its meter.' This may provide her with evidence that a certain phenomenon is present. But since she can see that this phenomenon is in fact not present, e_1 also allows her to know that h_1 is true: 'The instrument is not in working order.' Here, e_1 describes good evidence for h_1 because it describes evidence for a falsehood.

Some philosophers might object that when a measuring instrument is out of order its readings no longer serve as evidence concerning the range of phenomena that it normally measures. However, this issue would not arise concerning the following example:

(E 28)   *Mr. Spotter*: S receives a report from Mr. Spotter, who S
         knows to be a generally reliable observer regarding a certain
         range of phenomena, that Mr. Spotter looked at a phenom-
         enon in this range and observed some proposition, f_2, to be
         true of that phenomenon. However, other overwhelming
         evidence shows S that f_2 is false, and partly because of this,
         S knows h_2: 'Either Mr. Spotter did not look carefully or
         he did not pay special attention to what he saw.'[1]

Thanks to the fact that Mr. Spotter's report is some good evidence
for what S knows to be false, S knows h_2. The mere fact that Mr.
Spotter did not look carefully or with special attention is not enough
to make his report cease to be some good evidence in support of f_2.
For the range of phenomena about which Mr. Spotter is a generally
reliable observer may include many instances where he can accurately
report what occurs after a mere glance, while paying no more than
ordinary attention to what is before him. Yet when his report does
err, h_2 may provide S with the best explanation of why S is in
possession of misleading evidence.

(2) Someone might object that in the above example it is not *only*
because S has some good evidence a falsehood that S has good
evidence for h_2. For S also has good evidence for h_2 consisting in
the fact that what Mr. Spotter claims to have seen did not occur.
Should we then take Dreher's general requirement to be that there
is no false proposition, f, such that part of the explanation of why
e describes good evidence for h is the fact that e describes good
evidence for f? This requirement is also too strong. For it is not
satisfied by S's knowledge that h_3 is true: 'Someone is providing S
with good but misleading evidence that h_2 is true.'

(3) It would be too strong to require that a full, correct explanation
of why e describes good evidence for h can be given without mentioning any false proposition. For the false proposition h_2 does need

---

[1] This example, and most of the contents of the present section, appeared in Shope
1979c.

to be mentioned in order to give a full, correct explanation of why e_2 describes good evidence for h_2.

(4) If we only require that some correct statement (not necessarily a full, correct explanation) of why e describes good evidence for h can be given without mentioning any false proposition, then the requirement becomes useless. For one could purport that in the case of the clever reasoner (E 6) what makes S's evidence good evidence for the proposition, 'Someone in the class owns a Ferrari,' is that it is good evidence for some (unmentioned) proposition entailing that someone in the class owns a Ferrari. The requirement would not show why this is an improper claim.

(5) Perhaps it would be useful to require that a full, correct explanation of why e describes good evidence for h can be given without *asserting* any false proposition.[2] However, this will not allow us to deal with a clever reasoner who refuses to accept the false proposition, f_3: 'Mr. Nogot owns a Ferrari,' and who merely includes the following conjunct, c, in his explanation:

'Proposition e_3 (which describes Mr. Nogot's behavior and past general reliability) describes good evidence for h_4: 'Someone in the class owns a Ferrari,' because e_3 describes good evidence for f_3 and f_3 entails h_4.'

Notice that in asserting c the clever reasoner does not assert the false proposition f_3. Even if he does thereby assert the proposition that e_3 describes good evidence for h_4, and even if such an assertion should be false, the point of the requirement was to show why such an assertion is false, and this has not been done.

(6) Thus, we might be led to the following version of Dreher's requirement: There is some correct explanation of why e describes good evidence for h that either (A) has the form: 'e describes good

---

[2] Possibilities (i) and (v) were obliquely raised in a personal communication from Lehrer to Harman in which Lehrer suggested that we need to consider whether S would be able to completely justify S's belief in q without appealing to any false statement or to any statement that could only be "shown to support" q by "reasoning through" a false statement (Harman 1966, pp. 245-246).

evidence for x and x entails h,' where x is true; or (B) has the form: 'e describes good evidence for h because e describes good evidence for x and x describes good evidence for h,' where x is true.

Unfortunately, there is a defect in the phrasing of (A). This may be illustrated by an example where x is the proposition, 'Someone in the class owns a Ferrari,' and h_5 is the proposition, 'Either someone in the class owns a Ferrari or Brown is in Barcelona.' Suppose that S claims that his evidence concerning Mr. Nogot's behavior and reliability is good evidence for h_5 because it is good evidence for x and x entails h_5. The present wording of Dreher's requirement would not give a way of showing why this is an improper claim. For x is indeed true.

A similar defect occurs in (B), as may be seen by recalling the case of Relator-Nogot (E 17). Let e_4 describe the fact that S receives from the generally reliable Mr. Relator his report of Mr. Nogot's past reliability and recent conduct, and let x be that description of Mr. Nogot's reliability and conduct. If S claims to know h_4 to be true: 'Someone in the class owns a Ferrari,' the wording of (B) does not show why it is improper to say that e_4 describes good evidence for h_4 because e_4 describes good evidence for x and x describes good evidence for h_4.

Thus, if the type of approach we have been discussing is to help us deal with all Gettier-type cases, it will need to be formulated so as to generate a regress at each point of an explanation of the justified status of various beliefs and propositions, so as to expose at some point of the regress an improper reliance on a falsehood.

2. Sosa on Trees of Knowledge and Epistemic Explanations

Ernest Sosa attempts to construct the proper type of regress by means of a sequence of factors which explain why various propositions are evident for S. This sequence focuses simultaneously on issues about justification (in hopes of solving the Gettier problem) and on issues about one's "being in a position to know" (which takes account, among other things, of the social aspects of knowing) (Sosa 1974a). For, according to Sosa, philosophers should no longer interchange the phrases, "justified belief," and "evident belief," when discussing the justification condition in a standard analysis of S's knowing x. Instead, we should admit that when the condition requires that x be evident for S, "*two* conditions must be satisfied: (i) that S be rationally justified in believing x, and (ii) that S be in a position to know whether x is true" (p. 118). In addition, we must expand the statement of the justification condition so that it entails the existence of the proper type of regress concerning what is evident. The regress will, according to Sosa, be constituted by the existence of a 'tree of knowledge,' so that the standard analysis should be modified as follows:

S knows x if and only if
  (1) x,
  (2) S believes x, and
  (3) there is a tree of knowledge for S and the
      proposition x. (p. 122)

A tree of knowledge for S and the proposition x is defined by Sosa as beginning with a proposition, p_1, of the form: 'x is evident for S.' The next member of the sequence forming the tree is any set of propositions which offer an "epistemic explanation" of the truth of p_1. This explanation will be a set, I, of propositions $\{p_{11}, \ldots, p_{1n}\}$ such that the conjunction of the members of I entails p_1 not by itself but in combination with true epistemic principles (which do not by themselves entail p_1) (p. 121). In this sense, we may say that the joint truth of the members of I makes p_1 true.

Any member of I will be (a) a proposition whose truth helps to make it true that proposition x is something S is justified in believing, or (b) a proposition whose truth helps to make it true that S is in a position to know whether x is true. (We may leave open the possibility that some propositions are of both types.) Within these groups of propositions there is a further subdivision according to whether a given proposition describes other propositions as ones S is justified in believing or in a position to know, or fails to describe other propositions in these ways. When it does describe other propositions in one of these ways, the given proposition within set I contributes to the generation of portions of the next set, II, in the sequence that Sosa constructs, and we may say that the given proposition in I is an ''S-epistemic proposition,'' in the following sense:

> *S-epistemic propositions*: of these (i) some are to the effect that some other proposition x has some epistemic status relative to S (i.e., to the effect that S believes x and how reasonably); and (ii) others are to the effect that S is in a position to know whether a certain proposition is true. (i) and (ii) are varieties of ''positive S-epistemic propositions.'' Logical compounds of such propositions are also S-epistemic, but no other propositions are S-epistemic. (p. 120)

When a member, p_{ij}, of set I is S-epistemic, then the next set, II, in the sequence of sets which Sosa constructs contains as at least some of its members, propositions $p_{ij1}, \ldots, p_{ijm}$, whose joint truth makes p_{ij} true, i.e., provides an epistemic explanation in the above sense of the truth of p_{ij}. Subsequent sets in the sequence are constructed in an analogous fashion until we reach a set none of whose members is S-epistemic.

2.1 *Terminal Nodes*

The relations of the aspects of such a tree of knowledge may be illustrated by a diagram such as the following, fashioned after one offered by Sosa:

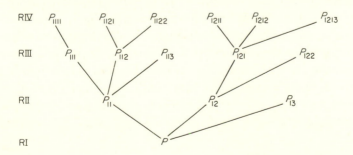

Suppose that this diagrams the beginning of a tree of knowledge which continues to grow beyond what is shown at the top of the diagram. The first four "ranks" of the full tree, I, II, III, IV, are the sets of propositions diagrammed to the right of the Roman numerals for those ranks. The bottom rank has as its only member proposition p_1: 'x is evident for S,' diagrammed by "P." The second rank is the set of true propositions whose truth makes it true that p is evident for S, i.e., makes p_1 true in the sense of providing an epistemic explanation of its truth.

Branches of the tree continue to grow only beyond those members (call them "nodes") that are S-epistemic propositions. Thus, the propositions that are diagrammed above by "P_{13}," "P_{113}" and "P_{122}" are shown as not being S-epistemic. For example, if S knows x: 'The tie is red,' simply by seeing the tie in front of him and knowing from its red appearance that it is red, then "P" diagrams the proposition, 'It is evident for S that the tie is red,' and the terminal node diagrammed by "P_{13}" would be a true conjunction of propositions entailing, among other things, that S is not red-green colorblind (where the latter proposition presumably helps to epistemically explain why S is justified in believing that the tie is red or why S is in a position to know whether the tie is red). Because the portion of the tree extending beyond rank IV is not shown, the diagram does not indicate whether or not the various propositions in rank IV are S-epistemic.

The diagram shows p_{11} and p_{12} as propositions of rank II that are not terminal nodes and are therefore S-epistemic propositions. If one of these is a proposition of type (i) then there is need to show in the diagramming of the next rank something that makes it true that such a proposition has the degree of justification it has for S, that is, there is a need to show the (true) "successors" of the proposition (which are diagrammed as connected to it by lines). Should the proposition in question in rank I instead be of type (ii), then the diagram will show as its successors on the next rank a set of true propositions whose joint truth makes it true that S is in a position to know that proposition. If the proposition in question is a logical compound of propositions of types (i) or (ii), then the diagram will show as its successors some true propositions the joint truth of which suffices to make the logically compound proposition true.

2.2 Being in a Position to Know

Sosa's use of the phrase, "being in a position to know," is not an opening in his analysis for circularity, for the phrase is intended to be understood by its role in a list of true epistemic principles. Sosa purports to describe only some principles in such a list: (1) One is not in a position to know x if (because of substandard performance in the use of one's cognitive equipment or because of defects in one's cognitive equipment) one is prevented from acquiring crucial information that a normal inquirer in the epistemic community would acquire in that situation; (2) One is not in a position to know x if one lacks[3] crucial information generally known to those in the epistemic community who have taken an epistemic stand on the question whether x (counting suspension of judgment as one way of taking an epistemic stand) (p. 119).

Thus, in our previous illustration where a normal person knows that the tie is red by seeing it in the usual way, some of the conjuncts in the proposition diagrammed by "P_{13}" will rule out cognitive defects of the type covered by epistemic principle (1), thereby helping to assure that S's cognitive equipment is adequate for a judgment on the question whether the tie is red. Sosa does not require that this conjunct, nor the one we considered earlier, c: 'S is not red-green colorblind,' are justifiably believed by S nor even that S believes them. This detail of Sosa's account is appropriate, since a child might know that the tie is red but be too unsophisticated to have a concept of his cognitive equipment's being adequate for the question at hand in the manner indicated by (1) or too unsophisticated to have the concept of red-green colorblindness. Thus, some philosophers speak of the conjuncts in question as propositions articulating back-

---

[3] For discussion of a modification Sosa introduced into principle (2), see Chapter 4, Section 2.1, below.

ground conditions required for knowledge, which need not be believed by the knower.[4]

However, in failing to place any further restrictions upon the conjuncts in terminal nodes, such as c, Sosa opens his analysis to counterexamples involving social aspects of the situation related to those nodes. Consider the following counterexample:

(E 29) *The Red Tie (Version One)*: S sees a tie in front of him at close range in broad daylight and responds by judging p: 'The tie is red.' However, S happens to be one of those who have recently undergone eye examinations in a clinic and is awaiting the results, never having had his vision tested before. S has just read the generally reliable town newspaper and has noticed that it contains a list purporting to be a report of those found during the testing to have defective vision and that it reports not-c: 'S is red-green colorblind.' S realizes that this justifies S in being quite suspicious as to the truth of p, but for no good reason decides to ignore the point, and continues to believe p. As luck would have it, owing to some accidental and unsuspected phenomenon which occurred during the testing in spite of the clinicians' best efforts, S was incorrectly diagnosed and his cognitive equipment is in fact not at all defective.

In order to treat S as failing to know p, Sosa may wish to impose a restriction on terminal nodes to the effect that S not be unjustified in refraining from believing conjuncts in those nodes to be false.[5] This could obviously be accomplished by altering the previous definition of an S-epistemic proposition to include propositions affirming that S has such-and-such a degree of justification in refraining from believing some proposition (where one way of refraining from believing is to neither believe nor disbelieve).

However, a counterexample that is more difficult to deal with is a variation of the above case in which c is placed in a position

---

[4] See Alston 1976, p. 168.
[5] Indeed, one of Sosa's earlier papers indicated the need to consider this type of issue (Sosa 1964, p. 5).

somewhat similar to the proposition, 'The assassination occurred,' in Harman's newspaper example (E 9):

(E 30)   *The Red Tie (Version Two)*: As in (E 29), except that S is unaware of the newspaper report, but most townspeople have seen it and accordingly have formed a belief to the effect that S's cognitive equipment, including his perceptual apparatus, is not adequate for determining whether something is red just by looking.

This case is relevantly similar to Harman's example, and a similar intuition would lead one to say that S does not know p.

To be sure, Sosa will be able to avoid this counterexample if he persists in defining "crucial information" in (1) and (2) in the following way, but only at the price of opening his account to a different counterexample:

Information is crucial relative to your knowing whether p provided that adding that information to your evidence base would induce a fall in the epistemic status of your belief either that p, or that not-p to such an extent that where previously that belief was rationally justified it no longer is so. (p. 119)

In (E 30), if we were to add to S's evidence base the information that the report in question appeared in the generally reliable town newspaper, that might very well prevent S from being justified in believing p. So epistemic principle (2) appears to be violated concerning S's being in a position to know whether p.

But this way of interpreting crucial information makes the following example run counter to Sosa's analysis:

(E 31)   *Knowing a Naïve Belief*: S believes some false proposition, f, without having any reason to think it false, and knows p: 'S believes f.' A generally known piece of information in S's epistemic community is that f is false.

According to Sosa's definition of crucial information bearing on p, epistemic principle (2) would be violated in this case and Sosa would incorrectly be led to treat S as failing to know p, unless the phrase, "induce a fall," in the definition is interpreted as requiring that the added information is relevant to the question whether p. Unfortunately, such an interpretation would make Sosa's definition incapable of providing any way of avoiding counterexample (E 30). For the presence of the report in the town newspaper is not relevant evidence concerning whether the tie is red.

It would be quite vague to respond to these difficulties simply by imposing a requirement on terminal nodes that S be in a position to know whether they are true (but not necessarily have any beliefs concerning their truth). For the relevant epistemic principles defining the application of the phrase, "in a position to know," would remain to be specified. We shall deal with this issue in a different fashion in the final chapter by requiring that propositions such as those which Sosa describes as terminal nodes be 'justified propositions.'

2.3 Gettier-Type Difficulties

Sosa adds a further detail to his definition of a tree of knowledge in order to deal with Gettier-type examples. He maintains that the most plausible attempts to construct a tree of knowledge for S and the proposition x in such examples would utilize false beliefs of S. For example, an attempt to construct a tree for 'It is evident for S that someone in the class owns a Ford' in a typical Nogot case would lead one to include on rank II a proposition of the form: 'S believes, with such-and-such a degree of justification, f_1: "Mr. Nogot is a person in the office who owns a Ford." ' Sosa topples such "pseudo-trees" by adding a requirement that a tree of knowledge must attribute no false belief to S (although S may have false beliefs not involved in the tree) (p. 122).

However, I have shown (Shope 1979d) that this requirement is not violated by the case of the clever reasoner (E 6). Sosa had denied that such an example involves justifiably believing x since such justification would depend upon whether the clever reasoner, S, sees a connection between S's evidence and x (Sosa 1974a, p. 116). But as Lehrer describes the case, S does indeed see such a connection.

The clever reasoner avoids believing the false f_1: 'Mr. Nogot is a person in the class who owns a Ferrari,' but has propositions of the following forms on rank II of his putative tree of knowledge:

p_{1i}: '*S* believes the following proposition, q, which is evident for *S*:

"The proposition, f_1: 'Mr. Nogot is a person in the class who owns a Ferrari,' is evident for *S*." '

p_{1k}: '*S* believes the following proposition, r, which is evident for *S*:

"The proposition, x: 'Someone in the class owns a Ferrari,' is entailed by f_1." '

On rank III of the clever reasoner's putative tree of knowledge, one of the successors of p_{1i} is a proposition to the effect that *S* believes, and it is evident for *S*, that Mr. Nogot has been generally reliable and has behaved in a certain manner concerning the Ferrari, etc. Thus, no false belief is attributed to *S*, yet *S* does believe in a certain connection between his evidence for f_1 and proposition x.[6]

Of course, Sosa's account can be supplemented so as to deal with the case of the clever reasoner by means of additional restrictions on epistemic principles, for example:

(R) For any false proposition, f, no epistemic principle permits the derivation of a proposition of the form, 'h is evident for *S*, and *S* believes h,' from a set of propositions, ϕ, when ϕ contains as a nonsuperfluous member a proposition entailing one of the form, '*S* believes, and it is evident for *S*, that f entails h' or of the form, '*S* believes, and is justified to such-and-such an extent in believing, that f entails h.'

But this does not indicate what additional restrictions would have to be invoked to deal with the following case, which involves mod-

---

[6] The view that something may be evident for *S* even when *S* does not believe it is explicitly held by Peter Klein (Klein 1971). The view seems to be at least implicit in Sosa's own earlier characterization of the evident (Sosa 1970, p. 64).

ifying the red-tie examples in a manner inspired by Russell's clock example (E 2):

(E 32) *The Perceptual Experiment*: *S* has volunteered for a scientific experiment, the nature of which has been concealed from her, save that it is harmless. *S* is now in what she takes to be a waiting room, seated upon an ordinary-looking chair, expecting the experiment to be conducted in another room. The chair is secretly connected to a machine that can, without being detected by the subject, randomly alter the subject's perceptual capacities in numerous fashions, including having them be normal, or having *S* become temporarily red-green colorblind. A monitor displays to scientists in a separate room what alterations are made, and at the moment, although the scientists are justified in supposing that the monitor is working properly, it is not, and it would indicate that *S*'s perceptual capacities are normal (in a manner which includes their nondefectiveness) no matter what the true setting of the machine. Looking at the monitor, the scientists accept *c*: '*S* is not red-green colorblind now.' As luck would have it, the machine has switched itself to a setting where *c* happens to be true because it leaves *S*'s perceptual capacities unaffected. Simultaneously, *S* glances at another subject who has just entered her room and she believes on the basis of seeing his tie, *p*: 'The tie is red.'

In this example, as in Russell's, it is the merest accident that those who trust a measuring instrument reach a true belief by so doing. This Gettierized aspect of the social setting in the example seems to me to prevent *S* from knowing *p*, but nothing in Sosa's analysis accounts for that fact.

We shall develop a way of coping with such details in the final chapter, which will acknowledge the importance of Sosa's emphasis on epistemic explanation as one type of explanation constructed by epistemic communities in their pursuit of epistemic goals. However, an understanding of the possible content of epistemic explanations will need to be enlarged by bringing in the concept of a justified proposition. By analyzing this type of justification in terms of the rationality of members of an epistemic community we shall also acknowledge the importance which the relativizing of knowledge to epistemic communities has played in Sosa's work.

4.

Additions to Standard Analyses III: Limitations on the Justifying Power of Evidence or Grounds

1. CHISHOLM'S REQUIREMENT THAT EVIDENCE NOT JUSTIFY BELIEVING FALSEHOODS

Roderick Chisholm has developed an analysis of S's knowing p which avoids relying on any subjunctive conditionals. He includes a fourth condition of knowledge which requires that p be "non-defectively evident for S" in the following sense: Either p is certain for S, or p is evident for S and entailed by a conjunction of propositions each having for S a basis which is not a basis of any false proposition for S (Chisholm 1957, p. 109). S's having a basis of some proposition, h, is understood in the sense of S's having at least one basis, which might be a proper part of some larger basis. Thus, Johnsen's strategy of 'gerrymandering' one's evidence is built into Chisholm's analysis in the form of gerrymandering, if need be, the full basis S happens to have of proposition p.[1]

Chisholm demonstrates that by concentrating in this fashion on actual rather than hypothetical epistemic relations we can deal adequately with a number of typical Gettier-type examples (pp. 109-113). The analysis may even stand up to the case of Tom Grabit's actual twin (E 10), if any basis sufficient to make it evident for S that Tom stole the book will also suffice to make a false statement such as the following evident for S: 'S could distinguish Tom's participation in the theft from that of any other nearby person who had an opportunity to steal the book.' Again, the case of the numb

---

[1] See the discussion of Johnsen in Chapter 2, Section 1.44.

96

pyromaniac (E 13) is one where S knows p: 'The match will ignite' because any basis sufficient to make it evident for S that he will perceive the ignition contains propositions not needed to make p evident for S.[2]

However, Chisholm errs in not constructing an analysis of the type that we considered in the previous chapter and will defend in the final one, roughly, an analysis restricting its attention to those false propositions that one might suppose are involved in a full account of the justification of p. His analysis permits the false proposition in question to lie outside any such account and to be justified by an independent route from S's basis. Indeed, Chisholm describes an example which appears to be of just such a nature and attempts to show that it is not a genuine counterexample to his analysis:

(E 33)   *Drawings from an Urn*: S is about to make a set of random drawings from an urn and knows p: 'Most of the drawings will be of balls that are black.' This is made evident for S by a basis which permits him to know e: '99 percent of the balls are black and many random drawings are about to take place.' Moreover, the following statement, f, is false: 'The next ball to be drawn will be black.' (p. 111)

Chisholm denies that the basis of e also makes f evident for S, arguing that it at most makes f acceptable or reasonable for S, in other words, that S does not have (adequate, complete) justification for believing f. Chisholm says that if we were in the same epistemic situation as S, we would readily grant him the right to assert that he knows p, but if he went on to assert that he knows f, "our reaction would be to reply: 'Either you're mistaken or else you have some evidence other than e that we do not have'" (p. 111).

A critic might insist that such a case becomes a genuine counterexample once the numbers are sufficiently large, say, by involving an urn containing a billion balls, only one of which is not black.

---

[2] Ralph Slaght defends Chisholm against certain putative counterexamples (Slaght 1977, pp. 31-33). Also see Chisholm's reply to Michael Hooker (Chisholm 1978; Hooker 1978).

But that objection leaves open the question whether knowing the outcome of a draw in advance makes the drawing cease to be a "random" one.[3] Moreover, it overlooks the gerrymandering strategy of dropping any evidence concerning the total numbers of various colored balls from S's basis of proposition e.

Instead, consider a counterexample concerning causation, which has a structure resembling (E 33). We may first acknowledge that our common understanding of a generalization of the form, 'A's cause B's,' does not lead us to regard the generalization as ruling out the possibility of interfering factors that can prevent an A, in a given situation, from bringing about a B (R. Clark 1973). For example, I may know the following causal generalization, g, to be true: 'Turning the key in my car causes it to start.' At the same time, I realize that if a micrometeorite had made an inconspicuous hole in the hood last night and punctured the wiring at a certain spot, then the efficacy of turning the key this morning would be cancelled. Further, I do not need to *know* that such a meteorological event has not occurred in order to know q: 'When I turn the key this morning, my car will start.'

Now consider the following example:

(E 34) *Starting the Car*: Let e be the proposition evident for me: 'g and I shall be turning the key this morning as well as a number of other mornings.' This allows me to know p: 'On one or more of those occasions, my car will start.' It so happens that q is false.

It appears that whatever basis I have of proposition e not only makes p evident for me but also makes q evident for me. On occasions when q is true, we commonly say that I know it to be true, thanks to knowing e to be true. However, when q is false, because a fleeting problem will unexpectedly prevent starting this morning but not on other mornings, we have a counterexample to Chisholm's analysis.

Suppose that, in a situation where q is true, someone says to me

---

[3] For related considerations see Bonjour 1980, pp. 69-70.

as I stroll to my car, "You don't know p unless you are appealing
to further evidence which shows that no micrometeorites have pen-
etrated certain wires, that nobody will detonate a nuclear device over
your driveway as you turn the key, and similarly for all physically
possible interfering factors." Such an attitude will indeed lead one
to reject the preceding counterexample, but will also lead us toward
the skeptical position that we never know what particular events will
cause others in everyday life. Philosophers who wish to avoid such
skepticism must look for a different means of dealing with Gettier-
type examples.

Of course, sophistication will lead the person in (E 34) already to
be aware of *some* possible interfering factors which we will hold
him accountable for knowing to be absent before being able to know
p. But the description of the example can be amended to take account
of such knowledge. Let us label the set of such factors, ϕ. Then we
may simply change the example so that the person's evidence includes knowledge r: 'On all the upcoming occasions the factors in
ϕ are absent.'[4]

An alternative way of attempting to resist counterexample (E 34)
is to point out that we have stressed the fact that any basis the person
has of proposition e will make both p and q evident, but that Chisholm
is actually only concerned with a different issue, namely, whether
every basis the person has of proposition p will make both p and q
evident. Perhaps gerrymandering the basis of e will still provide a
basis of p without providing a basis of e. Thus, we may gerrymander
so that the basis of p does not include a basis of r but only of
something entailed by r, namely, r': 'On at least one of the upcoming
occasions the factors in ϕ will be absent.'

This latter shift will not help if the example is described so that
the false proposition is q': 'When I turn the key this morning, if the
factors in ϕ are absent then my car will start,' where we construe
the example so that this morning the factors in ϕ do happen to be

---

[4] I shall not attempt to decide here whether the distinction I have drawn bears any
interesting relation to the distinction between relevant and irrelevant 'alternatives' in
situations where one knows; see Chapter 5, Section 6.13.

absent and the failure to start is due to some exotic, unsuspected factor.

However, the gerrymandering strategy might then turn to the issue of further details concerning the basis of *e*. If these are statistics concerning one's previous experiences with attempts to start the car upon turning the key in the absence of factors in φ, then Chisholm might try to whittle down the report of the statistics so that it is just barely strong enough to make *p* evident but not strong enough to make the false *q* or false *q'* evident.[5]

I believe that this strategy can be blocked by modifying the example:

(E 35) *Starting the Car (Modified Version)*: As in (E 34), except that the person knows *g* and knows *r'* only thanks to trusting the testimony of some expert known to be generally reliable, who has asserted that *g* and *r'* are true and that the factors in φ are the relevant ones in such situations bearing on whether the person knows whether *p*. It so happens that *q'* is false.[6]

If one pressed beyond the person's own bases of *p* and began to consider gerrymandering the basis of the expert, or the basis of a further expert upon whom that one relied, and so on, perhaps a way of dealing with (E 35) could be developed. The technique which we shall present in the final chapter to solve the Gettier problem would permit this type of gerrymandering (although it will be noncommital regarding the existence of what Chisholm calls a 'basis').

It would obviously backfire if Chisholm permitted too great a degree of abstraction in articulating the person's basis of *p* in the example in order to keep it from being a basis of the false proposition,

---

[5] I owe this point to Ernest Sosa.

[6] This case may serve better than Johnsen's example concerning additional reports (E 19) in order to refute analyses relying on (iv$_8$) (see Chapter 2, Section 1.44). For Johnsen's example overlooked the possibility that the difference in subject matter of the stories on different pages of a newspaper might affect the degree of reliability of the story. (Compare the discussion of Sosa's example of the vain wife [E 20], described in n. 24 to Chapter 2.)

q'. For example, suppose that he allowed the basis to be described merely as 'a basis sufficient to make evident for S something said by an expert known to be reliable, which itself suffices to make p evident for S.' Unfortunately, a similarly abstract description could be given in Gettier-type examples, e.g., in the Relator-Nogot case (E 17), which would deprive Chisholm's analysis of the ability to rule out knowledge in such an example.

This point bears on whether Chisholm can avoid having the piece of wax example (E 21) run counter to his present analysis. For if Chisholm were to describe S's basis in that example very abstractly, as 'propositions referring to phenomena making it evident for S that a piece of wax is present,' then a similarly evasive strategy would prevent elimination of Gettier-type cases.

A special problem arises for Chisholm in dealing with this example because his technical definition of 'a basis' treats every basis as a basis of a proposition describing itself (p. 138). This means that if S's basis is articulated in the inappropriate vocabulary of sense experience, then it will be the basis of a false proposition in (E 21), namely, the one that articulates it.

However, a restricted eliminative materialist is willing to say that the vocabulary which S is disposed to employ in describing a basis of S's judgment that a piece of wax is present yields false descriptions which nonetheless refer (in the wrong vocabulary) to material states of S that would be describable in the language of possible future scientific theories. So Chisholm might be able to present a plausible case for treating the basis S presently has as those material states and as describable by true propositions articulatable only in a presently inaccessible vocabulary. Under such an interpretation, S's basis does not form a basis of falsehoods such as 'S is having sense experiences.'[7]

---

[7] It is difficult to assess this point because Chisholm's definition of a basis in terms of what is "self-presenting" utilizes the problematic concept of necessity, and because the definition of what is self-presenting is subject to various problems that have led in the meantime to a series of revisions in that definition, a development which I shall not attempt to survey here.

An additional counterexample to Chisholm's analysis will be developed in the course of the next section. Moreover, as Slaght has noted, Chisholm does not adequately explain how to apply his approach to cases which involve the social aspects of knowing, e.g., where there is relevant evidence that S does not possess (Slaght 1977, p. 33).[8]

[8] One part of Fred Dretske's criticism of Chisholm (Dretske 1979) misfires because Dretske does not understand why the definition of p's being nondefectively evident speaks of (1) a *conjunction*, and (2) *entailment* by the conjunction.

Dretske thinks that Chisholm's treatment of inferential knowledge regards the conjunction as, in Dretske's words, a combination of "relevant" propositions "on the basis of" which one "concludes" that p, so that Chisholm is concerned to clarify the requirement that "one's evidence must be nondefective" and to discuss "our basis for believing" that p, something "on which we rely for our justification" when p is "made evident through the agency of . . . [an] intermediate set of evident propositions that jointly entail" that p (pp. 261-267).

But Chisholm explains the wording of his definition as a device for allowing that in a case such as that of Mr. Nogot (E 1) S knows the conjunction e, describing Mr. Nogot's past reliability and present conduct, even though e is sufficient to make evident for S the falsehood, f: 'Mr. Nogot owns a Ford.' Chisholm's point is that none of the individual conjuncts in e suffice to make f evident for e. But Chisholm does not require that e be spoken of as deduced from other relevant propositions, since e entails itself.

When formulating his analysis of 'S knows p,' Chisholm needs to cover both cases where p contains conjuncts and cases where p does not. Rather than resorting to the device of calling propositions involved in the latter cases 'conjunctions' in a technical sense or 'degenerate conjunctions,' Chisholm has chosen to cover both types of cases by speaking of p as entailed by a (genuine) conjunction. When p is itself a conjunction, as in the case just discussed, p entails itself. When p is not a conjunction, it is nonetheless entailed by a conjunction formed by conjoining it with any other true proposition, k, which is evident for S but which has a basis that makes no falsehood evident for S. But k need have no relevance to p.

Since Chisholm did not explain the latter detail, Dretske has misunderstood him as attempting to deal in the definition with intermediate steps in S's deductive reasoning to p. Accordingly, Dretske objects that this improperly denies S knowledge in many cases, since S would either be construed as accepting a false generalization as a premise in order to make S's inference deductively valid in those cases, or else S would be left with a probabilistic or statistical premise that is useless for any relevant deduction of p.

Dretske more appropriately criticizes Chisholm's analysis as having untoward consequences when it is combined with Chisholm's view that the 'concurrence' of a set of propositions may raise their epistemic status higher than the merely reasonable status which each conjunct possesses because of its own individual basis. Thus, p

2. SOSA ON EPISTEMIC PRESUPPOSITIONS

In his most recent account of knowing (Sosa 1979), Ernest Sosa again treats the standard justification condition for S's knowing p as entailed by the more complex condition that there is a tree of knowledge for S and the proposition p. But Sosa now diagrams a tree of knowledge more simply than he did in the account which we considered in Chapter 3. Sosa now describes the tree as growing from the starting point, 'S is justified in believing p,' rather than from 'p is evident for S.' As a result, the remainder of a tree of knowledge now becomes one type of a "tree of justification," where the latter is a tree in which successors to a node of the form, 'S is justified in believing p_i,' indicate what makes it true that S is justified in believing p_i.[9]

Thus, a tree of knowledge no longer includes any nodes saying that S is in a position to know whether p is true or false. Instead, Sosa treats the details involved in what he formerly called S's being in a position to know as a special case of various "epistemic presuppositions" which S makes in believing p on (a set of) grounds, G. One way in which a tree of justification for S and p will fail to be a tree of knowledge, according to Sosa, is when it contains a node that involves S in some false epistemic presupposition.

The full definition of a tree of knowledge is as follows:

A tree of justification, T, for S and p is a tree of knowledge for S and p if and only if

---

might be a true proposition made evident for S through concurrence with other false propositions whose individual bases only make them reasonable for S but not evident for S (p. 266).

Chisholm could avoid this objection by changing the ending of his definition of p's being nondefectively evident for S so that the definition reads: Either p is certain for S, or p is evident for S and entailed by a conjunction of propositions each having for S a basis which is not such that (necessarily) if it is evident for S then some false proposition is reasonable for S. But this unfortunately turns (E 33) into a counterexample to the resulting analysis of knowing.

[9] Once again, in order to deal with the first version of the case of the red tie (E 29), Sosa may wish to require that S not be unjustified in not believing terminal nodes to be false. (See Chapter 3, Section 2.2.)

(1) no node of T is to the effect that S is justified in believing q for any false q; and

(2) no node of T gives (the members of) a set G as S's basis for believing a proposition, r, such that some falsehood is an epistemic presupposition made by S in believing r on the basis of (the members of) G. (pp. 89-90)

Proposition r is an epistemic presupposition made by S in believing p on the basis of (the members of) set G if and only if

(i) grounds G would prima facie ground r for S; and

(ii) the combination of grounds G with not-r would fail to prima facie ground p for S; and

(iii) that S believes r would not prima facie ground p for S. (p. 89)

Sosa explains the grounding relation as follows: A set of propositions (or states of affairs) G would prima facie ground some further proposition r for S if and only if there is a set G' such that

(1) G' would prima facie justify r for S (i.e., the combined truth of the members of G' would justify r for S); and

(2) G' is composed of (a) a proposition that S's believing r is (causally) based on the members of G, and (b) for some or all of the beliefs attributed to S by members of G, propositions to the effect that S is justified in having such beliefs. (pp. 87-88)

Sosa's undefined concept of a set of propositions being such that it would prima facie justify h for S (i.e., the combined truth of its members would prima facie justify h for S) is not a subjunctive conditional. Sosa specifies that it is a concept of a justification-making relation akin to W. D. Ross's ethical concept of a right-making relation between, e.g., S's promising to do A and A's being prima facie obligatory for S to do.[10]

---

[10] Even if the following subjunctive conditional is true: 'If S had not heard Jones he would not be prima facie obligated to go on the mission,' his hearing Jones is not what made S obligated. Instead, volunteering to go made him obligated, and the

One of the motivations for Sosa's new account is to deal with cases such as the clever reasoner (E 6) and Feldman's version of the Nogot case (E 8), which, as we have seen, defeated Sosa's earlier account. In these examples, even if S fails to believe the false proposition, 'Mr. Nogot owns a Ford (Ferrari),' it does at least count as one of S's epistemic presuppositions in S's believing 'Someone in the office (class) owns a Ford (Ferrari)' on the basis of grounds including the evidence which S has obtained concerning Mr. Nogot.

Even though the relation of justification used to define the concept of epistemic presupposition is not explained in terms of subjunctive conditionals, its role in the definition of epistemic presupposition is somewhat analogous to that played by a conditional relationship in various defeasibility accounts, and a comparison allows us to notice further strengths of Sosa's analysis.

For example, condition (ii) in the definition of an epistemic presupposition is analogous to one of Swain's proposals, considered earlier (see Chapter 2, Section 1.461), which spoke of what would happen if S were to become justified in believing false certain false propositions S actually believes to be true. However, by adding condition (i), Sosa is able to deal with the counterexamples that I brought against Swain. For in those examples, S's grounds for believing p are insufficient, without supplementation, to prima facie ground the false propositions in question.[11]

Condition (iii) helps Sosa to avoid refutation by the Relator-Nogot example (E 17), which ran counter to Johnsen's defeasibility analysis of knowing. Because a tree of justification can include at each node what Johnsen called gerrymandering of evidence, Sosa is able to deal properly with the Shrink-Grabit case (E 14). Condition (iii) also saves the analysis from being subject to a counterexample when S knows p': 'S is justified in believing f,' where f is an unsuspected falsehood. In such an example, condition (i) is satisfied because any

former conditional is true only because the following one is true: 'If S had not heard Jones, he would not have volunteered to go.'

[11] For similar reasons, Sosa's new account yields the correct result regarding the Klein-Grabit case (E 23), which defeated Klein's revised defeasibility analysis.

basis sufficient to prima facie ground p' will also do so for f. And condition (ii) is satisfied because addition of S's justifiedly believing not-f to S's grounds for p' wrecks S's justification for believing f. But condition (iii) fails to be satisfied, because S's believing p' does suffice to prima facie ground f for S.[12]

Thanks to condition (ii), Sosa's analysis of knowing is not refuted by (E 35), the modified version of the example concerning my starting a car, which constituted a counterexample to Chisholm's analysis. For in discussing that example, we admitted that adding to my evidence the proposition, 'It is not true that when I turn the key this morning, my car will start,' does not prevent me from knowing p: 'On one or more of the upcoming occasions when I turn the key [only one of which is this morning's attempt], my car will start.'

Unfortunately, because of his reliance on (ii), Sosa's analysis of knowing succumbs to the example of lucky Mr. Nogot (E 22), which I employed in Chapter 2 in order to refute defeasibility analyses that rely on condition (iv$_9$). The relevance of this objection to Sosa's analysis is not surprising, since those defeasibility analyses are structurally similar to Sosa's present analysis. In the case of lucky Mr. Nogot, S fails to know but is nonetheless justified in believing the accidentally true proposition, p: 'Either Mr. Nogot owns a Ford or Mr. Nogot does not own any blue Ford that he drove in front of S.' But Sosa is unable to count the following false proposition, f, as an epistemic presupposition: 'Mr. Nogot owns a Ford,' for clause (ii) fails to be satisfied regarding f. Adding not-f to S's grounds for p gives S a new justification for believing p by grounding the second disjunct in p. Thus, Sosa is unable to count S as failing to know p, and his present analysis of knowing is too weak.

Reliance on (ii) also makes Sosa's analysis too strong, as may be seen from the piece of wax example (E 21), which I employed as an objection to defeasibility analyses relying on (iv$_9$). In that example

---

[12] Sosa also argues that (iii) is needed in order to cope with an example described by Harman (pp. 83-84). However, I am not sure that condition (i) is satisfied in Harman's example when gerrymandering is taken into account. Sosa's fourth footnote to his article also casts doubt upon whether (i) is satisfied in Harman's case.

(assuming that restricted eliminative materialism is correct), the evidence that some ordinary person, S, relies on in coming to know p: 'A piece of wax is present' suffices to justify S in believing the following false proposition (entailed by the vocabulary in which S articulates the evidence), f: 'S is having sense experiences.' Yet adding not-f to the beliefs on which S grounds p would so call into question S's contact with reality that Sosa's condition (ii) would be met.[13] But since condition (iii) also is met, Sosa would have to count S as failing to know p, contrary to the intuitions of a restricted eliminative materialist.

Another reason for regarding Sosa's analysis as being too strong is that clause (ii) may be satisfied in some cases only because of a Gettierized connection between not-r and a proposition incompatible with r, which cannot be avoided by gerrymandering of evidence or grounds. Perhaps the following example will demonstrate this difficulty, provided that we agree with certain intuitions of Keith Donnellan regarding the reference of definite descriptions (Donnellan 1966; cf. Suppe 1972).

(E 36) *Relator-Nogot (Donnellanized Version)*: As in (E 17), except for the following details: Mr. Relator is a notary or legal expert who knows that Mr. Nogot permanently divested himself of all property prior to time t. Relator also happened to recognize Mr. Nogot while looking in a window of the office at t, but without realizing it was the office. In fact, he justifiably took it not to be the office. Relator knows independently that the only other living member of the Nogot family is Mrs. Nogot, and that she was in the office at t and is sometimes referred to by people. [Following Donnellan's intuitions about reference we can allow that] Mr. Relator is able to refer to Mr. Nogot by the phrase, "the only living member of the Nogot family not in the office at t" and also

---

[13] Perhaps Sosa would be able to avoid this result by availing himself of the alternative construal of what constitutes S's basis which I mentioned in the preceding section.

by the longer phrase, "the only living member of the Nogot family either not in the office at t or never referred to by anyone." Thanks to a conversation between S and Relator, and to S's awareness of Relator's record as a source of information, S obtains the set of grounds, G, consisting in the following items: (1) S's (correctly) believing that Relator is a generally reliable informant for S; (2) S's (correctly) believing that Relator has made the particular assertion that he has in saying, "The only living member of the Nogot family who either was not in the office at t or is never referred to by anybody permanently divested himself of all property prior to t." On the basis of this set of grounds, S knows p: 'The person to whom Relator referred as the only living member of the Nogot family who either was not in the office at t or is never referred to by anybody did not own a Ford at t.'

There is no way to gerrymander G (or any basis of G sufficient to ground p for S) so as to prevent it from grounding for S the false proposition, f: 'The person to whom Relator referred was not a generally reliable person in the office offering e at t,' where e describes the usual charade by Nogot in front of the teacher. Thus, f satisfies condition (i) in the definition of an epistemic presupposition made by S in believing p on the basis of G. And f obviously satisfies (iii). To the detriment of Sosa's account of knowing, f also satisfies (ii), because the combination of G with not-f would justify, by means of a Gettierized connection, S's believing that the person to whom Relator referred owned a Ford at t, or at least would make believing this sufficiently reasonable for S that S would no longer be justified in believing p. (This example may also be seen to be a counterexample to the analysis presented by Chisholm that we considered in the previous section.)

2.1 *Being in a Position to Know; Harman on Available Evidence*

Sosa now regards the expression, "in a position to know whether p is true," as dispensable in a tree of knowledge for S and p. He believes that the relevance which being in a position to know has for a tree of justification's turning out to be a tree of knowledge is adequately characterized by speaking of false epistemic presuppositions. (He suggests that these epistemic presuppositions happen to be due to S's cognitive limitations.) Accordingly, Sosa offers the following definition:

> One is in a position to know with respect to the proposition p if and only if:
>
> (D_1) there is a possible tree of knowledge for oneself and the proposition that p, i.e., a tree of justification that involves one in no false justified belief or false epistemic presupposition. (p. 80)

This analyzes the concept which Sosa roughly characterizes as follows: "My notion of 'being in a position to know' is approximately that of [D_2] being in a position such that one has only to believe correctly and with adequate justification in order to know" (p. 80).

It will prove useful to notice that D_2 might apply in situations where the preceeding *definiens*, D_1, would not, as in the following example:

(E 37) *The Doxastiscope*: A reliable scientific instrument (a 'doxastiscope') is used by scientists surrounding S to detect S's beliefs, at least his epistemic beliefs. One piece of correct information they obtain is i: 'There are indications on the reliable doxastiscope that S has no beliefs about the justifiedness of any of S's beliefs.' In addition, S neither believes nor disbelieves p: 'S has a justified belief about the justifiedness of some of S's beliefs.'

In this situation, D_2 might be true of S. For if S were to believe p justifiably, perhaps that would make p true and S would be aware of the truth and justified status of p in a way that would allow S to know p.

Yet there is one way of understanding D_1 which would prevent it from applying to S in the above example, given Sosa's views about the epistemic presuppositions that we make in everyday life. For

Sosa suggests that we usually make the following important epistemic presupposition in forming a belief or assumption that h on the basis of our evidence:

ep: 'If anyone [who were to be in S's epistemic community][14] were to have a grasp of a richer variety of relevant facts than S and were to form a (justified) opinion on whether or not h is true on that broader basis and were not to make a false epistemic presupposition in doing so, then that person would (also) believe h.' (p. 86)

Sosa's view that ep is a common epistemic presupposition is appealing, because it appears to give us a way of dealing with various social aspects of knowing and with misleading defeaters of one's justification. For example, when S_1 knows h then someone, S_2, with more relevant information than S_1, who would disbelieve h or refrain from believing it because of the inclusion of what in fact is a misleading defeater, d, of S_1's justification, would make a false epistemic presupposition in taking such an epistemic stand on those grounds, namely, the presupposition that anyone, S_3, with an even richer grasp of relevant facts would not believe h unless S_3 made a false epistemic presupposition. The presupposition made by S_2 is false because the added information S_3 is imagined to have might merely be something that shows up d as misleading. (However, since the most informed *actual* inquirer might be S_2, Sosa needs to allow the sequence of inquirers to include merely possible [states of] inquirers; we shall consider the significance of this point shortly.)

If we understand the wording at the end of the description of ep and of D_1 as speaking of epistemic presuppositions which are *actually* false, then D_1 does not apply in the doxastiscope example. For in

---

[14] Presumably, Sosa wishes to include the qualification in brackets in light of A. J. Holland's insight that a quite different pattern of conditioning in some other epistemic community could account for its members reacting doxastically in a quite different fashion to evidence from the way S and the members of S's epistemic community react (Holland 1977). However, nothing that follows depends crucially on this qualification.

that example *ep* is an actually false proposition, either because it entails the falsehood that S believes p, or because it entails the falsehood that the scientists who possess information i would nonetheless believe p upon obtaining any actual relevant facts (which may be none) that S presently has regarding the truth or falsity of p.

We should not attempt to avoid this result by understanding the end of *ep* and of D_1 as speaking of epistemic presuppositions that *would* be false were S justifiably to believe p. Such an understanding saddles Sosa's analysis with the conditional fallacy because of the way in which it utilizes D_1. Consider the following examples:

(E 38) *Mass Drugging*: S_1 is in the unusual position of knowing p_1: 'I am the only person [or: the only person in my epistemic community] who is forming an opinion,' thanks to knowing that a drug has made all the others totally unconscious.

(E 39) *The Fact-Grasping Mavin*: S_1 knows p_2: 'Nobody [or: nobody in my epistemic community] has as wide a grasp of a rich variety of relevant facts about grasping facts as I do.'

According to Sosa, in each example S makes epistemic presupposition *ep*. However, satisfaction of the antecedent of *ep* regarding someone, S_2, other than S_1, would create a situation where p_1 and p_2 would be false, and S_2 might very well be aware of their falsehood and disbelieve them. So *ep* will be true only if S_2 would make a false epistemic presupposition in so doing. Yet the only apparent candidates for such a false presupposition are propositions that *would* be true in the hypothetical situation entertained by the antecedent of *ep* (although false in the actual situation surrounding S_1), e.g., the propositions, 'Someone other than S_1 is forming an opinion' or 'Someone grasps more relevant facts about grasping facts than S_1.'

So we must return to our former understanding of D_1 and admit that it treats S as failing to be in a position to know whether p is true in (E 37) simply because S does not at the moment—for whatever reason—happen to have any beliefs about the justifiedness of S's beliefs. The peculiarity of this result may prompt us to wonder whether D_1 really does capture the force of the role that being in a position to know played in Sosa's earlier views, and whether D_1 does succeed in helping Sosa to escape objections to those previous views. There is reason to suppose that it does not.

For example, Sosa had previously maintained that a defect in your cognitive equipment is one thing that may put you out of a position to know whether p is true even in cases where you justifiably believe p, and that "it must be a defect that prevents you from acquiring information that (1) a normal inquirer in the epistemic community would acquire in that situation *and* (2) makes a difference to what you can reasonably conclude on the question whether p (or at least how reasonably you can draw the conclusion)" (Sosa 1974a, p. 115). However, Sosa immediately altered this condition by allowing that because of the defect the person "misses or *is liable to miss* available information which may be highly relevant and important and may make a difference to what he can conclude on the question in hand" (emphasis added; p. 115). The latter wording covers a type of situation which the former did not:

(E 40) *Magoo's Murk*: Untying his bonds, and removing his blindfold, the extraordinarily nearsighted Mr. Magoo forms the true judgment, p: 'I am inside the airplane hangar,' on the basis of his murky visual percepts gained after a stroll in the middle of his hideout, an otherwise empty, large, white airplane hangar.

Magoo does not know p, and it was an accident that he made a correct judgment about his location. He was liable to have missed the information that he gathered, liable to have judged instead, e.g., that he was outside in a fog on the runway. Sosa's new account would force us to find a false epistemic presupposition made by Magoo, but it is not obvious what it is. Sosa indicates that he does regard Magoo as justified in making such judgments as p, and describes Magoo as a person whose "expectations are based on a long and varied background of successful experience, or so we may assume by supposing his defects to be congenital" because he "survives and indeed flourishes only by incredible luck" (p. 85). But surely Magoo's grounds for judging that *p* do not by themselves ground for him the false statement: 'Magoo is not liable to miss the information that *p*.'[15] And the mere fact that Magoo got the information is also insufficient to ground false statements affirming that Magoo's cognitive equipment is nondefective (just as the grounds which a child has when seeing something fail to ground a similar statement about the child's cognitive equipment). Of course, Magoo's grounds may also ground 'Magoo's cognitive equipment is normal,' but this proposition will not satisfy clause (ii) in the definition of an epistemic presupposition; for Magoo has no reason to suppose that any abnormality of his cognitive equipment tends in the direction of deficiency rather than superiority.

Sosa has argued elsewhere (Sosa 1974b) that justified identification of something as ϕ by the way it looks involves what Peirce called 'abduction,' for example, believing that the best explanation of one's data or experiences is that the thing is ϕ. But in Magoo's situation this belief is true, provided that Magoo realizes that fog is quite rare in his area. Only by considering what are good explanations in relation to information available to *S*'s epistemic community could we contest this explanation.

Thus, the only candidate for a false epistemic presupposition in this case may be *ep*. But Sosa's wording of *ep* appears to restrict the added information of which it speaks to what is relevant to whether or not Magoo is in the hangar. So the effect of any added information concerning Magoo's defects relates only to clause (ii) in the definition of an epistemic presupposition. Consequently, *ep* does not appear to be false in this example.

The example could be dealt with either by dropping the term

---

[15] A slightly different falsehood is *f*: 'Magoo has the ability to discriminate the state of affairs that *p* from the state of affairs that not-*p*.' Certain theories concerning discrimination will be noted in Chapter 5. It is difficult to decide whether Magoo's basis for *p* suffices as a basis for *f* until philosophers provide a satisfactory explanation of what constitutes such a discriminatory ability, capacity, or power.

"relevant" from the description of *ep* or by understanding that term as covering information which, while not directly relevant to the question at hand, at least makes a difference as to how justified *S* is in accepting an answer to that question.

However, this understanding of *ep* has several shortcomings. First, it fails to explain why *S* lacks knowledge in one of the cases that defeated Sosa's earlier analysis of knowing, namely, the perceptual experiment (E 32). In that example, the scientists surrounding *S* are normal inquirers yet they possess no information that bears negatively on *S*'s judgment or on how justified *S* is in making the judgment, nor do they lack information that bears positively on it and which is pertinent to clause (ii). The sequence of issues about justification which needs to be considered in order to deal with that example is, as we shall see in the final chapter, different from that which Sosa generates.

Secondly, both the above understanding of *ep* and the original one undercut the utility of Sosa's appeal to a sequence of inquirers as a means of ruling out the effect of merely misleading defeaters. Since some members of the sequence concern merely possible inquirers or merely possible states of actual inquirers, they include an inquirer's possessing information that no actual inquirer does possess in *S*'s situation. Thus, Sosa's account conflicts with Harman's claim that *S* knows *p* in the following situation:

(E 41)   *The Unobtainable Unopened Letter*: *S* knows *p*: 'Norman is in Italy,' thanks to being told upon phoning Norman's office that he is spending the summer in Rome. In addition, Norman tried to deceive *S* by having a friend in San Francisco mail a letter from Norman to *S* claiming that he is spending the summer in San Francisco. The letter will continue to lie unopened in a building to which the postman misdelivered it on its way from San Francisco to *S*. (Harman 1980, p. 164)

Harman contrasts this example with the following one, where *S* fails to know *p*:

(E 42)   *The Unopened Letter*: As in (E 41), except that the letter lies unopened on *S*'s hall table among the morning mail.

Whereas Sosa's recent account treats *S* as failing to know in both examples because of the unpossessed (relevant) information, Harman offers a necessary condition for knowing *p* which does not prevent *S* from having knowledge in (E 41):

(H)   One knows *p* only if there is no evidence one does not possess, possession of which would make acceptance of *p* unjustified, and which one can obtain oneself. (p. 165)

Indeed, Harman credits a quite early paper by Sosa as providing a condition "like" this (p. 179). Actually, two related requirements were implied in Sosa's paper:

(S)   One knows *p* only if there is no evidence one does not possess, possession of which would make acceptance of *p* unjustified, and which is readily available. (Sosa 1964, p. 5)

(S')   One knows *p* only if there is no evidence one does not possess, possession of which would make acceptance of *p* unjustified, and which one could reasonably be expected to have. (p. 7)

The contrast between the ending of H and of S raises questions about the former. The cooperation of others may be required for one to gain evidence. Obviously, if *S* is incapacitated in (E 42) and dependent upon others to carry the morning mail to her, that does not mean that the example turns into one where she knows *p*.[16]

---

[16] The need for *S* to rely on other people as conduits of available evidence raises a further difficulty for Harman's formulation of H. Harman describes the following case:

(E 43)   *The Unopened Letter with Enclosure*: As in (E 42), except that Norman's friend in California included an enclosure revealing the hoax. (Harman 1980, p. 164)

Harman allows that in this case *S* does know that Norman is in Italy, for H is to be understood so that "the obtainable evidence not be merely part of the evidence . . . [*S*] would obtain if she were to obtain evidence including that part" (p. 164). However, this would yield the wrong results in the above case if it just happens to

The contrast in wording between S and S' alerts us to a further question regarding H. For the contents of the letter misdelivered to the other building might be "readily available" to the extent that S, who is not incapacitated, needs but commit some immoral act, such as climbing in the unwatched, unlocked window of the apartment in which the letter lies in order to come across it. Yet we would not say that S "could reasonably be expected to have" this evidence, not only because of our moral reservations but because of standards governing the reasonable *search for* evidence. So when Harman speaks in H of what one "can" obtain, there must be a complex background involving assumptions about epistemic communities that we shall need to expose more fully in the final chapter.[17]

---

be true that the helper upon whom S relies to open and bring her the mail would accidentally overlook the enclosure and throw it away with the envelope before bringing S Norman's letter. We shall need to take more explicitly into account standards for S's acquiring evidence through the intervention of others. (Moreover, Harman's understanding of his subjunctive conditional may be improperly 'backward-looking' by considering what would have been involved in bringing about the acquisition of evidence by S at *t* rather than merely considering S's having the evidence at *t*; for discussion of 'backtracking' aspects of conditional contexts see Bennett 1974; D. Lewis 1973.)

[17] Harman's wording of the ending of H may be meant partly as a response to an article that Harman acknowledges (p. 179) by William Lycan, containing criticism of a principle akin to S (Lycan 1977). Lycan maintains that "the marks of accessibility . . . are evidently matters of degree" and that no procedure comes to mind for even beginning to decide where to draw the line in that regard between extraneous facts that undermine a knowledge claim and those that do not (pp. 120-121).

Lycan charges Harman with relying on such an objectionable principle in counting the case of Mrs. Grabit (E 12) as an instance of S's failing to know because the number of people who have heard Mrs. Grabit's testimony is a mark of ready accessibility of defeating evidence. But Lycan is forced to admit (p. 116) that Harman's original description of the case did not specify that many other people believe Mrs. Grabit's testimony. In Chapter 7, Section 5, we shall consider independent grounds for deciding how to treat the Grabit case.

Lycan himself characterizes evidence that is readily or easily accessible to me as evidence that I could—and will if events continue in their normal course—come to possess with a minimum of effort on my part (p. 116). The gradualistic overtones of the term "minimum" are avoided by Harman's wording of H but his use of the term "can" involves issues about the 'normal' course of the search for evidence in an epistemic community in a sense to be discussed in Chapter 7 (and which Hector-Neri Castañeda regards as involving methodological issues; see Chapter 5, Section 5). The wording of S' comes closer to acknowledging this point.

We can presently conclude, however, that some of the issues raised by the details of S and S' have been omitted by Sosa in his formulation of epistemic presupposition *ep*. It will not be appropriate to respond simply by modifying that formulation as follows:

ep': 'If anyone [who were to be in S's epistemic community] were to have a grasp of a richer variety of relevant facts than S which are readily available to S or which S could reasonably be expected to grasp and were to form a (justified) opinion on whether or not *h* is true on that broader basis and were not to make a false epistemic presupposition in so doing, then that person would (also) believe *h*.'

This proposition happens to be true in an example such as the following:

(E 44) *The Newspaper in Solitary*: As in (E 9), except that S is locked in solitary confinement with no source of information about the assassination other than the newspaper accidentally left behind by a guard, and the denials have been heard by the rest of the prison community. (Harman 1980, p. 165)

Harman plausibly describes this as a case where S fails to know that the assassination occurred. So a more explicit reference needs to be made to the social aspects of knowing than is provided by *ep* or *ep'*.

In addition, in spite of their suggestive power, conditions H, S, and S' each involve the conditional fallacy, as the following example demonstrates, an example that all three conditions would incorrectly fail to count as constituting knowledge:

(E 45) *Knowing One's Limits*: S knows p_1: 'S possesses only *n* pieces of evidence [or: possesses exactly such-and-such evidence] regarding who possesses evidence,' and S knows p_2: 'S fails to understand psychological theory T about understanding.' There is additional evidence bearing favorably upon p_1 which S can obtain himself. There is also some evidence formulable only in terms of theory T bearing favorably on p_2, evidence which is readily available to S and which S could reasonably be expected to learn how to understand in seeking to do so.

One cannot avoid this difficulty by adding to H, S, and S' the stipulation that acquisition of the new evidence would not change the truth value of p. For there might be a case just like the above one except that S does not know p_1 or p_2 because S fails to possess some genuinely defeating evidence whose possession would also change the truth values of those propositions. We shall see in the final chapter that these types of difficulties can best be avoided by ceasing to ground the relevance of the social aspects of knowing on egocentric considerations.

At that point we shall also find a way to deal with one additional peculiarity in Sosa's wording of ep. Sosa's description puts no restriction on the psychological makeup of the other inquirers who are imagined as grasping the additional facts. It seems implausiblé to believe that they all would arrive at the same conclusion. There are various types of somewhat irrational mental functioning that could lead some of the inquirers to disagree with the others. It is not obvious that this would always show up in a false epistemic presupposition made by those who disagree with S when S does know h. Even when one's rationality is being manifested, one's manifestation of it in forming a justified belief may involve an admixture of other factors, some unconscious, leading to variations in details of those manifestations (e.g., consider the intrusion of what Freudian psychoanalysts call primary process associations; see Shope 1983). Perhaps we shall be able to deal with this point by speaking of the extent to which people might manifest rationality in accepting propositions rather than speaking of what they in fact would accept or of the extent to which they in fact would manifest rationality.

5.

Causal Analyses, Conclusive Reasons Analyses, and Reliability Analyses

1. EARLY CAUSAL ANALYSES

Some philosophers add a clause concerning causation as a fourth condition of knowledge, while others substitute such a clause for the justification condition in a standard analysis.

It is generally agreed that the following simple condition yields an analysis that is too strong:

(c_1)   the state of affairs (fact) that p is a cause of S's believing p.

For example, Alvin Goldman has remarked that when S knows that something is a dog by seeing that it is, S's percept (and thus S's belief) is not caused by the animal's being a dog. Instead, the molecular properties of the animal's surface are causally responsible for the transmission of light, which, in turn, brings about S's percept (Goldman 1976; and see Audi 1980, p. 77). Nor do these surface properties "*ensure* that the object is a dog, either logically or nomologically. Something could have that surface (on one side) and still have a non-dog interior and backside" (Goldman 1976, p. 785n; and see Armstrong 1973, p. 165). Goldman's latter remark, however, seems to require that causes be necessary conditions, and to overlook the very broad sense of "cause" that he employed in his own early causal analysis of knowing, according to which a cause is anything that "leads to" or "results in" another event or state (Goldman 1967, p. 360n).

To be sure, in that earlier paper Goldman also admitted that (c_1) fails to cover empirical knowledge of existential or universal generalizations. For such generalizations do not describe states of affairs

119

that cause belief in them. Goldman originally proposed to deal with such knowledge by extending the sense of causal terminology by means of the following principle:

(GP)   If q is logically related to p [by either entailing or being entailed by p], and if [the fact or state of affairs that] p is a cause of [or causally connected with] z, then [the fact or state of affairs that] q is a cause of [or causally connected with] z.[1]

Mark Steiner has pointed out that applying (c_1) and GP to mathematical knowledge stretches the ordinary sense of causal terminology too far. He suggests that a causal theorist might wish to include the following condition for knowledge, instead:

(c_2) the sentence "p" must be used in a causal explanation of S's believing that "p" is true. (Steiner 1973, p. 60)

But Peter Klein has shown that if we agree with Steiner's additional view that the axioms of number theory and analysis are contained in any theory utilized in causal explanations, then (c_2) will be too weak to rule out knowledge of those axioms due to a bizarre, Gettierized causal sequence leading to belief in them. For any causal explanation of the belief would still include those axioms (Klein 1976, p. 796).

Moreover, Klein shows that GP is violated when the conjunction $a\&b$ entails c, where the state of affairs that c is a causal consequence of the state of affairs that b but not of the combined states of affairs that a and that b, because the latter have interfering effects (p. 797).

An example that may run counter to (c_2) is the following:

(E 46)   *The Bumpkin*: S, ignorant of magicians, happens to see one transfer a coin in the middle of a sleight-of-hand routine in which, prior to S's entrance, the magician has sometimes only given the appearance of doing so—as the audience is

---

[1] The need for bracketed modifications of Goldman's principle is explained by Peter Klein (Klein 1976) and Louis Loeb (Loeb 1976). Loeb also defends Goldman against Brian Skyrms's example of the beheaded corpse (Skyrms 1967, pp. 385-386).

well aware. On the basis of the present appearances, S forms the true belief, p: 'The man has transferred the coin.' (Carrier 1971, p. 7)

Even though S does not know p, John Barker claims that the case does not run counter to (c_2), on the grounds that the actual movements consisting in transferring the coin are not necessary for S's believing p, since it is impossible for S to detect that they are taking place (Barker 1972, p. 317). Barker maintains that the same appearances would, even if deceptive, have caused the same belief. However, if Goldman's point about the dog is correct, such an objection is too strong. For when one visually perceives a dog, one does not detect its inside and backside, even though one knows the dog is present.

There are other, less controversial, counterexamples against (c_2), including one offered by Goldman:

(E 47)   *The Careless Typesetter*: On a newspaper known to be generally reliable, a typesetter carelessly misprints details of a story which S misreads because of eyestrain in such a fashion as to believe the true story. (Goldman 1967, p. 363)

Goldman's response to this example was to add a further condition to the causal analysis of knowledge requiring that S be able to reconstruct all the "important" links in the causal chain leading to S's belief, and that S be justified in this reconstruction (Goldman 1967, p. 363). Commentators have regarded this addition as vague and counterintuitive, and, as we shall see, it fails to prevent the analysis from being too weak.

Certainly, justification or a workable substitute for it needs to be mentioned somehow in any plausible causal analysis of knowledge in order to avoid counterexamples such as the following:

(E 48)   *The Beloved Speck*: From wishful thinking, and not because of reliable information, S forms the true belief that a speck which S sees on the horizon is a boat bearing S's approaching lover. (Ackermann 1972, p. 96)[2]

---

[2] See also the prophet of doom example (Morawetz 1974, p. 368). Goldman has explained that his original causal analysis of knowing only intended to count "Carte-

2. CONCLUSIVE REASONS ANALYSES

L. S. Carrier has attempted to include acknowledgment of justification by requiring that the causal chain involve a connection between the state of affairs that p and S's reasons for believing p, where those reasons are causes of the belief (Carrier 1971, p. 5). In analyzing empirical knowledge, Carrier describes the connection between belief and the corresponding state of affairs by substituting certain subjunctive conditionals for the traditional justification condition:

(c_3)   (a) the reasons for S's believing p are such that, in S's circumstances, if it were not the case that p then S would not believe p, and (b) the reasons for S's believing p are such that, in S's circumstances, if S were not of the belief that p, it would not be the case that p. (p. 6)

Not every philosopher agrees that causal connections can be rendered by such simple conditionals. However, it is convenient to discuss this causal analysis together with certain varieties of what have come to be called conclusive reasons analyses, namely, those varieties that propose a necessary condition for knowledge (or, at least, for knowledge of particular matters of fact, as opposed to general truths) either entailing (a), or entailing one of the following: (a′) There is some subset H of existing circumstances that are logically [and causally][3] independent of the truth of p, such that unless p were the case, S would not believe p; or (a″) . . . unless p were the case, S would not have the reasons S does for believing p.[4]

---

sian'' accounts of justification as irrelevant to knowing (Goldman 1979, p. 1). See n. 36, below.

[3] Ernest Sosa points out (Sosa 1974b, pp. 390-391) that it is best to delete this component of the condition, since, for example, a reliable instrument might be used by S to know that someone else is awake in a case where that very employment of the instrument happens to be causally responsible for the person's being awake.

[4] For brevity, I shall allow a broader and a narrower reading of (a″). When S has reasons described by "R," the narrower reading regards (a″) as saying in its consequent that S would no longer possess those reasons (whether or not "R" were to remain true). On the broader reading, (a″) is saying in its consequent that "R" would no longer be true (whether or not S continued to believe R).

A conclusive reasons analysis[5] is one variety of what has been called a reliability analysis of knowing. The latter is an analysis which presents the knower as reliable concerning the question whether p, in the sense that some of the knower's cognitive or epistemic states (not analyzed in terms of knowledge) are such that, given further characteristics of the knower (possibly including relational ones), it is nomologically necessary or at least in a certain way probable or likely that p.

We cannot refute analyses requiring (a), (a'), or (a'') by appealing to Goldman's point about seeing a dog. For in the usual contexts of perception, no appropriate substitutes for the dog's interior and backside would have occurred, had those portions of the dog been missing yet other circumstances been as described in (a), (a') or (a'').

Analyses including one of these requirements correctly rule out knowledge in the bumpkin example (E 46) because the magician is so disposed that even were he not to transfer the coin "he would still have made the bumpkin believe he did" by giving the same appearances (Carrier 1971, p. 8). However, this way of describing the magician allows us to see why Carrier himself was forced in a

---

Fred Dretske's understanding of conclusive reasons is the narrower one (Dretske 1971). That Dretske intends (a'') to be understood as saying: 'If p were not the case, then S would not have the reasons S does for believing p' rather than as saying: 'If S were to have the reasons S does for believing p, then p would be the case' is clear from his discussion of a lottery example where S possesses only one among the thousands of tickets. Dretske says that S does not know p: 'S is not going to win' because condition (a'') is not satisfied, and in this context he words the condition as follows: "If S were going to win the lottery, his chances of winning would not be $1/m$ (m being the number of tickets sold)" (p. 4).

George Pappas and Marshall Swain mention difficulties in other types of conclusive reasons analyses (Pappas and Swain 1978, pp. 18-22). However, their discussion of Peter Unger's analysis is too limited (see Chapter 6, Section 2.1).

Some conclusive reasons analyses add further necessary conditions or include qualifications of (a), (a'), or (a''). For example, David Armstrong requires that conditional (a') be supported by true laws of nature (Armstrong 1973; also see Harrison 1978-1979) and makes several additions to the conditional, some of which will be considered below. For a general discussion of Armstrong's qualifications, see Pastin 1977 and for additional qualifications that would be needed in order to meet certain objections to Armstrong, see Bonjour 1980.

[5] Except for one depending on the broader reading of (a'').

later paper to admit that the following example is a genuine counterexample to any analysis which includes either (a), or (a'), or (a''):

(E 49)   *Eloise's Phone Call*: Talking on the telephone, Abelard knows *p*: 'Eloise is wishing me happy birthday.' But, unsuspected by Abelard, an actress, set to give a perfect imitation of Eloise's greeting and hired by Abelard's concerned psychiatrist lest Eloise forget to call, was attempting to get through on the telephone at the same time as Eloise, and would have performed but for Eloise's dialing. (Carrier 1971, p. 9; see Carrier 1976, p. 242.)

Such an example of knowledge involves alternative causation.[6] The following counterexample to (c_3) and to (a') is significantly different. It also serves to call into question Carrier's view that reasons causally explain a belief:

(E 50)   *The Explained Hologram*: *S* initially believed *p*: 'There is a vase in that box' because he was tricked by seeing an illuminated hologram rather than the vase. But *S* presently knows *p* for the following reasons: Mr. Promoter has cogently explained that the box is part of a machine that alternates between displaying the hologram and the real vase contained in the box. (Lehrer and Paxson 1969, p. 236)

Here, the etiology of *S*'s belief may be irrelevant to *S*'s eventual knowledge after hearing Mr. Promoter's explanation. For *S*'s belief may be from the start "so firmly and unequivocally fixed that the subsequent revelations neither altered nor reinforced it" (p. 236).

John Barker criticizes this type of example by saying that if *S*'s belief had been "so insensitive to the real state of the world" that,

---

6 Notice that if we refuse to count such a case as constituting knowledge, we may then be burdened with the consequence that one commonly fails to know that one knows propositions of the form '*a* caused *b*' or of the form '*a* was involved in the causation of *b*.' For one would have to know that it is false that God or a Cartesian deceiving demon would have intervened to bring about *b* because of the absence of *a* or *a*'s failure to cause *b* (Carrier 1976, p. 242).

had subsequent revelations shown there really was no vase in the box, S would still have persisted in his belief, then S does not know p (Barker 1972, p. 317). But this does not show that the presence of the vase is a necessary condition in the existing circumstances for the actual belief. It only shows that changed evidential circumstances plus absence of the vase would have been sufficient for absence of the belief.[7]

The following example may show that analyses utilizing (a) or (a$'$) are too strong because they commit the second version of the conditional fallacy, assuming that certain speculations about possible developments in the future of science are plausible:

(E 51)   *Noncompulsive Belief:* S is one of our descendants who knows, thanks to future scientific discoveries, p_1: 'Some beliefs are noncompulsive, i.e., might be otherwise' (or knows p_2: 'Some of S's beliefs about beliefs might be otherwise').[8]

Before turning to Carrier's second analysis, it is worth noting that Barker and Brian Skyrms have shown that (c$_3$) yields an analysis that becomes too weak if we merely drop condition (a) (Barker 1972, p. 314; Skyrms 1967, p. 385). In addition, even as it stands such an analysis is too weak to rule out knowledge in the following case:

(E 52)   *Judy's Mole:* S believes the true statement, p: 'Judy is present' on the basis of how Judy looks. But until today, S's 'perceptual schemata' of Judy and of Trudy have been

---

[7] When addressing George O'Hair's analogous case of the prejudiced parent, who already believed his child to be innocent before acquiring adequate evidence of it, Armstrong maintains that the parent does not know the child is innocent; we may say of the parent that "from his point of view" the evidence is "unnecessary confirmation" (Armstrong 1973, p. 210). But Armstrong's latter remark actually shows that a new cognitive attitude is present, for the parent regards himself as possessing (additional) evidence in support of the believed proposition.

[8] This may be turned into a counterexample to analyses relying on (a$''$) by considering S's (present-day) knowledge that p_3: 'Some reasons for believing something about beliefs might have been otherwise' (or: 'Some of S's reasons for believing something about beliefs might have been otherwise').

indistinct, and S is now only able to discriminate the twins because (1) S has fallen down and hit his head so that, unknown to him, a new feature has been added to his Judy-schema, a mole-associated feature, and (2) again unknown to S Judy happened today to develop just such a mole. (Goldman 1976, p. 789)[9]

Some who believe in a creator of the universe may find (c_3) too weak to rule out knowledge in the following example:

(E 53)   *Belief of the Elect*: S is one of the Calvinist elect, and God compels S to believe p: 'God exists.'

I suspect that few religious believers wish to count S as knowing p, yet they would regard clause (a) of (c_3) as being satisfied in this case, since they would presume that S would not even exist if there were no creator. They would also allow that clause (b) is satisfied if they believe that there is a sufficient reason for God's actions.

3. CARRIER'S SECOND CAUSAL ANALYSIS

Carrier's more recent causal analysis (Carrier 1976) deals with the case of the explained hologram (E 50) by allowing that acquisition of reasons may help to "sustain" a belief even when it does not enter into the causal origin of the belief. (Which is not to say that the acquisition of reasons need reinforce the belief in the sense of making it stronger.) Carrier includes the following condition:

(c_5)   mention of p alone provides at least a partial causal explanation of S's believing p. (pp. 238-246)

Carrier says that this condition accounts for S's failure to know in the case of the careless typesetter (E 47). For "if it is asked what caused the reader's coming to believe that p, I doubt whether anyone would be satisfied with the answer that the reporter's observations

---

[9] See also the televised sheep and candles on a seesaw examples (Swain 1972b, pp. 297-298; Williams 1978, p. 260).

did'' (p. 244). Thus, we should not regard the reporter's observing that p as a member of the same causal chain that contains the newspaper reader's coming to believe that p. Instead, when tracing back the chain we regard the reader's misreading as explained by eyestrain, and in explaining the eyestrain we are led in a direction away from the state of affairs that p (p. 246). A similar point holds regarding the case of Judy's mole (E 52), since we are eventually led to explain why S's present Judy-schema has a mole-associated feature.

The new analysis also has the advantage of being able to deal with the following case:

(E 54)   *The Belief-Chemical*: A causally necessary condition for anyone to have a belief is the presence in his or her brain of chemical C, and S, without any evidence, happens to believe p: 'C is present in my brain.' (Armstrong 1973, pp. 178-179)

Carrier can treat S as failing to know p because the standing condition of C's being present would not be selected as a cause when one explains S's believing p.[10]

Carrier deals with knowledge of a priori truths by saying that the event of one's learning such a truth is a reason in a causal chain leading to one's belief in the truth, and that an explanation which mentions the learning ipso facto mentions the truth (pp. 239-240). Again, when one gains knowledge of a universal empirical statement from observation of instances, the generalization explains why the observations occurred which formed part of a chain of reasons leading to (or sustaining) one's belief (p. 240). In contrast, no causal ex-

---

[10] Armstrong attempts to modify (a') so as to deal with this case by requiring that whenever believing p would nomologically ensure that the state of affairs that p obtains, then believing p would ensure that subset H obtains. However, in the case of the belief-chemical, H trivially obtains and is merely the condition of S's being someone capable of beliefs. Armstrong can avoid this objection by insisting that H be ensured by a nomological necessity which is not (also) a logical necessity. However, this has the untoward upshot of ruling out one's knowing that one exists or one's knowing that one has beliefs. See Mark Pastin's critique of Armstrong for a related criticism (Pastin 1977).

planation of S's belief would mention merely the axioms of number theory and analysis in the Gettierized example sketched by Klein.

Furthermore, Carrier's account has the virtue of being compatible with the fact that a dog's presence is not ensured by its light-reflecting properties. For it is plausible to say that the presence of the dog does explain the presence of the surface which reflects light in a certain way toward S.

The difference between the example of Eloise's phone call (E 49) and the bumpkin case (E 46) consists, on this view, in the fact that the explanation of why certain appearances were presented to the bumpkin is not that the magician did transfer the coin, but that a magician was involved who would have produced the given appearances whether or not the coin was transferred. Whereas, the explanation of Abelard's belief that he is speaking with Eloise is her calling and speaking, inasmuch as that blocks the causal intervention of the actress.

In spite of these virtues, Carrier's account becomes obscure when he attempts to deal with the following example, which is significantly different from the case of the belief-chemical:

(E 55) *Brain Damage*: S suffers brain damage which happens to affect his present state of mind so that he believes p: 'S has brain damage.' (Sosa 1969, p. 39)[11]

Carrier says that "if there is a chain of reasons connecting his belief to his brain damage, then the case is one in which his belief in brain damage is perfectly reliable . . . [although] we are unaware of this chain of reasons . . ." (Carrier 1976, p. 249). Moreover, Carrier reduces reliability to the fact that "in those specific circumstances it is not at all accidental that one got it right, since there was a chain of reasons present insuring that one would," where reasons are simply "causes which, if discovered and articulated, can be used to provide an explanation for one's coming to have the belief one has" (pp. 248, 246).

---

[11] See also the case of the hallucinating paranoid (Collier 1973, p. 351).

Apparently, what Carrier means is that a hypothetical scientist who had enough (presently unavailable) knowledge about S's brain and mind could explain S's belief in his brain damage by mentioning the fact that the damage has befallen S. The scientist would have the necessary background information, including laws concerning brain and mind, to permit the mention of the brain damage to constitute an explanation for the scientist of S's belief.

Construing reliability in this fashion leads, however, to counter-intuitive results. For example, S would be accorded knowledge in Harman's newspaper example (E 9). Carrier accepts this upshot on the grounds that "to insist on a 'social condition' for knowledge paves the way for common prejudice to hold sway over one's true and justifiable beliefs" (p. 250). But this remark ignores the differences between justified and unjustified beliefs held by members of the epistemic community surrounding S.

In addition, Carrier would have to accord S knowledge in the case of Tom Grabit's actual twin (E 10), which does not depend upon social aspects of knowledge. Carrier himself would not be disturbed by this result, for he even allows that a person who believes the boy who cried "Wolf!" succeeds in gaining knowledge from the boy's testimony on the occasion when the beast finally appears. Indeed, Carrier attributes knowledge to S in the following case:

(E 56) *The House of Illusion Tomato*: While passing through an amusement park fun house in which many appearances are deceiving, S spots a real tomato and believes it is real. (p. 249)

In contrast to the bumpkin case, nothing is set to replace the real tomato with a fake one, were it to be missing, and a partial causal explanation of S's belief could merely mention the presence of the tomato.[12]

---

[12] See also the case of the clever auto thief (Klein 1976, p. 801n). Laurence Bonjour describes a related case concerning a lottery, which serves to remind us that the person going through the fun house knows that someone will be somehow visually deceived in visiting it but not who or how (Bonjour 1980, p. 69).

4. Morton's Causal-Reliability Analysis

Adam Morton's causal condition for knowledge avoids such counterintuitive results by giving a different account of reliability, and by adding a clause concerning false beliefs:

(c_5) S's belief in p is [produced or] sustained by a reliable process, that is, by a process which produces [or sustains] no false beliefs, and which is such that there is an explanation, in terms of the laws of nature and the facts of the case, why on this occasion it produces [or sustains] a true belief. (Morton 1977, p. 58)

By demanding that the process produce no false beliefs, Morton is able to rule out knowledge in the bumpkin example, provided that we construe S as reasoning by falsely believing that the person who is providing appearances that intimate that the coin is being transferred is not trying to be deceptive about conveying information of this general type. Likewise, someone who trusts the boy who cried "Wolf!" may falsely believe from the boy's manner that he is one not prone in general to jest about such matters. Again, Keith Lehrer and Bredo Johnsen have suggested that certain false beliefs may be generated in Harman's newspaper example (Lehrer 1974, p. 225; Johnsen 1974, p. 280).

But all these examples could be modified as in the case of the clever reasoner (E 6), where it is implausible to attribute false beliefs to S. In response, Morton would be prepared to argue that "although we can explain why this process did produce a true belief . . . we cannot explain why it is that this process *should* have produced a true belief" (Morton 1977, p. 59; cf. p. 61).

Our discussion of Carrier's views might lead us to interpret Morton's remark as meaning that knowledge is absent when a statement of the process by which the belief in p was produced fails to provide a partial causal explanation of S's belief, i.e., of the belief's having the *content* that it does. The trouble with such an interpretation lies in the fact that explanation is relative to those giving or receiving it. The hypothetical scientists mentioned above who have more background information than we do concerning S's brain damage might indeed give just such an explanation of the content of S's belief that he has brain damage, and we would be led to the same counterintuitive result as Carrier's own analysis produced.

But Morton rewords his point as follows: "To put it differently, the process . . . could as easily have produced a quite different belief, which might have been false" (p. 59). To say it could have done this is not meant to deal with statistics but with "a causal matter; it depends on whether there are good reasons, in the workings of the mind and the routes by which information comes to it, why true beliefs should result. In fact, a process can be reliable in this way, even if it operates only once and cannot be repeated," as in the following case:

(E 57)   *The Retina-Rotting Drug*: S, who was blinded after initial development of his visual system, is given an experimental drug that allows him to know something about his surroundings by looking at them for just a few moments before it destroys his retinas. (p. 58)[13]

Morton's perspective accords with D. S. Goldstick's view that reliability concerns causal mechanisms which obey the following conditional: "The conclusions to which the method *would* generally lead from true data, *would* be true conclusions" (Goldstick 1972, p. 240).

Thus, in the bumpkin example (E 46), Morton would say that the

---

[13] Armstrong opposes the admission of unrepeatable processes on the grounds that knowledge is a "pragmatic concept"; we are interested in the distinction between knowledge and mere true belief because "the man who has *mere* true belief is unreliable. He was right this time, but if the same sort of situation crops up again he is likely to get it wrong. . . . But if it is empirically impossible or even very unlikely that the situation will crop up again, then the distinction loses almost all its *point*" (Armstrong 1973, p. 173). Armstrong provides a reason why we are interested generally in the distinction, but that does not prohibit us from admitting that some applications of the distinction lack this pragmatic consequence, especially if we admit that there are also theoretically significant aspects to the existence of knowledge.

magician "was not out to provide S with true information" and so was not, in the above sense, "a reliable factor in the process" (Morton 1977, p. 60). The same might be said of the process of gaining information from perceptual appearances when in a house of illusion, as in (E 56), where appearances are not generally set up to provide one with true information. Again, in the case of Tom Grabit's actual twin (E 10), trusting one's perceptions when there are other people around whom one could easily mistake for those concerned in one's belief is a process that would not generally lead to true beliefs, at least, not if we are imagining a hypothetical sampling among various physically possible similar situations involving roughly equal proportions of participation by the different people.

Three other cases that Morton's analysis is able to handle are the following:

(E 58)   *The Degenerating Memory Trace*: Over time, S's memory trace of the fact that p degenerates, but an accident restores the original encoding, which now accounts for S's believing that p. (Armstrong 1973, p. 157)

(E 59)   *Veridical Hallucination*: S is in a hypersensitive and deranged state where almost any considerable sensory stimulus would cause S to believe p: 'A sound of such-and-such a sort is present.' By coincidence, just such a sound happens to be present now and S comes to believe p. (Armstrong 1973, pp. 158, 171)

(E 60)   *Frequent Undetected Hallucinations*: Driving through the countryside, S has been having frequent hallucinations of the state of affairs that p: 'A barn is present,' but she does not suspect that they are hallucinations and has no reason to do so. Right now, however, she is not in a state tending toward hallucination,[14] and believes that p because she sees a real barn. (Audi 1980, p. 76)

---

[14] I have added this detail to Robert Audi's description of the case in order to make it differ more fully from the veridical hallucination example. Mark Pastin describes

In these three cases, S fails to know p and Morton can explain the fact. He may say of the first case that trusting beliefs arising from memory traces markedly altered by accidents is not a reliable process, and say of the second case that it, too, involves a process that would not generally lead to true beliefs concerning a wider range of sensory stimuli. Although the third case may not be compared to the tomato in the house of illusion example (E 56), since S lacks reason to suspect her perceptions, it does involve the process of trusting senses appropriate to forming the belief that are liable to provide incorrect cues concerning one's surroundings (see Audi 1980, p. 86).

Morton therefore has an advantage over David Armstrong's conclusive reasons account, which relies on clause (a') (see Section 2, above), and which rules out knowledge in the first two cases only on the ground that there is not much empirical possibility of a recurrence of possession of characteristics H, that is, the characteristics which are such that when combined with believing p nomologically ensure that p. Armstrong simply says that the description of H must not be "too specific" (Armstrong 1973, pp. 173-178). But Robert Audi has noted that this fails to rule out knowledge in the third of the above cases, where S's sensory faculties are not presently in a state of readiness to provide incorrect cues (Audi 1980, p. 78).

Morton's analysis unfortunately leaves the meaning of the phrase, "on this occasion," in (c_5) unexplained. Why, for example, should we not be forced to admit of the final time that the boy cries "Wolf!" that on this occasion the speaker does intend to provide true information and that trusting *such* testimony would generally lead to true beliefs. Perhaps, Morton might deal with this objection as he does with a case similar to the newspaper example. He might say that the occasion includes people surrounding S who know of additional evidence concerning the boy's previous pranks, and that "had things been essentially no different" S would [in a good proportion of imaginary cases similar to this] have paid attention to the additional

---

a somewhat similar case that includes the presence of frequent trickery exercised upon members of S's epistemic community concerning questions similar to the question whether p (Pastin 1977).

evidence and would have disregarded the source of S's actual belief, thus counting it as "not completely reliable" (Morton 1977, p. 60).

A. J. Holland argues that we should not confuse the issue of whether a source of information is reliable upon a given occasion with the issue of whether the source is [better: would be] generally reliable on such occasions, that is, whether it "typically" generates true beliefs in circumstances where the fact that p explains why S's belief had the content that it did (Holland 1977, p. 564). Holland says of a case modeled on the newspaper example that it is not typical that true beliefs are formed. For even when a true belief happens to occur, "the circumstances are such that it might so easily have been otherwise" (p. 563).

But in order to deal with the newspaper example, we need to consider a problem raised by D. Goldstick, namely, that we are able not only to gerrymander evidence but also to gerrymander the process of acquiring belief: "one and the same sequence must always exemplify many different process types, some of which might conceivably be reliable and some not" (Goldstick 1972, p. 244). Accordingly, Goldstick suggests that it is necessary to include the following condition within a causal analysis of knowing:

(c₆) the process by which S's belief in p has been arrived at and [better: or] sustained falls under at least one description that describes a type of process of arriving at and sustaining beliefs which would be generally reliable, and there is no description of this process which logically entails the above description without being logically entailed by it and which does not describe a type of process that would be generally reliable. (p. 247)

Thus, in the newspaper example, the process may be narrowly described as not merely consulting a news source but consulting one when other news sources contain contrary information. However, it is not clear in the case of Judy's mole (E 52) what it means to speak of a "typical" employment of a process of utilizing a perceptual schema whose details have partly been formed by falling down and hitting one's head. Nor is it obvious what is the typical upshot of forming beliefs caused by brain damage, as in (E 55).

Further, Holland shows that sufficient imagination concerning the range of typical situations creates difficulties. One's additional beliefs, prejudices, or previous exposure to gross maltreatment or prolonged suggestion can lead by familiar processes to unfamiliar beliefs (Holland 1977, p. 568). Holland concludes that a causal theory of knowledge should require that the process through which S's belief in p is acquired [or sustained] is one in which the belief is at least sensitive to the way the world is, that is, beliefs resulting from such a process would vary systematically in content with variations in the states of affairs encountered, even if S's past history makes the range from which he selects beliefs unfamiliar (p. 569). Perhaps we may acknowledge that this requirement is not met in the brain damage example.

The analyses presented by Holland, Morton, and Carrier are defeated by counterexamples that show them to be both too strong when combined with Goldstick's proposal and too weak even if not combined with it:

(E 61)   *The Pointed-to Sheep*: S knows p: 'There is a sheep in the field' because his attention was directed by a farmer's pointing to the animal. Unsuspected by S, the farmer was simultaneously fooling a city slicker by saying that the item is just an artificial replica that stimulates wool production. (Paxson 1974, p. 60)

(E 62)   *The Sports Fan's Surmise*: On a quiz show, S cannot remember who won a certain sports award, but S makes a correct educated guess on the basis of fragments of information which he can remember. (Olen 1976, p. 151)

In the former example, as Thomas Paxson remarks, the farmer's pointing causes S to see the sheep and is an integral part of the testimony to the city slicker, which, if known to S, would keep his evidence from justifying his belief in p. So, a narrow description of the process by which S reaches the belief mentions the presence of evidence capable of blocking S's justification and the case meets Goldstick's condition of failing to know. But S would also fail to know according to the accounts offered by Holland, Morton, and Carrier when supplemented by Goldstick's condition. For it would not be generally reliable to form beliefs by this type of process.[15]

In (E 62), S justifiably believes the best explanation, or most reasonable hypothesis, one that coheres best with his other beliefs, and he relies on no false beliefs. S does not *know* who the winner of the award was, not until, for instance, he checks the record books. Yet the example involves a process of belief-formation that satisfies the characterizations of reliability provided by Holland, Morton, and Carrier.

One might attempt to improve these reliability analyses by combining them with Goldman's account of what it is for S's belief to result from a reliable process in a manner that is necessary for the belief to be justified. He suggests that a process be construed as a functional operation generating a mapping from "input" states onto "output" states (Goldman 1979, p. 12). For reasons that I shall consider in a moment, Goldman argues that the input states should be restricted to events within the organism's nervous system. This would prevent us from describing any process in the case of the pointed-to sheep (E 61) mentioning the factors external to S concerning the farmer's remarks to the city slicker, and would remove the impediment to saying that S knows p. It would also no longer be necessary to speak of being struck on the head as an aspect of the process of belief-formation in the case of Judy's mole (E 52), so we would not need to puzzle over the frequency of true beliefs resulting from any such process or the propensity of such a process to yield true beliefs.

But Goldman's reason for this restriction is unconvincing. He

---

[15] Adding a requirement that there be no even narrower description of the process, e.g., a description mentioning that the extra evidence is misleading, under which the process again becomes generally reliable, will lead to a problematic regress analogous to that explored by Steven Levy concerning misleading defeaters (Levy 1977).

writes, "Justifiedness seems to be a function of how a cognizer deals with his environmental input, i.e., with the goodness or badness of the operations that register and transform the stimulation that reaches him. . . . But *'cognitive'* operations are most plausibly construed as operations of the cognitive faculties, i.e., 'information-processing' equipment *internal* to the organism" (pp. 12-13). Goldman has not shown that justifiedness is *only* a function of dealing with environmental input and never concerns self-knowledge. Nor does the fact that a cognitive faculty is itself internal prevent it from being partly constituted by dispositions or propensities toward thought or conduct within one type of environmental situation rather than another (e.g., see Goldman's own mention of the problem of "biased sampling," p. 10).

Moreover, the modification of reliability theories which we are now considering would have the disadvantage of providing no way of ruling out knowledge in the case of Judy's mole (E 52) or the newspaper example (E 9) once reference to external factors is omitted. And the strategy is helpless to rule out knowledge in the case of brain damage (E 55) if the damage is due to an internally provoked hemorrhage, or in the case of the belief-chemical (E 54).[16]

Let us return to the case of the sports fan's surmise (E 62). Is

---

[16] Indeed, Goldman admits that in the latter case we provide no reason to regard *S*'s belief as justified if we merely point out that it is "nomologically necessary that if anyone believes he is in brain-state *B* then it is true that he is in brain-state *B*, for the only way this belief-state is realized is through brain-state *B* itself" (p. 7). Yet his own analysis of justified belief fails to count such a belief as unjustified. Goldman may think that this type of case is handled by his additional requirement that the relevant processes "are required to admit as input beliefs (or other states) with *any* content," a requirement that he introduces in order to rule out having to count as a process, e.g., inferring *x* whenever the Pope asserts *x* (p. 12). But, of course, the concept of content here is propositional content, which is irrelevant to (E 54) and to (E 55), even though these examples do speak of input from a physical state with a particular chemical or neurophysiological content.

The case of the degenerating memory trace (E 58) shows that the analyses of knowledge provided by Morton and Holland remain too weak even if supplemented by Goldman's understanding of processes. For the description of that case specified that the trace gets restored, albeit by a biological fluke. Carrier, at least, can deal with this example as he does with the case of the careless typesetter (E 47).

there any interesting sense in which we can say that the process of belief-formation involved is not generally reliable or that this is so of at least some narrower characterization of the process?[17]

We can only provide such a narrower characterization by going beyond a strictly causal analysis of knowledge. We may take as a clue Morton's willingness to rephrase his description of unreliability in the following way: "To put it differently again, knowledge of how the belief came about would not give one much reason to believe that it is true" (Morton 1977, p. 59). Morton may be speaking of whether members of S's epistemic community would be rational in accepting p because S does, and may be hinting at the account of 'justified factual knowledge' that I shall defend in the final chapter. It is one that, roughly put, requires S's belief to be justified through its connections with a chain of propositions which themselves are justified in the sense of being ones it would more manifest the rationality of members of the epistemic community to accept in place of competing propositions when pursuing epistemic goals (Shope 1979d).

In situations resembling (E 62), the epistemic community requires further processes of confirmation before allowing that it more fully manifests the rationality of its members for them to accept educated guesses, whether those guesses are arrived at by individuals or groups. But only empirical considerations which take (improving) scientific methodology as one important guide will help to provide the contextual considerations that are needed in order to apply the terms "rational acceptance" and "justified proposition." And only some of those contextual considerations are approximately described by the conditions in causal and reliability analyses of knowledge.[18]

---

[17] After describing several other cases of this type, Jeffrey Olen notes that it will be difficult to specify an independent way of determining what more is needed for knowledge, considering the vast number of contextual considerations that bear on such determination (Olen 1976, p. 152).

[18] See also Morton's acknowledgment of a difference between "healthy" and "pathological" means through which beliefs are caused (Morton 1977, p. 59).

5. CASTAÑEDA'S RELIABILITY ANALYSIS

We can further appreciate the need for this perspective by considering Hector-Neri Castañeda's reliability analysis of S's knowing p at t (Castañeda 1980). Castañeda's justification condition requires a certain type of reliable connection between S's evidence, described as e, for p and the fact that p. Because he does not emphasize reliability of belief-forming processes, Castañeda is able to allow S to have knowledge in cases such as the explained hologram (E 50) and the retina-rotting drug (E 57). However, Castañeda does not regard the connection between the fact that p and S's evidence as being in every case a causal connection. Nor does he believe that it is adequately characterized by subjunctive conditional (a″) previously mentioned in Section 2. Instead, his justification condition focuses on a conditional of the form, 'If e then p,' which indicates a nomological (but not necessarily causal) regularity holding within a certain context. This context involves additional conditions, Z, concerning certain respects in which the subject matter connected with the fact that p happens to be normal or abnormal. The context also involves certain regularities, s, which hold concerning other factors connected with Z. We shall clarify these details momentarily.

The form of Castañeda's justification condition is as follows:

(1) given Z and s, if e then p; and
(2) both s and e are true; and
(3) at t, S believes that e and believes that *ceteris paribus* if e then p. (p. 227)

It may assist our understanding of this suggestion to draw an analogy to a context in which I believe something of the form, j: '*Ceteris paribus* the cause of b is a,' where, for example, b is a peculiar sort of noise (which I sometimes hear in my Ford) and a is lack of lubrication in a particular engine part. My believing j does not require me to believe that a causes b in all contexts. I may allow, for example, that there are modified Fords which lack this engine part and which make a similar noise for other reasons. But since I do not think of them as a normal Ford, my *ceteris paribus* clause rules them out of consideration. Nor do I have to believe that my Ford is completely normal; I can allow that it is in some respects abnormal, even to the extent of having abnormalities that are contributory conditions which cooperate with *a* in bringing about *b*. The presence of such abnormalities is covered by my *ceteris paribus* clause.

The set of normal and abnormal factors that one has in mind in making judgment *j* is analogous to set Z in Castañeda's justification condition. He defines Z as a set of circumstances relevant to the truth or falsity of *p* which obtain in S's situation and which are either normal or normal except for respects of abnormality $r_1, \ldots, r_n$. In a part of the analysis outside the justification condition, Castañeda adds the following requirement:

(4) S believes that the circumstances are normal or that they are normal except for respects $r_1, \ldots, r_n$.

In the causal analogy, further contextual assumptions lie behind my judgment *j*. When I make *j*, I presume that certain types of interactions do not occur as part of the way in which the previously mentioned factors get connected with *b*, e.g., I assume that the connection of those factors, and the lack of lubrication, with the noise is not accomplished through the intervention of mediating mechanisms external to my car. For example, I am not prepared to make judgment *j* on the hypothesis of the intervention of an orbital monitoring device placed above the earth by aliens, which senses a lack of lubrication in my engine part and sends a beam of energy into my engine, leading to vibration in the part struck by the beam and thus to the noise I hear.[19]

The analogous assumptions in Castañeda's justification condition concern *s*, which Castañeda describes as a set of "structural" presuppositions and assumptions such that S "has the propensity to

---

[19] For a less fanciful illustration of this point see Shope 1967, p. 315.

make inferences in accordance with the members of s'' (p. 226).[20] The members of s are presumed to be relevant to the nomological connections between (A) the truth or falsehood of p (or of competitors to p[21]) and (B) factors which are either existing abnormalities or existing facts, including the evidence described by e, presumed to pertain to the issue whether p (or to issues of the type whether p[21]).

Just as there is a sense in which judgment j presumes that there is a reliable connection between a and b given the other factors and assumptions, so Castañeda's justification condition characterizes a type of reliable connection between S's evidence and the fact that p given Z and s.

If we initially allow ourselves some flexibility in what we count as 'abnormal,' the above justification condition plus requirement (4) gives the analysis considerable power in dealing with the examples we have previously considered. In a number of those examples, S would fail to know because S fails to believe some relevant abnormality to be present. These are abnormalities such as: the presence of a typographical error (and, perhaps, the eyestrain) in the careless typesetter example (E 47); the discrimination-enhancing accidental change in S's perceptual schema in the case of Judy's mole (E 52); and the degeneration and restoration process affecting the memory trace in the case of the degenerating memory trace (E 58).

In other examples that we have discussed, there are unsuspected

[20] This phrasing means to leave open whether S consciously formulates beliefs in s and to leave open the possibility that in some cases the relevant inferences occur unconsciously.

[21] I speak here of competitors, and of issues of the type whether p, as a rough way of indicating a complex dimension to Castañeda's analysis which I shall not discuss. He makes the attribution of knowledge that p relative to the attributor's having in mind a set of questions and a set of possible answers to those questions which are related in an intricate way that suffices to deal with various methodological constraints on S's manner of finding answers and also to deal with certain interesting points about knowledge attributions made by Fred Dretske (Dretske 1972; 1975a). I shall also avoid discussion of an "epistemic powers" clause which Castañeda includes in his analysis of knowing, and which appears to commit the conditional fallacy in cases where S knows that S will die in a moment or will have no thoughts for an immediately ensuing duration (Castañeda 1980, p. 227).

abnormal factors which do not enter into the nomological connections that obtain in the example, but S nonetheless fails to know p because, if S had believed those factors to be present then S would not have judged that *ceteris paribus* if E then p. For they are factors not excluded by the *ceteris paribus* qualification, yet which figure in some members of s relating to inferences to competitors to p. This is true in the newspaper case (E 9) concerning the 'abnormal' presence of surrounding inquirers in the epistemic community who hold different epistemic stances from S regarding the issue whether p. The same may be said of the presence of a nearby look-alike in the case of Tom Grabit's actual twin (E 10); of the magician's proclivities in the bumpkin example (E 46); or of the recent past history of deception about issues of the type at hand on the part of the boy who cried "Wolf!"[22]

In other cases, S fails to know according to Castañeda's account not because S fails to be aware of the relevant abnormalities, but because S does not in fact believe that *ceteris paribus* if E then p. This is true of S in the tomato in the house of illusion example (E 56), since S believes that the conditions nomologically connecting visual evidence and the objects of perception have been to a great extent tricked-up.

However, it is clear that the justification condition proposed by Castañeda does not, even when combined with requirement (4), explain why S lacks knowledge in the case of the sports fan's surmise (E 62).[23] Accordingly, Castañeda adds further clauses to his analysis of knowledge which relativize attributions of knowledge to "constraints" imposed by the attributor, constraints which may include "methodological" aspects of S's accepting p. I shall argue in the

---

[22] In the latter case, if abnormalities are picked out in relation to the particular boy involved, then the factor which S fails to believe to be present yet abnormal is the boy's intending to convey true information about the presence of wolves. If abnormalities are picked out in relation to boys in general, or informants in general, then S fails to believe that this boy has a history of lying about the presence of wolves. (However, see n. 29.)

[23] Also see Sosa's example of the diagnostic palmreader (Sosa 1974b, pp. 392-393).

final chapter that methodological issues be brought into the analysis in a less direct way. But even Castañeda's analysis, which is one of the most sophisticated reliability accounts, has found it necessary to deal with them separately from its condition concerning justified belief.

There are some disadvantages even to Castañeda's conception of reliability. He is forced to insist that all knowledge is based on evidence separate from the state of affairs known to obtain. Epistemologists who believe in the existence of immediate knowledge will find this objectionable.[24] Castañeda needs to rely on this detail in order to relate his justification condition to the brain damage case (E 55), and to the belief-chemical case (E 54). In each example, S would lack knowledge because S has no evidence supporting S's belief in p (presuming that we refuse to count the null set as evidence).[25]

At least one of Castañeda's requirements (1)-(4) will need modification in the face of merely misleading evidence S does not possess. For instance, this is true in the case of the pointed-to sheep (E 61); for in contexts where one's perception of x indicates that x is present, there is normally nobody pointing to x and denying that it is x. Yet S fails in the example to believe that this abnormal condition is present, and it is a *type* of condition that S takes to be relevant to

---

[24] Castañeda acknowledges this implication of his view, although he initially expresses the point by saying that the knower's "beliefs" must guarantee that p (p. 195). But he reiterates the view by saying instead that "the knower's beliefs (whether we call them evidence or not) guarantee in a very strong way the truth of what he believes and knows" (p. 196). This wording implies both (A) that the guarantee comes from the *content* of the beliefs and (B) that the facts characterized in that content might not always be labeled "evidence" in the everyday sense of that term. His final wording of clause (1) of the justification condition confirms that he intends implication (A), as does his reference at one point to evidence as a set of "propositions" (p. 202). That he intends implication (B) is confirmed by his speaking of what the belief that p is "grounded on" (p. 203).

[25] Each of these cases might be modified so that the brain damage or brain-chemical or probing by a surgeon also causes S to have some flimsy evidence that p, described by e, and to have the beliefs mentioned in clause (4). We can refuse to count these as cases of knowing according to Castañeda's account only by presupposing some 'constraints' not specified in the account.

whether *ceteris paribus* if he has his present perceptions then a sheep is nearby. Of course, there is an additional factor present in light of which the farmer's remark is merely misleading, namely, the farmer's intent to use his statement to deceive someone concerning the issue at hand. But S is also unaware of this factor. If Castañeda tries to qualify (4) to allow lack of awareness of such factors, he may need to move in the direction of some type of defeasibility account.

Certain philosophers would fault Castañeda's neglecting to require that the beliefs in (3) or (4) not be unjustified for S.[26] But even if Castañeda did require, e.g., that S not be unjustified in believing e, the question remains whether 'Gettierization' of e can occur in a manner that thwarts the utility of Castañeda's justification condition and requirement (4). It is not obvious that what is abnormal relative to the question whether p includes all that is abnormal relative to the question whether e, or to the question whether the belief mentioned in (4) is true.

Certainly, Castañeda's justification condition deals successfully with the standard Gettier-type cases considered thus far. For instance, the intent to deceive in the usual sorts of Nogot case is an abnormal factor which S fails to believe to be present and which is relevant to situations where one utilizes evidence of the type that Nogot provides in deciding whether someone owns the type of car in question. For the same reason, the analysis successfully deals with the following variant:

(E 63) *Compulsive Mr. Nogot*: As in (E 1), except that Mr. Nogot has a compulsion to trick people into believing true propositions by getting them to believe [or to have evidence that would justify them in believing] false propositions, and Nogot provides his evidence to S because Nogot is aware of Mr. Havit's owning a Ford. (Lehrer 1979, p. 76)[27]

---

[26] For example, see Laurence Bonjour's discussion of related issues (Bonjour 1980).

[27] This type of Nogot case has been used by Lehrer in order to show that analyses of knowing which rely on the existence of a nomological connection between what makes p true and S's believing p fail to rule out every Gettier-type example by such a device (Lehrer 1979, p. 76). (Contrast Fred Dretske's case of the meddler and the

In this case, there is no undetected, rare intention to deceive S regarding the question whether p. But there is an undetected compulsion which we believe to be rare in contexts where evidence is gathered on the basis of testimony in order to decide questions of this type, at least in relation to testimony of the typical informant.

The latter belief is relevant to whether Castañeda will encounter difficulty in dealing with a somewhat similar case:

(E 64)   *Compulsive Mr. Nogot (Modified Version)*: As in (E 63), except that Nogot's unsuspected compulsion is ostentatiously to appear to keep up with his fellow students regarding expensive items. Having learned that Mr. Havit owns a Ferrari, Mr. Nogot's compulsion makes him borrow or steal a Ferrari in order to supply the evidence he does to S, who responds to it by believing p: 'Someone in the class owns an item of the type Nogot is flaunting.'

Because of the change in the content of p in this example, it is not rare but common for the undetected compulsion to be present in contexts where there is inquiry into questions of the type whether p. Even though S fails to know p, conditions (1)-(4) appear to be satisfied.[28]

Volkswagen [Dretske 1975a, p. 800], where the person communicating with S is not nomologically connected to what makes p true.)

[28] Our intuition that S lacks knowledge in this case calls into question Castañeda's claim that S knows in the following example:

(E 65)   *The Cross-Wired Rememberer*: Whenever S very clearly perceives a date written in a book, his peculiar memory mechanism causes him to remember the date as ten years later than what was actually printed. S's only source of information about a given historical date has been his having carefully read and memorized a particular history book in which, unsuspected by S, the date was misprinted as ten years earlier than the correct date, D. S now believes p: 'The date was D,' thanks to S's peculiar memory mechanism. (pp. 202-203)

Castañeda's view that S knows p in this example indicates that Castañeda regards abnormality not as relative to a typical inquirer's finding answers to questions of the type whether p, but instead as relative to S's finding such answers. So it is unclear

But Castañeda may reply that appearances are deceiving, and that abnormality must be regarded as relative to the "constraints" which we presuppose when we attribute knowledge. Perhaps we deny that S knows p in the above case simply because we impose constraints that presuppose as a normal or contrasting context one which is free of compulsions dominating the testimony of those providing relevant information. As Castañeda remarks, in practical life we adopt an "attitude of trust" and in "basic epistemology" we assume "that if a person attempts to communicate he or she will, if successful, communicate candidly" (pp. 201, 196). This would mean that S does fail to believe one of the abnormal conditions to be present in the above case. Perhaps it is only after application of constraints that normality becomes a mere function of statistics.

Such a move does bear an analogy to our procedures when picking out the cause of b as a. Ever since the ground-breaking study of

---

why our intuitions would be different concerning this example and that of the compulsive Mr. Nogot (E 63). (However, it may be that Castañeda is imagining an attribution of knowledge which only satisfies constraints involved in what counts as knowing "in a television quiz show" or similar context [p. 217]. Such a context has been considered in certain discussions of whether the analysis of knowing should contain any belief condition; see Chapter 6, Section 1.3.)

Castañeda says that in (E 65) S's belief is fully justified because it is "grounded on" false beliefs (p. 203). But this does not mean that what is falsely believed makes the belief justified or justifies it. Indeed, the original false belief is now gone and is replaced by the incorrect memory, and does not function now to justify S's belief (compare Pappas 1980).

Again, Castañeda's cross-wired rememberer is not significantly different from the following person who lacks knowledge:

(E 66) *The Consistent Represser*: S has a memory mechanism such that whenever S very clearly perceives a scene where sexual organs appear to be displayed S remembers the scene as not containing a display of sexual organs. Today S encounters a scene where people simulate such a display in a visually realistic way. S's memory mechanism works in its usual fashion and S forms the true belief that p: 'No sexual organs were displayed.'

If Castañeda objects that the simulation of such a scene is itself abnormal in S's surroundings, the same may be said concerning the typographical error mentioned in his own example.

causal selection by H.L.A. Hart and A. M. Honoré (Hart and Honoré 1959), it has been realized that we conceive of *a* as a 'differentiating factor' whose addition to an otherwise 'normal' situation, or 'contrast situation,' in which *b* is absent turns it into one like the actual situation containing *b*, but that we do not always conceive of the contrast situation wholly in terms of what is statistically normal. Indeed, the latter type of normality may be less directly relevant than even Hart and Honoré suggested, and the contents we conceive to be in the contrast situation may be dictated by many types of interests.

However, one of the puzzles about causal selection is to clarify the extent to which any conceptual limits are set on either the interests pertaining to choice of the contrast situation or the standards of interaction between the differentiating factor and the contrast situation. (Can one, to take the extreme case, make a true judgment that *a* was the cause of *b*, or was a cause of *b*, when one quite arbitrarily picks the contents of the contrast situation and standards of interaction?) Analogous puzzles would arise concerning Castañeda's relativizing abnormality to 'constraints.' This obscurity becomes even more important once we realize that the following example may lead us to place all statistical considerations on the side of the constraints which are presupposed by one who makes the knowledge attribution:

(E 67)   *The Pyromaniac (Modified Version)*: As in (E 7), except that the match is going to light not because of any rare Q-radiation, but partly thanks to a chemical composition that the Sure-Fire match company uses in their matches only rarely, when the usual supplies are unavailable, and which has rather seldom been the composition of a Sure-Fire match that *S* has struck in the past. (Shope 1979c, p. 403)

It is not implausible to say that *S* knows *p* in this example, or in ones which might be constructed where *S*'s memory or perception is presumed to work by a variety of alternative brain-paths, some of which are employed much more rarely than others. But we can hardly require *S* to be aware of the rare links when they occur. Thus, it is questionable whether Castañeda's analysis can give any automatic role to considerations of statistical normality.[29]

The upshot of these difficulties is the danger that the concept of abnormality may figure in Castañeda's account, or in any simple modifications of it, not as a way of illuminating knowing, but as parasitical on our intuitions about knowledge, so that the concept of abnormal conditions turns out partly to be the concept of conditions which, when unsuspected, are conducive to lack of knowledge.[30]

[29] Indeed, Castañeda will also have to resort to prior imposition of methodological considerations if he is to permit S to have knowledge in the case of Eloise's phone call (E 49). In that example, the presence of the actress is abnormal, unsuspected by S, and yet relevant to the truth or falsity of competitors to p. Granted, it is not relevant to the truth or falsity of p itself, but if Castañeda's account were amended to consider only abnormal factors relevant to the truth or falsity of p then the account would not be able to deal with a number of examples in the way we had supposed (e.g., [E 9], [E 10], [E 46], the case of the boy who cried "Wolf!"; also see examples [E 87] and [E 88] in Chapter 7).

It is of no use to suggest concerning (E 67) that we might say that at least it is normal for one or the other of the paths in question to be followed. If we permitted that degree of flexibility regarding Castañeda's conception of normality we would remove the ability of his analysis to deal with many cases which it otherwise succeeds in counting as situations where S fails to know p. For example, in Gettier-type examples one would be able to say that a normal condition is for a non-Gettierized or Gettierized path to exist leading to belief in p.

[30] This point has relevance to the analysis which Fred Dretske has defended in a quite recent book, published after the completion of the present manuscript, in which a particular category of "knowledge is identified with an information-caused belief" (Dretske 1981, p. x). When there is a positive amount of information associated with item a's being F, Dretske suggests that we analyze 'S knows that a is F' as follows: 'S's belief that a is F is caused (or causally sustained) by the information that a is F' (p. 86).

Dretske's treatment of Gettier-type cases characterizes them as involving the formation of belief, e.g., that the office is holding a Ford-owner on the basis of another false belief, e.g., that Mr. Nogot is in possession of a Ford, where gaining the latter belief cannot constitute receipt of information (cf. pp. 96-97). However, Dretske could manage to deal with Gettier-type cases (E 5), (E 6), and (E 8), which involve no false beliefs, by pointing out that the state of affairs that someone in the office owns a Ford is not a source of information transmitted to S.

Yet, if the case of the compulsive Mr. Nogot is also construed so as to avoid the presence of actual false beliefs, so that the compulsion is simply to trick people into believing truths by getting them to have evidence for a false proposition, Dretske will need to appeal to his view that "whether an existing condition is stable or permanent

Finally, two difficulties concerning the role of normality in Castañeda's analysis may be noted. First, since we never are aware of all statistically normal relevant conditions, Castañeda's account covers them not by a list of the conditions but under the rubric "normal." But that means that conditions (3) and (4) will only be satisfied by knowers who possess the concept of normal conditions. Castañeda regards it as a strength of his account that it allows us to speak of young children and pets as knowing various things because it does not require them to have any concepts of mental states or of probability. Yet what reason is there to suppose that the concept of normality is possessed by young children and pets?

Secondly, Castañeda overlooks the fact that, thanks to being abnormally keen-sighted, a child may know a certain object is approaching but have no beliefs about being abnormally keen-sighted. The abnormality may obtain not only in relation to the general population but even in comparison to the person's own childhood if a disease will soon reduce the child to the same level of visual acuity as the typical child.

6. SWAIN'S CAUSAL-DEFEASIBILITY-RELIABILITY ANALYSIS

In view of the strengths that causal and defeasibility analyses of knowing possess, we may expect that philosophers will explore the possibility of overcoming the deficiencies of each type of account by combining them in some fashion. Indeed, Marshall Swain has attempted to do this in one of the most complex analyses of knowl-

---

enough to qualify as part of the channel" for the transmission of information is "a question that may not have an objectively correct answer," and may involve issues which are "in part at least, responsive to the interests, purposes, and, yes, values of those with a stake in the communication process" (pp. 132-133). But it is highly artificial, or at least insufficiently illuminating, to say that compulsive Mr. Nogot fails to form a "channel for the communication of the information" that p, just as it would be insufficient merely to remark that he is not a "normal" channel.

It should also be noted that Dretske's subjunctive characterization of something's causally sustaining a belief (cf. pp. 88-90) is subject to difficulties of the type which I point out concerning Harman's and Swain's views. (See Chapter 2, Section 2.2, and this chapter, Section 6.12.)

edge yet presented (Swain 1978; 1979). Let us consider a number of problems which arise from the way in which he unites causal and defeasibility considerations, and then determine whether a reliability theory of justification which he adds to this account provides any means of solving those problems.

6.1 *Knowing*

Swain concentrates on the causal ancestry of some of S's reasons for believing p (or the causal ancestry of S's having those reasons), where "reasons" are construed not as evidential data but as states of S, including, but not necessarily restricted to, S's belief-states. According to Swain, those reasons (or the set of those reasons) constitute that upon which S's belief is based. We shall later discuss Swain's causal account of the basing relation which connects belief in p with S's reasons. Let us first consider Swain's independent requirement that the causal ancestry of S's reasons be "nondefective" in a manner which involves defeasibility considerations.

The overall form of Swain's analysis is as follows:

(SA) S knows p at t if and only if
   (1) p; and
   (2) there is some set of reasons, R, such that
      (a) R is (or the members of R are) that upon which S's belief that p is based at t,
      (b) S's believing that p on the basis of (the members of) R is justified at t,
      (c) S has R as a result of at least one nondefective causal ancestry, and
      (d) if, at t, S has [or has had] any other reasons, R', that are relevant to S's justifiably believing that p, then S would be justified in believing that p on the basis of (the members of) the set of reasons formed by the union of R with R'.

Clause (2d) is added in order to deal with the possibility that S might suppress some relevant considerations bearing on whether p

or might omit basing belief that p on some relevant reasons which S possesses. I have added the phrase in brackets to deal with reasons S fails to have at t only because S has, for example, forgotten them.[31]

In explicating clause (2c), Swain distinguishes what he calls primary knowledge from secondary knowledge (defined as any knowledge that is not primary). We shall initially concentrate on primary knowledge since it is only regarding this type of knowledge that Swain attempts to offer necessary and sufficient conditions for nondefectiveness of a causal ancestry. Primary knowledge is defined as "knowledge of noncompound propositions that designate occurrent, causally efficacious events or states of affairs . . ." (Swain 1978, p. 229).

In order to discuss the causal ancestry of the relevant reasons, Swain divides S's reasons into background reasons, which "consist of believed generalities arrived at on the basis of past experience, information concerning the reliability of any witnesses involved, and other data which tend to remain relatively invariant from case to case," and local reasons, which "consist of data that are peculiar to the specific proposition" p (p. 231). It is only regarding the latter subset of S's reasons that Swain imposes special requirements in explicating (2c) for primary knowledge; he insists that besides being nondefective, each of the local reasons, L, must have any one of the following three types of causal ancestry:

TYPE I: The ancestry includes the state of affairs that p as a cause of (S's having) L. For example, when the state of affairs that p is a particular state of affairs on the stock exchange, L may be the complex visual perceptual state S has when reading the report of that state of affairs on a television news service ticker tape.

TYPE II: Some cause, C, of (S's having) L is also a cause of the state of affairs that p. For example, when the state of affairs that p is the occurrence of the television image of the news service report on S's downstairs television, L may be the complex visual perceptual state S is having while watching the report on the upstairs television,

---

[31] The force of clause (2d) might be covered in Castañeda's account by his allowance for methodological considerations and by some of the content of s.

and the common cause, C, is the particular state of affairs in question on the stock exchange.

TYPE III: Some cause, O, of (S's having) L is a "pseudo-over-determinant" of the state of affairs that p. This possibility will require further discussion, but Swain describes an example similar to the following:

(E 68)   *Mr. Dunfor*: S observes Mr. Dunfor taking a clearly fatal dose of poison, and S, who is a doctor well-acquainted with the poison's properties, and who knows that Dunfor is not going to receive an antidote, comes to believe p: 'Mr. Dunfor will soon die.' But before the poison finishes him off, Dunfor is killed by a truck. This accident is not at all due to the poisoning. (p. 243)

Here, O is Mr. Dunfor's ingestion of the poison and L the complex visual perceptual state S has in observing O.

6.11 DEFECTIVENESS OF CAUSAL ANCESTRY

Swain invokes defeasibility considerations in order to explain what it is for any of these three types of causal connections to be defective in a way that precludes S's knowing p. His explanation is quite complex, and utilizes further technical terms which we shall need to clarify.

When one considers an *actual* connection between a cause, X and an effect, Y, such as those involved in I or II or that which holds in III between O and (S's having) L, then the following conditions are said by Swain to be necessary and sufficient for defectiveness of the causal connection:

(DA)   *Either* (1)   both (a) there is some event or state of affairs, U, in the causal chain from X to Y such that S would be justified in believing that U did not occur, and (b) it is essential to S's justifiably believing that p on the basis of (the members of) R that S would be justified in believing that U did not occur,

or (2) there is some significant alternative to the causal
chain from X to Y with respect to S's justifiably
believing that p on the basis of (the members of)
R. (pp. 238-241)

When we are instead considering the connection in III between O
and the state of affairs that p, Swain suggests that the following
condition is necessary and sufficient for defectiveness of the connection:

(DO)   If an actual causal chain from O to the state of affairs that p
had occurred then it would have been defective [in the manner
defined in DA] with respect to S's justifiably believing that
p on the basis of (the members of) R. (p. 243)

In the case of the pointed-to sheep (E 61), a connection of Type
I occurs, yet Swain can allow that S has genuine knowledge. To be
sure, in that case clause (1) of DA is satisfied if we let U be the
following event in one of the causal chains leading from the state of
affairs that a sheep is in the meadow to S's complex visual perception
of the sheep: the farmer's pointing to what he claims is not a sheep.
But since the case is also one where a nondefective connection of
Type I occurs between the presence of the sheep *after* S's attention
is directed to it and the reasons constituting his visual perception of
the sheep, clause (2c) of SA permits us to say that S knows p.

Swain discusses a contrasting case similar to (E 50), the explained
hologram, where S is tricked by a televised image of a vase in the
box into believing the truth, 'There is a vase in the box.' Swain
suggests that this causal connection of Type I may be seen to be
defective by letting U be the televising of the image of a vase on
the front of the box (p. 237).

However, this sort of application reveals a difficulty for Swain's
account. For when S is an infant, a primitive adult, or even a typical
adult prior to the widespread awareness of television and holograms,
S will lack the concepts required to conceive of U's occurring, and
thus to be justified in believing U did not occur, at least when U is

specified in the degree of detail Swain has provided. It would seem that Swain needs to resort to a more abstract description of U. Perhaps, he could do so by moving closer to Castañeda's approach and by letting the description of U have the form: 'Something abnormal other than $c_1, \ldots , c_n,$' where $c_1, \ldots , c_n$ are abnormal events S believes to have occurred. Then the issue will arise as it did for Castañeda whether infants have the relevant concept of abnormality.

Further difficulties concerning clause (1) of DA arise because of its vagueness regarding the basis for the belief, call it B, in the nonoccurrence of U, which S would be justified in having. The resulting analysis may be too weak if we allow that new reasons for belief B may be brought into existence by the addition of B.[32] Again, suppose that B is an actual belief that S already has. Shall we not have to add to (1) some clause akin to (3) of SA, so that genuine knowledge will not be ruled out in cases where S's believing B on the actual basis S uses omits additional relevant reasons possessed

---

[32] In a very recent book, published after the present manuscript was completed, Swain acknowledges this difficulty but none of the others with which my present discussion is concerned (cf. Swain 1981, pp. 191-192).

Swain now proposes to rule out S's acquiring new reasons for belief by first defining what it is for a set of reasons to be essentially the same as another with respect to the justification of a specific belief:

> The set of reasons R' is essentially the same as the set of reasons R with respect to S's justified belief that p if and only if:
> some subset of R' is identical with that subset of R which results from the deletion from R of all members that are inessential to S's justifiably believing that p. (p. 193)

He then offers the following defeasibility account of justification:

> S's believing that p on the basis of R is indefeasibly justified at t if and only if:
> (1) S's believing that p on the basis of R is justified at t; and
> (2) S's belief that p would have been justified and based upon essentially the same set of reasons as in the actual world if
>   (a) for every false proposition such that S would have been justified in believing it, S had instead believed its negation; and
>   (b) S's epistemic situation had otherwise been the same except for some minimal set of changes given (a). (p. 193)

The corresponding defeasibility account of knowing is still subject to the counter-example which I cited in Chapter 2, Section 1.461, concerning S's knowledge that S believes f, where f happens in fact to be false.

by S that would turn the existence of a candidate for U into a merely misleading defeater.

Even if these difficulties are resolved, certain problems must be noted concerning Swain's explanation of the technical concept of a defective pseudo-overdeterminant. Swain initially characterized a pseudo-overdeterminant as follows: "To say that P is a pseudo-overdeterminant of H is to say that P would have been a cause of H had the causal chain that actually results in H not occurred" (p. 242). This was an ill-formed definition because Swain wished in some cases to speak of pseudo-overdetermination even if there happen to be several causal chains which actually result in H (i.e., where H happens to be genuinely overdetermined as well). Moreover, one way for the actual causal chains resulting in H not to have occurred might have been through absence of relevant standing conditions which would be necessary even for O to be a cause of H. In addition, the definition fails to capture Swain's intention that there is no actual causal chain from P to H. For in a case where H was part of an actual causal chain leading to P, one way for the actual chain to be imagined as not having occurred is for the portion of it before H not to have occurred yet the portion of it from H to P still to have occurred.

A weakness corresponding to the latter difficulty appears in definition DO of a defective pseudo-overdeterminant. The antecedent of the conditional needs to incorporate a clause that stipulates the removal of all the actual causal chains leading to the state of affairs that p, or at least all portions of those chains nonidentical with the hypothesized chain from O to the state of affairs that p.

In his later discussion, Swain avoided the above deficiencies in the definition of a pseudo-overdeterminant by characterizing it as follows:

(DPO) Where c and e are occurrent events, c is a pseudo-overdeterminant of e if and only if:
      (1) c is not a cause of e; and
      (2) there is some set of occurrent events $D = [d_1, d_2, \ldots, d_n]$ (possibly having only one member) such

> that (a) each d_i in D is a cause of e; and (b) if no member of D had occurred, but c and e had occurred anyway, then there would have been a causal chain from c to e, and c would have been causally prior to e. (Swain 1979, pp. 36-37)

This definition has marked formal similarities to conditional C, proposed by Harman, which was criticized in Chapter 2, Section 2.2. Analogous difficulties affect Swain's definition DPO. As I pointed out when discussing Harman, if some of the actual causes of a certain result had not been effective, then a new factor might have occurred which would have blocked the remaining actual causes from being causes. A similar point holds *mutatis mutandis* regarding the blocking of the possible influence of that factor which Swain wishes to pick out as a pseudo-overdeterminant if all the actual causes of the state of affairs that p were to be omitted. For example, it may be that if Mr. Dunfor had not been hit by the truck, he would have been injured by a car, and in the course of being treated would have been given a sedative which just happens to be an adequate antidote to the poison, and yet would have died anyway because of a terrorist attack on the hospital. Nonetheless, since S knows that in the *actual* situation no antidote will be received, I believe that we would still want to say that in the actual situation S does know p: 'Dunfor will die soon.'

6.12 BELIEF-BASING

Indeed, Swain encounters the same difficulty at a second point when he offers the following causal analysis of the basing relation between S's belief in p and S's reasons R for the belief:

(B) S's belief that p is based upon the (members of) the set of reasons R at t if and only if
    (1) S believes that p at t; and
    (2) for every member r_j of R, there is some time t_n (which may be identical with or earlier than t) such that
        (a) S has (or had) r_j at t_n; and
        (b) either (i) S's being in reason state r_j at t_n is a

cause of S's believing that p at t, or (ii) S's being in reason-state r_j at t_n is a pseudo-over-determinant of S's believing that p at t. (pp. 26, 30)

The loss-of-intellectual-nerve counterexample (E 27) which affected Harman's account also affects clause (2bii) in Swain's analysis of the basing relation because of the way Swain has defined a pseudo-overdeterminant.

However, since Swain does not work under precisely the same constraints as Harman and is not aiming at a purely 'functional' account of basing relations, he may be able to deal with this difficulty in one of two ways. First, Swain might substitute for (2bii) the following:

(2bii′) S's being in reason-state r_j at t_n causally sustains S's believing p at t.

But since Swain wishes to analyze causal relations in terms of counterfactual conditionals, he may find this unilluminating. Moreover, George Pappas has described an example which may challenge the above requirement:

(E 69) *Belief Inducement and Back-up Systems*: S is performing a task in a future experimental situation where surrounding technicians have from time to time induced particular beliefs in S through electrical stimulation. Given the history of the experiments, S is adequately justified in believing that the technicians are not inducing his particular true belief in p: 'The correct place for this puzzle piece is the corner.' Moreover, S has evidence adequate to justify believing p and even justifiably believes that he has arrived at his belief in p as a causal result of his beliefs in the evidence. But, in fact, it is only stimulation applied by some of the technicians that has induced his belief in p. In addition, had those technicians not induced the belief, other technicians would have done so because of a sequence of back-up mechanisms being applied as a precaution against failure in the electrical circuitry. (Pappas 1979a, pp. 57-58)

The force of this example depends upon the assumption that the technicians do indeed succeed in preventing S's belief in the evidence from even being part of the process causing his belief in p. If we allow, for the sake of argument, that this degree of fantasy still abides by the laws of nature, the example would constitute an objection to the use of (2bii'), provided that Pappas is correct in claiming that S does know p.

A second replacement for (2bii) may succeed in avoiding this objection:

(2bii″)   there is some set of occurrent events $D = [d_1, d_2, \ldots, d_n]$ (possibly having only one member) such that (a) each d_i in D is a cause of e; and (b) *if* no member of D had occurred, but S's being in reason state r_j had occurred at t_n and S's believing p had occurred at t anyway without being caused by any event not identical with S's being at t_n in reason state r_j, *then* there would have been a causal chain from S's being at t_n in reason state r_j to S's believing p and the former would have been prior to the latter.

It is not obvious how to ascertain experimentally the truth value of the peculiar conditional in clause (b) of this emendation, but perhaps it is not more difficult than ascertaining the truth value of (2bii'). On the other hand, if the truth of (b) is entailed simply by the truth of the principle of determinism, then clause (2bii″) may be too easily satisfied.

6.13 ALTERNATIVES

We have thus far been considering only the first disjunct in Swain's definition DA of defectiveness of a causal chain. The second disjunct concerns issues arising from Alvin Goldman's views concerning perceptual discrimination.

6.131 Goldman on Relevant Alternatives in Perceptual Discrimination

Goldman points out that in an extended or figurative sense we speak of an electric-eye door as knowing something is coming. He claims that we say this because "the door has a reliable mechanism for discriminating between something being before it and nothing being there," a mechanism by which objects standing in certain relations to it have differential effects on its internal state (Goldman 1976, p. 791). Goldman suggests that this accords with his account of the literal sense in which we speak of S as knowing p. According to Goldman, "a person is said to know that p just in case he *distinguishes* or *discriminates* the truth of p from relevant alternatives" thanks to certain causal processes or mechanisms involved in the formation or sustaining of his beliefs (pp. 772-773, 783).

Goldman characterizes discriminability, at least for cases of perceptual knowledge, by means of a conditional which affirms that the causal process or mechanism "would produce true beliefs, or at least inhibit false beliefs, in relevant counterfactual situations," which we may technically call relevant alternatives to the actual situation confronting one (p. 771). For example, suppose Sam spots Judy and identifies her as Judy, even though she has an identical twin, Trudy. In saying that Sam knows that it is Judy, we are implying that thanks to some causal process involved, "if the person before Sam were Trudy (rather than Judy), Sam would believe her to be Trudy" (p. 778). Or, in view of Goldman's remark about inhibiting false beliefs, at least Sam would refrain from believing her to be Judy.

In order to have an account that is strong enough to deal with example (E 52) Judy's mole, Goldman adds the further requirement that, roughly, S's propensity to form the type of belief in question has "an appropriate genesis" (p. 789). Goldman does not go on to propose an account of such appropriateness.

But Goldman's previous counterfactual conditional yields an analysis of knowledge that is too weak to deny S knowledge in the following example:

(E 70)   *The Two Nurses*: *S* is a patient who is regularly but separately
attended by identical twins, Judy and Trudy. Unsuspected
by *S*, Trudy's duties, but not Judy's, include the responsibility of immediately administering to *S* a drug which has
the side effect of almost instantly making *S* highly attentive
to differences in his percepts. At the moment, *S* looks and
forms the true belief *p*: 'Judy is present.' But he does not
know *p* since he is very dulled and inattentive to details of
his present percepts; had he remained so, he would even
have identified Trudy as Judy, while still being able to tell
that at least one of them is present. It happens that the
difference in dress and behavior of the twins is so subtle
that it takes a certain period of close scrutiny even for their
close acquaintances to tell from their percepts which one is
present.

Goldman's counterfactual conditional is satisfied in this example
because Trudy's presence would lead her to administer the drug,
which would, in turn, lead *S* to be so alert during the period of
scrutiny typically required for discrimination that *S* would indeed
notice the difference. We cannot deal with this example simply by
adding to the antecedent of the conditional a clause that in the hypothetical situation no change in *S*'s degree of attention should occur
and that the causal mechanism be exactly as it actually was. For that
would eliminate genuine cases of knowledge where the presence of
the alternative perceptual object would itself naturally produce a shift
of attention that permits its discrimination.

In addition, there are cases of knowledge where Goldman's conditional is satisfied for reasons irrelevant to knowing (although we
cannot use the brain damage example [E 55] to show this since it
does not involve perception):

(E 71)   *The Unsmashed Brain*: *S* is still conscious after a head trauma
and is lying on the operating table while seeing his exposed
brain in a mirror. He is able to recognize it as his brain but
believes *p*: 'It is unsmashed' on the basis of a blurred portion

of his visual percept, which is too indistinct to indicate many features of the brain. Further, S's scientific background is insufficient for S to realize that people with smashed brains see nothing.

If, contrary to fact, the object that S takes to be unsmashed were smashed, then a difference would, indeed, be made to S's beliefs, namely, S would have none. But here the satisfaction of the conditional seems irrelevant to what S knows in the actual situation.

Goldman's account, in addition, would rule out Abelard's knowledge that he is speaking with Eloise in (E 49). Of course, Goldman might deny that the possibility of Abelard's speaking with the actress on the telephone is a relevant counterfactual alternative. But there is no characterization of relevance in Goldman's discussion that implies this.

I believe that Goldman has misunderstood the significance of the extended sense in which we speak of nonhuman entities as knowing something. Such remarks take note of the fact that those entities have the power to tell the difference between the presence and absence of something. As with a thermometer that tells the temperature, the telling involves the fact that the device's behavior represents the state of affairs in question. But I suspect that the concept of an ability or power to produce or to become involved in something which represents a state of affairs will not be easily characterized by means of conditionals.

Indeed, if conditionals are at all relevant to the sense of "knowledge" with which we are concerned, they may be conditionals about the hypothetical behavior or beliefs of S in the presence of the state of affairs that p, rather than in its absence. This point is suggested by Holland's and Morton's discussions, and is at least implicit in Goldman's remark that if Sam "regularly" identifies Trudy and Judy correctly he apparently has a way of discriminating them (p. 778). However, recent discussions of abilities indicate that it is too strong to conclude, as Goldman does, that S would make no mistake on the present occasion, were the twins reversed. For a slip might be due to bad luck, or be in keeping with the fact that abilities can permit occasional nonperformance.[33]

6.132 Swain on Significant Alternatives

Partly inspired by Goldman's views, Swain explains clause (2) in DA by employing a conditional concerning S's believing p in the presence of causal chains differing from actual causal chains:

(S) An alternative causal chain, C^*, to the causal chain from X to Y is a significant alternative with respect to S's justifiably believing p on the basis of R *if*

    (1) it is objectively likely that C^* should have occurred rather than the causal chain from X to Y; and

    (2) if C^* had occurred instead of the causal chain from X to Y, then there would have been an event or state of affairs U in C^* such that S would not be justified in believing p if S were justified in believing that U occurred. (Swain 1978, p. 240)

Swain admits that he cannot presently offer a complete explication of clause (2) in DA. He says that subjunctive S only provides a sufficient condition for a significant alternative in view of the following example in which S fails to know p (an example that Gail Stine says Goldman credits to Carl Ginet):

(E 72) *Barn Facsimiles*: S believes p: 'Here is a barn,' because he sees a barn from the front while driving. He is unaware that this area of the countryside is full of paper-mâché constructions that look just like the other barns in the area from the front. (Goldman 1976, pp. 772-773)

Swain says that as we modify the example and imagine fewer facsimiles or imagine them further away from the immediate vicinity, our intuitions become vague as to whether S knows p. Swain treats S as only a sufficient condition for significance of an alternative,

---

[33] For further discussion of Goldman see Audi 1980.

since "it is not clear just *how* objectively likely an alternative must be in order that it be significant" (Swain 1978, p. 241).

Swain does not consider the possibility of answering this latter question in a manner that captures some of the vagueness built into our concept of knowledge by changing clause (1) of S as follows:

(1') it is not objectively unlikely that C^* should have occurred rather than the causal chain from X to Y.

Indeed, Goldman's concerns about discriminating Judy and Trudy merely seem to construe it as not unlikely that S be confronted with Trudy. They do not rule out, for example, that each encounter be equally likely.

Robert Audi has suggested that the following example shows that S is at best a sufficient condition for significance of an alternative:

(E 73) *Judy's Mole (Informed Version)*: The same as in (E 52), except that someone has given S excellent reasons to suppose that the accidental change in his perceptual schema has occurred. Nonetheless, S stubbornly rejects those reasons. (Audi 1980, p. 91)

Audi says that S would not be justified in believing that the accidental change did not occur as part of the causal ancestry of S's believing p: 'Judy is present,' so that clause (1) of DA is not satisfied. Of course, clause (2) might be satisfied if we count the imaginary state of affairs Trudy-with-a-mole as a significant alternative. But Audi maintains that the objective likelihood of this state of affairs may be low, so that S provides only a sufficient condition for significance.

If Audi's treatment of this example were correct it would equally apply to the modification of S involving (1'). (Indeed, it would show in addition that many of the defeasibility accounts discussed in Chapter 2 up to and including that involving [iv$_9$] to be too weak to rule out S's knowing in (E 73) that Judy is present.) However, Swain may plausibly claim that S fails to know because clause (2b) of analysis SA is not satisfied. Inasmuch as S refuses to accept the reason's concerning the existence of the accident, these are not reasons upon which S's belief in Judy's presence is based. So the latter belief does not appear to be justified. It is not obvious how to construct an example where the evidence tendered to S and which S resists is not enough to keep S from being justified in believing p yet is enough to make it true that S would not be justified in disbelieving in the existence of the relevant causal state of affairs.

However, S actually fails to be even a sufficient condition for significance of an alternative.[34] The difficulty is akin to one mentioned above concerning clause (1) of DA regarding merely misleading defeaters. S might fail to be justified upon believing in one step of the hypothetical alternative causal chain but remain justified upon believing in a further step which reveals the misleading nature of the former step, as in a case where a warning light would shine on a console but a second light would quickly indicate that the warning is to be disregarded.[35]

In addition, David Annis has suggested that the following example shows that S fails to provide sufficient conditions of significance of alternatives:

(E 74)   *Would-Be Druggers*: S believes p: 'There is a cup on the table' because S sees one there. But it was objectively likely that S have believed p due to receiving an hallucinogenic drug that, unsuspected by S, many people were attempting, but failing, to administer surreptitiously to S.[36]

6.14 SECONDARY KNOWLEDGE AND THE GETTIER PROBLEM

The most unsatisfactory aspect of Swain's analysis for the purposes of the present survey is the manner in which it deals with Gettier-type examples. Swain offers no general explanation of clause (2c)

---

[34] *Mutatis mutandis* for Audi's analogous description of what makes an alternative significant on pp. 91-92 of Audi 1980.

[35] For related examples, see Lycan 1977, p. 117 and Castañeda 1980, p. 208.

[36] Described by Annis in remarks delivered at the Seventy-Sixth Annual Meeting of the Eastern Division of the American Philosophical Association in New York City, December 29, 1979.

in SA for secondary knowledge, but he suggests that "defectiveness of an ancestry is to be accounted for in much the same way as the defectiveness of causal chains in . . . primary knowledge" (Swain 1978, p. 247). As an illustration, he considers the following Gettier-type case:

(E 75)   *The Repossessed Ford*: As in (E 1), except that (1) S's evidence e concerns Mr. Havit rather than Mr. Nogot, (2) S draws the true conclusion, p: 'Either Mr. Havit owns a Ford or Brown is in Barcelona,' where S knows nothing of Brown's whereabouts, and (3) while Mr. Havit is presenting evidence e to S, Mr. Havit's Ford is unexpectedly repossessed by the finance company. (p. 248)

Swain points to the event consisting in Mr. Havit's "mistakenly saying that he owns a Ford" and suggests that it is essential to S's justifiably believing p on the basis of e and his awareness of Havit's past reliability that S would be justified in believing that this event did not occur (p. 249). But in any ordinary sense of "causal," the *mistakenness* of the student's speech is not part of a causal ancestry of S's reasons or of S's belief in p. The mistakenness concerns noncausal relations between the student's speech and the repossession. If such 'external' relations could permit factors to be technically called parts of causal chains, then Swain's approach would treat Gettier-type cases as did earlier defeasibility analyses, which failed to deal properly with misleading defeaters. For example, why should we not in this technical sense say that in the following case a similar event involving external relations occurs in the causal ancestry of S's belief:

(E 76)   *Relayed Televising of a Sheep*: S believes p: 'That sheep was in the field,' thanks to viewing a videotape of the sheep relayed by a technician whose job is to provide S with a viewing of the day's happenings in the field. While flipping the switch to relay the images, the technician says to a visitor but unheard by S just what the farmer said in (E 61), and for similar motives.

Even though S knows p, Swain would have to deny this because any causal chain from the state of affairs that p to S's belief in p passes through an event consisting in the technician's flipping the switch while saying what he did to the visitor (and, *mutatis mutandis*, the same may be said of the causal ancestry of S's reasons, if what S came to believe was, 'There was a sheep in the field'). Indeed, unless a limit is set on admissible external relations, almost any case involving misleading defeaters can be similarly described.[37]

It is also clear that Swain's treatment of secondary knowledge will require elaboration in order to deal with some of the social aspects of knowledge, where S fails to know because of surrounding factors not involved in the actual causal chains of which Swain speaks or in relevant alternatives.[38]

6.2 *A Probabilistic-Reliability Model of Justification*

The difficulties uncovered in Swain's analysis of knowing do not seem to be resolved by the start that he has made on developing an

---

[37] In his recent book (Swain 1981), he deals with example (E 75) by insisting on the detail that S believes that Mr. Havit owns a Ford, and by pointing out that because this fails to constitute primary knowledge, S does not satisfy the following necessary condition for having (secondary) knowledge that p based upon S's reasons, R:

some (proper or improper) subset, B, of R is such that (1) every member of B is an instance of primary knowledge; and (2) the set consisting of $R - B$ would not be a set of reasons upon which S's belief that p would be indefeasibly justified. (p. 231)

But this overlooks the possibility of modifying (E 75) á la Feldman, so that, without believing that Mr. Havit owns a Ford, S uses the existential generalization from the occurrence of e as a basis for believing that p: 'Either someone in the office owns a Ford or Brown is in Barcelona.' For similar reasons, Swain's new approach would not correctly deal with Feldman's version of the original Nogot case.

[38] Annis has pointed out (see n. 36) that when S gains justified, true belief in p through a scientific experiment, e.g., involving randomizing, S may fail to know p simply because S is unaware of contrary results gotten by other scientists who are performing the same experiment elsewhere.

account of justification in terms of the reliability of belief as an indication of truth.

Swain suggests that people are in some respects like an instrument such as a barometer. When such an instrument has the characteristics, C_1, which constitute being well-constructed and in good working order, the instrument's reading is a reliable indicator of the way the world is. Swain treats this as a probabilistic fact about, e.g., the barometer: "the *probability* that the atmospheric pressure is P, *given* that the barometer registers P and the barometer is well constructed and in good working order, is greater than the probability that the atmospheric pressure is other than P, given those same facts" (Swain 1979, p. 43). Analogously, a person's believing p is said to be a reliable indicator of the fact that p by the first two conditions in the following "tentative formulation" of the "probabilistic-reliability model of justification":

(PR) S's believing that h on the basis of R is epistemically justified if and only if there is some relevant set of characteristics, C_2, such that

  (1) S has C_2; and

  (2) For every competitor q of h, the probability that h is true, given that S has C_2 and that S believes that h on the basis of R is greater than the probability that q is true, given that S has C_2 and that S believes that h on the basis of R; and

  (3) For every belief state Bsp_i ($i = 1, 2, \ldots, n$) of S which is a member of R and which is such that $h \neq Bsp_i$, there is some relevant set of characteristics C_i and some set of reason states R_i such that

   (a) S believes that p_i on the basis of R_i; and

   (b) S has C_i; and

   (c) For every competitor q_i of p_i, the probability that p_i is true, given that S has C_i and that S believes that p_i on the basis of R_i is greater than the probability that q_i is true, given that

S has C_i and that S believes that p_i on the basis
of R_i. (pp. 45-46)

I shall pass over condition (3), which is meant to acknowledge
the common view that "if a person's belief is to be justified on the
basis of some other belief, then the latter belief must itself be justified" (p. 45).[39] Let us instead consider certain serious objections
to clause (2).

Let h_1 be any proposition entailed by 'S has C_2.' Since one would
suppose that the probability spoken of in clause (2) that h_1 is true
will be 1 and that h_1 is false will be 0, the account renders S's belief
in h_1 justified whatever S's reasons may be. Is it obvious that each
characteristic involved in C_2 because of its 'relevance' is something
S is aware that S possesses?

One might avoid this difficulty by dropping "S has C_2" from (2)
and by regarding it merely as an aspect of the situation in which the
probabilistic fact mentioned by such an emendation of (2) obtains.
Whether this is open to Swain is not easy to decide, since he refuses
to commit himself in this discussion to any particular theory of the
nature of probability.

But neither this emendation, nor the hedging term "relevant,"
help to prevent the account from rendering S justified in believing
h_2: 'Some statements have probabilities of being true' regardless of
S's reasons for such a belief. The same may be said for S's believing
h_3: 'Causal connections exist.' For Swain's account of the latter
belief's being *based* on reasons entails the existence of causal connections. Again, if S has C_2 and believes something of the form, 'I
am ϕ' only because of very silly reasons, it may be that clause (2)
is satisfied if only a ϕ person would believe anything for such silly
reasons; yet that hardly seems contributory to S's being justified in
his or her belief.[40]

[39] For a few exceptions to the clause, see Swain 1981, pp. 119-120.

[40] Swain succeeds in ruling out only some of these in his new book when he adds
the requirement:

If h is contingent and is entailed by 'S believes that h on the basis of R,' and the
probability that h, given that S has C and given that S believes that h on the basis
of R, is greater than the probability that not-h, given those same facts about S,

Finally, Goldman has suggested that S is not justified in believing h_4 in the following example:

(E 77)   *The Brain Probe*: A surgeon intentionally manipulates S's brain to create belief h_4: 'S is in brain-state B_n.' It happens to be nomologically necessary that anyone with such a belief holds it partly through being in brain-state B_n. (Goldman 1979, p. 7)

Even if these objections can be avoided, it is far from clear that a suitable exposition of the force of the term "relevant" in PR or a proper understanding of the concept of probability has any significant bearing on the main questions we raised earlier concerning Swain's account of knowing: (1) whether children have the concepts involved in the description of U, (2) how to deal with the possibility that U is a merely misleading defeater, (3) difficulties in analyzing causal connections by counterfactuals, (4) the need to deal with social aspects of knowing, which do not all bear on whether S's belief is justified, and (5) the reliance on 'external' relations in order to incorporate factors into causal chains when coping with Gettier-type examples.[41]

---

then the probability that h, given (only) that S believes that h and given that S has C, is greater than the probability that not-h, given (only) those same facts about S. (cf. pp. 115-117)

[41] Equally unhelpful for Swain's purposes is the reliability account of justified belief offered by Alvin Goldman (Goldman 1979). However, Goldman's view of justification does succeed in setting aside the difficulties concerning h_2, h_3, and h_4, since it takes into consideration the processes or methods by which S arrived at S's belief. Goldman first offers definitions of several technical terms: A belief-forming process is conditionally reliable if and only if a large proportion of the time the beliefs it produces are true given that [or would be true if it were true that] the beliefs forming (part of) the input to the process are true (p. 13). A belief-(in)dependent process may be defined as one some (none) of whose inputs are belief states (p. 13). Goldman adds that 'cognitive' events are ones within the organism's nervous system, and that cognitive operations are operations of faculties that register and transform in the nervous system the stimulation reaching the organism (pp. 12-13). Goldman utilizes this terminology in a recursive definition of S's having justified belief in p at t. The base clause of the definition is the following:

(1) *If* (a) S's belief that p at t results ('immediately') from a belief-independent cognitive process that is (unconditionally) reliable; and

(b) there is no (unconditionally) reliable or conditionally reliable process available to S which, had it been used by S in addition to the process actually used, would have resulted in S's not believing p at t,

then S's belief that p at t is justified.

The recursive clause in the definition is the following:

(2) *If* (c) S's belief that p at t results ('immediately') from a belief-dependent cognitive process that is (at least) conditionally reliable; and

(d) the beliefs (if any) on which this process operates in producing S's belief that p at t are themselves justified for S; and

(e) there is no (unconditionally) reliable or conditionally reliable cognitive process available to S which, had it been used by S [in connection with beliefs (if any) that are themselves justified for S and used] in addition to the processes actually used, would have resulted in S's not believing p at t,

then S's belief that p is justified. (pp. 13-20)

Clauses (b) and (e) would help to show why, in the examples I employed against Swain, S fails to be justified in believing h_2 and h_3, provided that we assume that techniques to detect the silliness of the reasons for the beliefs are available to S and that S is not hardened against them.

However, there are problems with the present wording of Goldman's account which he himself acknowledges (p. 20). It is also both too weak and too strong as an account of justified belief. It is too strong because it commits the second version of the conditional fallacy in a case where S is justified in believing at t, 'I have not applied by t the cognitive process C,' where C is an alternative cognitive process available to S which, had it been applied, would have led to S's refraining from believing that it was not being applied.

Without further strictures on the nature of a process, Goldman's reliability analysis is too weak to rule out S's being justified in believing disjunctions of any of the following forms in cases where S neither believes q nor believes the second disjunct but does believe the disjunction:

(A) 'q or S has performed a cognitive process';

(B) 'q or S has a nervous system';

(C) 'q or some beliefs have causes.'

For one might at least be tempted to speak of a process of forming a belief by conjoining one of these second disjuncts with a randomly selected proposition, q.

It is clear that Goldman does not intend his account of justification to provide a key to the Gettier problem. It obviously does not prevent S from having justified belief in a number of Gettier-type cases, e.g., (E 1) or (E 4).

6.

Deletions from Standard Analyses

1. ATTACKS ON THE BELIEF CONDITION

Critics of a standard analysis of knowing have sometimes faulted it for including the belief condition. Some of their objections depend upon the differing linguistic roles played by "know" and "believe." Additional objections concern the possibility that knowledge may sometimes be ascribed on the basis of powers or capacities other than ones directly connected with belief.

1.1 *Some Linguistic Facts*

Merrill Ring has argued that the belief condition is not only unnecessary in a suitable account of knowing, but that it is never satisfied in any case of knowing (Ring 1977). Before alluding to various linguistic facts as a basis for his contention, Ring attributes to supporters of a standard analysis a view of knowing which, it is important to notice, goes beyond the content of what I have called a standard analysis.

According to Ring, in discussions of the proper analysis of knowledge and belief, "the usual format for discussions is to say that knowledge is (something like) true justified belief. Then the disputes arise as to whether belief is an occurrence or a disposition . . ." (p. 57). Ring thereby focuses on the nouns, "knowledge," and "belief," and on issues concerning their reference, mentioning Ayer's talk of situations "where the belief is refused the title of knowledge" (Ayer 1956, p. 31) and Socrates' analogy in the *Meno* comparing belief to an untethered statue and knowledge to the statue when tied down. We are, in Ring's words, concerned with the issue of whether "to be an X is to be a Y" (p. 51). Ring then persuasively shows that certain arguments are fallacious which have been offered in support of the view that, in this sense, "knowledge is a kind of belief" or that "knowing is a species of believing" (pp. 51-56).

However, we have not articulated the content of a standard analysis so that it reveals anything about the function of the noun forms of "know" and "believe." Even if some standard analyses do employ "S believes p" as a way of saying that S has the belief that p, where "the belief that p" is understood as referring to a psychological entity, this does not force us to regard "S knows p" as being tantamount to "S has (the) knowledge that p" in a sense in which "(the) knowledge that p" occurs as a referential expression. So we are spared any obvious need to regard a proposition of the form 'S has (the) ϕ knowledge that p' as entailing one of the form 'S has a ϕ belief that p.' A defender of a standard analysis may allow that some instantiations for "ϕ" make sense regarding knowledge but not belief, and conversely.

Indeed, if the kind of analysis envisioned by a given standard analysis of knowing is not intended to be what some call a conceptual analysis, nor intended to specify the sense of the word "know" and its cognates, then it need make no attempt to explain the reasons why the same instantiations for "ϕ" are not linguistically permissible for knowing and believing.

Nonetheless, even such an analysis must not misuse the relevant terms (or, if you will, concepts), and Ring has urged that there are so many linguistic differences between the use of the terms "know" and "believe," or between the use of cognate terms, that we have reason to suppose that knowing excludes believing. So it will be interesting to survey a large portion of the list of such differences which Ring and others[1] have unearthed, and to see how many can be explained away by taking the three conditions of a standard analysis either (1) as conceptually or semantically necessary for knowing, or (2) as statements which are so obviously true of one who knows, that the very obviousness of this connection motivates linguistic

---

[1] For recent summaries of these facts and references to earlier discussions of them see Hartnack 1970; MacIntosh 1979-1980; Ring 1977.

conventions aimed at avoiding the communication of redundant, contradictory, or misleading information.

Possibility (1) seems to be Roderick Chisholm's concern when he maintains that there is a sense of "knowing" which entails believing, but that we must not think of knowing as being "in any sense a species of believing" (Chisholm 1957, pp. 17-18). He suggests that the relation of knowing to believing "is not that of falcon to bird or of airdale to dog; it is more like that of arriving to traveling" (p. 18). Ring objects that the example tends more to support the view that knowing excludes believing, since a person who has arrived is no longer traveling (Ring 1977, p. 59). I have suggested (Shope 1979d) that Chisholm might find the following analogy more useful: One's getting married entails someone else's possession of certain intentions regarding oneself. (Depending on the customs of the country, the other person will be the prospective spouse, or the spouse's parents, or some authority, or all of these.) Yet one's getting married is not a kind or species of possession by someone else of intentions regarding oneself.

Let us now illustrate the relative ease with which a large number of the putative linguistic facts that critics have cited may be reconciled with the view that the conditions in a standard analysis of knowing are at least necessary ones.

By appeal to possibilities (1) or (2), the existence of a truth condition for knowing can be used to explain the following facts:

(f1) It is redundant to speak of true knowledge (but not of true belief).

(f2) We may speak of false belief (but not of false knowledge).

(f3) We may say that what is false is what we believed (but not what we knew).

(f4) When we admit it to be false that p, we need not say that a statement attributing a belief that p to someone is false (but must do so for a statement attributing knowledge that p).

(f5) It is odd, and seems to be redundant, to say, "I know p and I believe p."

Again, if S's knowing p involves a justified status for S's belief that p, then the following linguistic facts are explained:

(f6) We may speak of making a claim to knowledge (but not to belief).

(f7) In certain contexts, an answer to "What's your evidence?" after one has said, "I believe p," cannot be evidence relevant to whether belief is present but only evidence for the truth of "p" (but after having said, "I know p," will also be evidence relevant to whether knowledge is present).

The following is a more controversial linguistic fact which would be similarly explained, provided that we acknowledge a convention, c_1, of ordinary conversation not to provide irrelevant information needlessly:

(f8) In some contexts, we may initiate a conversation with "I believe p" (but not with "I know p," unless we anticipate being challenged).[2]

If we add that it is a convention, c_2, of ordinary conversation not to fail to provide relevant (epistemic) information, we may explain

(f9) If asked, " 'p'—Is that something you believe?" I may, for a variety of instantiations of "p" reply, "No, I know it."

For ordinarily the context is one in which " 'p' " expresses a rumor, a controversial view, or something similar, about which a

---

[2] Carolyn Black has said, "In all the cases I can think of, when I actually know that p, I do not and would not claim to believe that p" (Black 1952, p. 156). However, she qualifies this overly strong view when rephrasing it as follows: "In first-person knowledge claims, one does not claim to have belief when one is *ready to claim* to have knowledge. There is no point in claiming to have both" (emphasis added; p. 158). In calling attention to f8, Justus Hartnack points out that there would be no point in *claiming* knowledge when we reach for the television knob and remark to a family member, "I believe there is an interesting program on television tonight" (Hartnack 1970, p. 119).

Hartnack also maintains that it is a fact that we speak of belief behavior but not of knowledge behavior, but since this way of speaking sounds rather technical, I shall not appraise this putative fact or its background here.

number of people in the epistemic community are only in a position to take an epistemic stand falling short of knowledge. One could imagine a different context in which a psychologist or an anthropologist indicated that she was surveying common-sense opinion in a variety of cultures and would like you to cooperate, saying, "Let me see . . . 'p'—Is that something you believe?" In that case, convention c_1 would make it appropriate to reply, "Yes," rather than to reply as indicated in f9.[3]

Once we allow that the justified status of S's belief must be of a certain degree, additional linguistic facts are explained:

(f10) We may speak of believing (but not of knowing) naïvely, foolishly, superstitiously, irresponsibly, or obstinately, or as something the person cannot help.

(f11) In an epistemically relevant sense of "ought," we may say that one ought not to believe p (but not that one ought not to know p).

(f12) We may be asked both to reveal our evidence and to find more for what we say we believe (but only to reveal it for what we say we know).

Some things that we say about knowing and believing might be explained, according to David Annis, by admitting that we regard the following principle as defining the normal case in which we appraise a person's epistemic and doxastic state with regard to a proposition:

Presumption of Epistemic Normalcy: (1) The agent S is rational, that is, satisfies the standards of epistemic rationality[4] . . . and (2) the agent S has no special cognitive powers (as do *idiots savants* or seers). (Annis 1977, p. 224)

[3] I first heard this suggestion from Roderick Firth. See also H. P. Grice's conception of a cancellable implication (Grice 1961).

[4] An example of one such principle that Annis proposes is: "If S is in a knowledge-giving evidential position with respect to h, then from an epistemic point of view S ought to believe that h; that is, to withhold or disbelieve is irrational" (Annis 1977, p. 220).

In fact, Annis suggests that f5 concerns a merely apparent redundancy, and that the above principle explains the oddity of the remark in question, since epistemic rationality requires believing what one takes oneself to know. We may note that this would also explain what some have taken to be a linguistic fact:

(f13)   It is odd to say one disbelieves p (but not to say one fails to know p) after admitting that one has good reasons for believing p and no reasons against it.

For principles of epistemic rationality might, at least in some circumstances, prohibit disbelieving when a proposition is reasonable enough, even before one becomes justified in believing it in the way required for knowledge.

Facts concerning the degree or type of justification relating to knowing may make certain remarks about knowing inappropriate because they void a presupposition that is involved when parallel remarks concern a state of belief. It may be that we presuppose a lower degree of justification of belief when concerned with terminology such as that mentioned in the following point:

(f14)   We may speak of a person's belief (but not knowledge) that p as sensible versus silly, or as mature versus childlike.

A similar observation might be made concerning the following fact:

(f15)   We may ask, ''What makes you believe p?'' (but not ''What makes you know p?''—at least when not prone to add, ''when so-and-so does not'').

For the query about having a belief may be about S's reasons for holding it, but to ask such a question with such a presupposition about S's knowing p seems to clash with counting the possible presence of such reasons as already somehow involved in the justification condition. Thus, to ask what makes one know may be as odd as saying, ''I realize that what holds back the ship is the anchor, but what holds back the anchored ship?'' This also helps to explain the next two facts:

(f16)   We may ask, ''Why do you believe p?'' (but not, ''Why do you know p?''—at least when not prone to add, ''when so-and-so does not'').

(f17)   We may ask, ''How do you know p?'' (but not, ''How do you believe p?''—at least when this is not an improper way of asking, ''How can you believe p?'').

One might plausibly regard the ''how'' question as making sense because it deals with the way in which the justification condition comes to be satisfied, and the ''why'' question as making sense because it deals with reasons for one's belief (reasons whose presence or acquisition may partly explain how one knows what one believes).[5] In response to the following point, similar observations may be made about the way that terms applied to belief concern the nature of reasons for it or their effect on it:

(f18)   We may speak of one's belief (but not one's knowledge) as firm versus wavering, intelligible versus unintelligible, well-versus poorly-grounded, hesitant, or reluctant.

Even the following linguistic fact can be reconciled with a standard analysis of knowing (although it would be more difficult to reconcile with the view that knowing is a ''species of'' believing):

(f19)   We may speak of beliefs (but not of 'knowledges').

This fact does not appear to count against the view that knowing requires believing, once we notice the following linguistic analogy:

[5] Talk of knowing what one believes has been rejected by Zeno Vendler on the grounds that certain linguistic facts show that knowing and believing 'take different objects' (Vendler 1967; 1972). But critics have argued that those linguistic facts do not support the latter thesis, and that the thesis fails, in any event, to prove the exclusivity of knowing and believing. For discussion, see Aune 1975; Baier 1976; Dunn and Suter 1977; Jones 1975; Margolis 1976; Munsat 1977; Peterson 1977; Rosenthal 1976; Vendler 1975a; 1975b; 1978.

A necessary condition for S's having indigestion is that S has ingested something; nonetheless, although we can speak of a number of ingestions of chili which occurred during S's dining in the past week, we may not speak of 'indigestions' that S had, and must speak instead of various "cases of indigestion." Analogously, one speaks of "instances of knowledge," or "instances of knowing."[6]

1.2 Mannison on Seers

A number of philosophers have used examples such as the following in order to criticize the inclusion of a belief condition in a standard analysis of knowing:

(E 78)   *The Horserace Prognosticator*: On many occasions, for many years, S has picked the winner of every race at the track. Yet because S lacked special information about horses and racing, S initially justifiably regarded himself as having good reasons for disbelieving propositions of the form P: 'Horse n will win.' Indeed, S had no degree of confidence or of belief in such propositions, and only bothered to pick a horse to be sociable. (Mannison 1976a, pp. 141-142)

When discussing this example, D. S. Mannison slides from holding that (a) S may be said "to know how to pick winners," to holding that (b) S may be said "to know how to know that a particular horse will win" (pp. 144, 146). S's repeated success does justify (a).[7] But (a) means that S may be said to know, on certain occasions when a particular horse will win, how to pick that horse as a winner. This is different from saying that S knew a proposition of form P to be true.

Instead of defending this slide, Mannison proceeds to argue that (b) attributes to S an ability to know the winner and that we have

---

[6] For further remarks concerning f19, see Section 1.5 of this chapter.

[7] As time passes, S himself may come to affirm (a). Mannison has misled some critics (Almeder and Arrington 1977) by focusing on S's self-description throughout the period, but he does point out that this detail is not crucial (Mannison 1976a, p. 142).

no reason to deny that S's choices long ago manifested the same ability. Thus, S knew, even at the start, the relevant propositions of form P to be true (p. 146). Moreover, in keeping with our usual linguistic practice concerning abilities, we may say that the ability described in (b) "enabled" S to know those propositions of form P to be true and that S knew "in virtue of" having that ability, even though S did not believe those propositions (p. 146).

Mannison does not entirely succeed in clarifying his views in a later paper. He remarks that his earlier mention of *knowing how* was misleading, and that he had really been concerned with *knowing which*. He suggests that he would have expressed himself more clearly had he employed the phrase, "knowing which horse will win a race," instead of the phrase, "knowing how to pick winners" (Mannison 1977, p. 147). In addition, he implies that certain of S's abilities are identical: "picking the winner . . . is an exercise of his ability always to pick winners, i.e., the ability to know which horse will win" (p. 148).

These remarks illuminate the relation of (a) to (b). Rephrased accordingly, they become: (a') S may be said to know which horse will win, and (b') S may be said to have the ability to know that a particular horse will win. Once it is allowed that S's repeated success justifies (a'), Mannison's reason for also granting (b') is the following: "*knowing which*, and, as well, *knowing what*, are the sorts of abilities which, perhaps necessarily, issue in instances of *knowing that*, when they issue in anything at all" (p. 148).

But three peculiarities remain in Mannison's explanation: (1) At one point, he identifies the ability to pick the winning horse, not with the ability to know which horse will win, but instead with knowing which horse will win (p. 148); (2) Given Mannison's interpretation of (a'), he does not make clear why S's repeated success should support (a') rather than the more restricted statement, 'S may be said to know how to pick winners,' which does not seem to entail, 'S knows that a particular horse will win'; (3) In retrojecting S's ability on the grounds that at the track today "he does nothing that he did not do earlier," we must already grant that S not merely picks the winner today but knows today (independently of inductive grounds) that a particular horse will win.

All three peculiarities are understandable if we again take up the possibility mentioned in Chapter 5, Section 6.131, namely, that we are willing to speak in an extended sense of nonhuman entities as knowing something because they have the ability or power to produce or become involved in something which represents the state of affairs in question. Perhaps there is a literal sense in which the prognosticator in Mannison's example may be said to know that something is the case which amounts to S's having a certain type of ability or power to manifest, produce, or become involved in something that represents a state of affairs. In picking a horse as a winner, S so unfailingly represents states of affairs consisting in a horse's winning that we may plausibly attribute to S at least some kind of ability or power to, e.g., produce utterances or engage in actions which represent those forthcoming states of affairs rather than merely attribute his performance to luck. If Mannison is speaking of this type of ability or power as knowing which horse will win, then because such an ability is manifested in the picking, it will indeed be otiose to speak of S's capacity or ability to have this ability. The basic question then becomes whether we are prepared to treat such cases of *knowing which* as instances of *knowing that*.

1.3 Radford on Remembering

Whether an instance of knowing *which* is also an instance of knowing *that* seems to be the fundamental issue regarding Colin Radford's example of knowledge without belief:

(E 79)   *Unwitting Remembrance*: Tom playfully quizzes S on English history after S sincerely asserts that he never learned any. S believes each of his answers to be a mere guess. In spite of numerous errors and constant hesitancy, S answers about the Tudor and Stuart monarchs are right except for one error that is almost right. After Tom points this out, S finally thinks he remembers that he once did have to learn some dates about kings and queens and thinks it was indeed those dates. (Radford 1966, pp. 2-3)

The end of the conversation makes it less plausible to speak here of a "mysterious intuition" than to say that during the quiz S still remembers some English history. According to Radford, this entails that when S answered the corresponding question S did know, for example, "the date of James I's death, viz. 1625; that is to say, he knew that James I died in 1625 . . ." (p. 4).

O. R. Jones charges that if S really thinks he is just guessing then S was just as likely to have given a different answer and did not know p because S was not a reliable source of information (Jones 1971, p. 22). Radford has responded by saying that S may be prepared to stick to his answers, not because he believes them to be correct, but because it occurs to him that he could be calling upon information which he has without realizing it (Radford 1971, p. 171). A difficulty with this response is that it would lead some philosophers to say that S has at least a low degree of belief that the dates are correct, so that we lack a pure case of knowing without believing (Barker 1976a). Perhaps an appropriate reply to Jones is that the likelihood of an alternative answer may not be solely a function of S's belief that he is guessing but also partly a function of the lingering, temporarily unsuspected memory.

Even so, Keith Lehrer has criticized Radford for equating remembering the date of James's death with knowing *that* James died on that date. Because Lehrer says that S's "memory only functions well enough to yield a correct answer" (Lehrer 1974, p. 73; cf. 1975, p. 6), Radford has charged Lehrer with being committed to the contradiction that S does and does not know that James I died on that date (Radford 1975, p. 2). Radford admits that Lehrer tries to show that there is no contradiction, but Radford misrepresents Lehrer's argument: Lehrer says that there are contexts in which a person merely guesses the correct answer and yet is said to know the correct answer, e.g., a quizmaster does not exclude mere lucky guessing when he says, "George, if you know the answer to the question I am about to ask you will win that 1973 Ford'' (Lehrer 1974, p. 57). Radford inappropriately replies that Lehrer "equates" S's guess about a date in English history with "any lucky guess," and then Radford observes that "to know the answer in the way S does is not merely to give a fortuitously right answer" (Radford 1975, p. 2). However, it is only the *sense* of the phrase, "knows the correct answer," that Lehrer equates in the two examples, not the source of the guesses.

This point notwithstanding, Radford can distinguish these cases because he is prepared to say something about S, even though we would not say something analogous about George, namely, S knows *which* date James I died on.[8] Suppose that George's wife fretted over his initial hesitation, and even afterwards realizes that he was only making a lucky guess. She could not properly exclaim, "Wonderful! So he did know which date it was, after all!"[9]

Thus the fundamental questions regarding both Mannison's and Radford's examples are whether it is appropriate to say that they are cases of *knowing which*, and whether such cases of knowing which (or perhaps all cases) are properly spoken of as ones of *knowing that*.[10] These issues appear to me presently to rest on linguistic in-

[8] This is not to deny Lehrer's point that we offer *some explanation* of S's answers simply by saying that memory produced them (Lehrer 1974, p. 73).

David Annis attributes to *idiots savants* an unknown process by which they gain their mathematical "knowledge" (Annis 1977, p. 223). Lehrer might reply that the process is instead one which gives them an inclination to blurt out certain sentences and that when Annis maintains that their possessing knowledge is the "most reasonable explanation" of their behavior, Annis is ignoring relevant disanalogies to most cases of knowing.

[9] The quizmaster's phrasing is somewhat ritualistic, since people's winning answers are not usually mere guesses. Again, the quizmaster may be using "know" to refer to one's being *acquainted with* the *content* of the answer, and his remark may be elliptical for saying that George will win upon formulating a thought of this content aloud.

[10] We may say of a dog that it knows which bag holds the meat or knows that there is meat in this bag, without thereby implying that the dog accepts propositions. (Some, however, are willing to attribute beliefs to dogs, and even to ticks [Goldman 1977].) John Saunders regards such attributions of knowledge as metaphorical, because we are prepared to say similar things of information storage machines (Saunders 1966). Such issues also arise when we say that *idiot savants* know which number is the sum of various other numbers.

tuitions, and mine are in sympathy with those of Mannison and Radford.[11]

Yet Lehrer objects that if belief is compatible with the absence of conviction in Radford's example, then Radford cannot cite S's conviction that the belief is absent as proof that S does lack belief (Lehrer 1974, pp. 64-65). Radford has persuasively responded by pointing out that S would not bet on his answer if the issue were quite serious,[12]

---

[11] Peter Unger rejects Radford's example on the grounds that the following sentences give the impression of inconsistency: "S really knows that James I died in 1625, but S isn't certain of it," "S really *knows* that James I died in 1625, but S isn't certain of it," "S *knows* that James I died in 1625, but S isn't certain of it." Unger claims that these sentences do not alter the relevant sense of the phrase, "S knows," but only serve to focus our attention on what it expresses in Radford's example (Unger 1971, 1975). Indeed, Unger proposes that we analyze 'S knows p' as follows: 'that p is clear to S' (1975, p. 137).

But B. L. Blose has retorted that Unger's sentences actually alter the sense of "S knows" by restricting its employment to the best knowledge possible (at least, the best for philosophical purposes, where we focus on critical debate concerning articulated positions). Blose compares this to one way of using the phrase "really red," e.g., in saying of the auto, "It is really *red*," thereby restricting consideration to its being "fire-engine red, bright-bright red, ooh-la red, rather than maybe maroon red or wine red or dusky red" (Blose 1980, p. 185).

One reason to accept Blose's diagnosis is that we can focus attention on what the phrase, "S knows," expresses by saying, "It is (actually) knowledge which S has that James I died in 1625," i.e., knowledge as opposed to a mere temptation to guess. Yet I sense no contradiction in saying, "It is (actually) knowledge which S has that James I died in 1625, but S isn't certain that James I died in 1625." S simply does not confidently employ that knowledge and, perhaps, does not even realize that he has it. Because of that, it is not clear to S that James I died in 1625. Similarly, Freud regarded a person who carries out a posthypnotic suggestion as still having knowledge of the earlier actions of the hypnotist even though what happened during the trance is not clear to the person (Shope 1983).

For further discussion of Unger's views on knowledge see Barnes 1973; M. Black 1974; Cargile 1972; Dicker 1974; Hamlyn 1976; Johnson 1979; Miller 1978.

[12] This may be true of the horserace prognosticator at the start of the string of successes. It is incorrect for Lehrer to claim of such people, "If we ask such a man 'Do you know whether the answer you have given is correct?' the only right answer is 'No' " (Lehrer 1974, p. 58). As John Schumacher has noticed, Lehrer here confuses a justified answer with a true one, and the most careful, proper response for S to Lehrer's question would be, "I don't claim to" (Schumacher 1975, p. 252).

Schumacher presents his own argument against Radford's claim that S lacks belief in (E 79), which depends upon treating belief solely in terms of giving answers to and that during the quiz, S has even forgotten his learning of the relevant dates (Radford 1975, p. 2).

D. M. Armstrong maintains that if we allow the possibility of unconscious beliefs which may contradict conscious ones, the very same grounds that lead Radford to say that (E 79) is a case of knowledge should lead him to say that it is also a case of belief (Armstrong 1969-1970, p. 26). Armstrong bases this charge on a two-part argument. The first stage of the argument supports the intermediate conclusion that the following example is a case of false belief:

(E 80)   *Unwitting, Muddled Remembrance*: In the quiz, S gives Tom incorrect answers, which S takes to be mere guesses but are caused by memory traces which encode incorrect information because they have degenerated from traces encoding the correct dates acquired when S was taught the relevant English history. (pp. 30-31)

Armstrong notes that we can obtain (E 80) if we begin with an ordinary case of muddled memory where a person does not take himself to be guessing, and we make certain deletions and additions. The same alterations suffice to turn an ordinary case of (conscious) knowledge that p (e.g., that James I died on a certain date) into case (E 79): "The subject fails to take the words that he utters as being manifestations of belief and/or knowledge, but instead thinks they are mere guesses" (p. 31). Armstrong concludes that if Radford

---

questions. Rather than consider, e.g., S's preparedness to act upon or bet upon his answer's being true, Schumacher only considers whether it is a good bet (for us) that S will give those answers. Schumacher suggests that "S believes that p" should be taken to mean that it is a good bet that S will give p as an answer to appropriate questions provided that S tries to answer these questions, whether or not S is aware that this is the case (p. 265). This definition commits the conditional fallacy. For it entails that any person who is capable of understanding the question whether p and who is not severely distracted, say, by intense pain, will, even at times when the person is not actually being asked the question, believe p for instantiations such as the following: 'I am being asked a question,' 'Some question is being posed,' 'I am about to try to answer a question.' For it is an excellent bet that if the person is asked the question whether p and tries to answer it, an affirmative response will be given.

treats (E 79) as a case of knowing p, "he can hardly deny" that (E 80) is a case of false belief that p (although Armstrong admits that he has only supported this conclusion and not deduced it from his premises).

The second stage of Armstrong's argument compares the preceding examples to the following case:

(E 81)   *Unwitting, Unmuddled Remembrance*: As in (E 80), except that the correct information leading to S's correct answers is temporarily restored in the course of the degeneration of the trace. (p. 32)

Armstrong suggests that for reasons similar to those he gave regarding (E 80), we should regard (E 81) as a case where S believes p. He then says that it is plausible to regard the cognitive states in (E 79), (E 80), and (E 81) as having a common factor. He finishes the second stage of his argument by asking: "And what can this common factor be except that . . . the subject *believes*" p (p. 33).

Armstrong goes on to express confidence that against any case which is claimed to be one of knowing p without believing p, considerations arise similar to the ones brought against Radford. For example, consider the commonly cited case of a woman "who knows her husband is dead—she has all the proofs, and acknowledges their force—but at the same time is 'unable to bring herself to believe it' " (pp. 33-34). Armstrong says that we may construct a case comparable to (E 80), where either somebody "persuades her that her husband is dead" but he is not dead or else the evidence the woman has is faked. We may then regard it as a case of belief and ask what is common to this case and to the woman's situation in the original example. "The only answer can be that they both involve belief in the same proposition" (p. 34).

But Armstrong has affected our reaction to the latter illustration by saying that the woman is "persuaded that" her husband is dead and "acknowledges the force" of the arguments that he has died. In dealing with Radford's example, Armstrong instead needs to lean on his device of trimming down ordinary examples, and we may notice its limitation by returning temporarily to a consideration of hypothetical 'seers.' I have noted (Shope 1979b) that Mannison's example (E 78) is not made significantly different by supposing that S is paid to participate in a long-run experiment which does not require S to pick a winner in the races, but in which S is merely asked whether S has anything to say about the race ahead of time. Suppose that on each occasion S says, "I wonder whether H might win," where H is some entrant, but S never picks any horse as a winner. If the horses about which S muses always win and S does not say similar things about other horses in the races, then after a while we might be inclined to say that even in the initial stage of the experiment S knew which horses would win, and perhaps willing to say that S knew that a particular horse would win. (The same considerations apply if the future is represented merely in the visions or dreams of the seer.)

Thus, a process of trimming which is identical to the one described by Armstrong would convert an ordinary case of, e.g., musing about the possibility that James I died on the given date into case (E 79), and would also produce the same result in a number of other types of ordinary situations—the subject fails to take the words that he utters as being manifestations of belief and/or knowledge and/or musing and/or wondering and/or imagining and/or entertaining an idea and/or . . . , but instead thinks they are mere guesses. Thus, there is no good reason for Armstrong to respond to Radford's example by placing special emphasis on belief, among all the cognitive states on this list.[13] Moreover, Radford does not defend his intuition that (E 79) is a case of *knowing that* by producing the example through a process of whittling down an ordinary example of knowing. Thus, we are left only with Armstrong's objection to Radford's intuition, which amounts to a warning that the example is not "one of those clear cases that can be used as a test of a philosophical analysis" (p. 35).

---

[13] This also suffices to undercut the brief additional argument that Armstrong constructs on p. 33 by redeploying the sort of consideration used in the course of his main argument.

Lehrer has commented on Radford's interpretation of the example[14] by maintaining that the example either (1) is a borderline case of knowledge in the sense that there are equally conclusive considerations for and against applying the term "knows" in the example; or (2) utilizes a different sense of the term from that which concerns Lehrer; or (3) involves conflicting criteria for the application of the term in a univocal sense. According to Lehrer, all three possibilities reveal "inconsistent ordinary usage," so that he may choose to speak of knowledge in a sense that entails belief for his own philosophical purposes (Lehrer 1974, p. 67).

But Lehrer has overlooked three additional possibilities, which I shall note but not pursue here, namely, (4) "knows" is used in a univocal sense which can be rendered by means of Michael Slote's 'theory of important criteria,' where something would be an instance of knowing if and only if it had 'all the important criteria' of knowing (Slote 1966, p. 215); or (5) "knows" is what Richard Robinson calls a dismantling word, one that "has a complete use in which every element of a complex concept is intended . . . and then a number of different incomplete uses where parts of the possible meaning are not intended . . ." (Robinson 1971, p. 22); or (6) "knows" is used most broadly to attribute the type of representational power or ability which I mentioned earlier, where such an ability is typically, but not in every case, shown to be present by S's having some kind of justified belief. Each of these possibilities deserves discussion in future extensions of debate concerning the belief condition.[15]

1.4 Margolis on Informality of Epistemic Ascriptions

Joseph Margolis presents the following example of knowledge without belief:

[14] As well as E. J. Lemmon's interpretation of a similar example (Lemmon 1967, p. 63).

[15] For appraisal of Arthur Danto's argument in Danto 1968 that knowing does not entail believing, see Coburn 1971.

(E 82)   *The Uncontemplated Entailment*: S knows the date of Hannibal's crossing the Alps and the date of Washington's crossing the Delaware, but has never thought about the entailed
consequence, *p*: 'Hannibal's crossing happened before
Washington's.' (Margolis 1972b, pp. 405-406)

Margolis says that S cannot believe *p* because S has never thought
of that proposition and belief is a disposition to perform or to respond
appropriately, whose onset is dated from a relevant occurrence of
thought (Margolis 1972a, p. 79). Nonetheless, S is said in our society
to know *p* because knowledge may be ascribed as a "*capacity* to
provide the right information in the right way" on the condition of
possessing certain relevant skills, rather than on the condition of
dispositions to perform or respond, where the ascription of such a
capacity depends on variable "norms of a conventional sort" (Margolis 1972a, p. 78; 1973b, p. 7).

John Barker maintains that in (E 82) S has "virtual knowledge,"
that is, "the subject has only to think about the relevant proposition
to acquire actual knowledge . . ." (Barker 1975, p. 144). But to
suppose that "knowledge" has such a sense is to commit the first
version of the conditional fallacy. For Barker's characterization incorrectly leads us to say that S knows p_1: 'S is thinking of, pondering,
or entertaining proposition *q*,' where *q* is any proposition S could
understand but is actually not thinking of, pondering, or entertaining.

This type of objection might be avoided by adopting Mannison's
characterization of (E 82) as an example in which *p* could be known
without S's discovering or unearthing additional data, information,
or facts (Mannison 1976b, p. 558). For when S becomes aware of
thinking about *q* in the above example, that may fairly be called
acquisition of additional data. Mannison charges Margolis with confusing what could be known in this way with what actually is known.

Certainly a person who recovers from amnesia regains knowledge
that *h* without discovering new data, and the persistence of a memory
of its being the case that *h* (versus consciously remembering that
state of affairs) permits the eventual return of the knowledge that *h*,

even though the memory is not itself knowledge that *h* (Shope 1973). Mannison forces us to consider whether the presence of a *capacity*, e.g., to extract an entailment from what one already knows, should be regarded as analogous to the persistence of a memory, rather than as being knowledge of the entailed proposition. Here, present discussion again seems to depend on linguistic intuition, and mine accords with that of Margolis.

However, Mannison also objects to (E 82) by pointing out that I may be said to believe, e.g., that the internal mechanism of the typewriter upon which I am now typing has not turned to butter, even though I have had no such thought (Mannison 1976b, p. 554; cf. Barker 1975, p. 144). (It is notable that in [E 82] *S is* prepared to bet on *p* if the issue should become serious.) Margolis makes no response to this objection except to remark that "if it is said that under such circumstances, we might just as well claim that *S* does believe" the entailed proposition, "then we should have increased the informality with which epistemic ascriptions are made—by basing ascriptions of psychological states on what accords with *S*'s abilities, beliefs, and orientation" (Margolis 1977a, pp. 14-15).[16]

Margolis discerns a corresponding informality regarding ascription of knowledge when he characterizes knowledge, variously, as being

(1) a *capacity to provide* the right information in the right way (Margolis 1972a, p. 78); or
(2) a *belief as* graded in a relevant way (pp. 77, 78); or
(3) a normative *grade* or *status* assigned to *beliefs* or to beliefs and skills, as of inference (1973a, p. 467; 1973b, p. 4; 1977b, p. 126); or
(4) a *status* given certain psychological states *conceding* certain skills (1973b, p. 5); or
(5) a status of cognitive *agents* based on an *appraisal* of their beliefs and skills (1972a, p. 76; 1973b, p. 7; 1977a, pp. 12, 14).

---

[16] Margolis says that it is "gratuitous" to assume the existence of unconscious inferences to the proposition in question (Margolis 1977a, pp. 8-9).

A combination of (1), (4) and (5) may yield the most interesting interpretation of Margolis' view, namely, that S's knowing p is

(6) a capacity to provide the information that p in particular ways such that the capacity has a certain normative status in virtue of S's skills and beliefs (not necessarily including a belief in p).

The reference to cognitive agents in (5) appears to confuse the terms "knowledge" and "knows."[17] Both (2) and (3) concern the possibility of saying, e.g., that S's belief may "count as" knowledge or be graded as "constituting" knowledge (Margolis 1972a, p. 77; 1973b, p. 23). But it may be more revealing to say that the state of affairs of S's-believing-p, i.e., the belief's obtaining, may count as or constitute an instance of the state of affairs of S's-knowing-p. Knowledge itself, that which S *has*, might be said to be the capacity mentioned in (6).

Nonetheless, speaking of a "capacity" fails to take account of the amnesiac who has a capacity but not the ability to provide information. Furthermore, I suspect that speaking of S as "providing information" is too restrictive to cover some of the uses of "know."[18] It may be preferable to analyze knowing as some type of ability or power to manifest, produce, or become involved in something that represents a state of affairs.

If such an ability or power is a state of a person, it is not what we usually mean by "a state of mind," nor need it always be introspectible, since it typically involves a relation to an external state of affairs, as does, e.g., the ability to sink short putts. Combining such a treatment of knowledge with an analysis of x's representing something which explains the latter in terms of what observers of x are, under certain conditions, justified in accepting on its basis would,

---

[17] " 'Know' is an appraising term when applied to subjects . . ." (Margolis 1972a, p. 76).

[18] Not only is this true regarding, e.g., "knowing how," but it is also true in the example described in the previous section where a seer's musings or visions represent the future but the seer is not providing information in the sense of affirming or guessing.

indeed, stress an informal aspect of knowledge. It would do so because standards of justification are standards concerning what is more rational for those observers to accept and our present views of rationality are not entirely formal. But differences of the sort that Margolis mentions between ascriptions of knowledge, e.g., in law courts versus in common life (Margolis 1973b, p. 7), or differences among standards of various epistemic communities, need not be viewed as matters of "taste" or "fashion" (Margolis 1973a, p. 468). They may be different opinions concerning when it is rational for members of the epistemic community to depend on a person or aspects of the person's thought or behavior as a source of information.[19] (See Chapter 7, Section 5.) Our present rather crude grasp of the nature of rationality may make hypotheses concerning its manifestations sufficiently corrigible for some, like Margolis, to suspect that there is nothing behind the trappings. Should that be the case, perhaps there is no knowledge behind our behavior.

The preceding considerations imply that the analysis of knowing anticipated at the end of Chapter 3, and which will be elaborated in the final chapter, deals with only one way in which we can acquire knowledge as a representational ability. Accordingly, such an analysis may be said to cover what can technically be called 'justified factual knowledge,' knowledge whose possession partly involves justified belief or acceptance.

1.5 Why Are There No 'Knowledges'?

Analyzing a broad category of knowledge as a power or ability may help to explain linguistic fact f19, mentioned at the end of Section 1.1, above, which Merrill Ring has cited as evidence that knowing and believing are categorically exclusive (Ring 1977). Suppose that

---

[19] Margolis refers to a "schema of rationality that all particular ascriptions of knowledge and belief presuppose" (Margolis 1977a, p. 9; cf. 1973a, p. 467).

Relativizing to epistemic communities in the *analysans* (e.g., a community of experts versus a community including laymen—see Chapter 7) may permit a defense against J. Kellenberger's rejection of any necessary and sufficient conditions for knowledge (Kellenberger 1971).

speaking of instances of knowing is speaking of instances of having some type of ability or power to manifest, produce, or become involved in something that represents a state of affairs. This phrasing carries no implication that the state of affairs is the same in each instance or that the abilities are different in different instances. But to speak of 'knowledges' would be to speak of abilities to manifest, produce, or become involved in something that represents a state of affairs, and would be to mislead by implying several different abilities related, perhaps, to one and the same state of affairs.

2. ATTACKS ON THE JUSTIFICATION CONDITION

Any rejection of the belief condition will also constitute a rejection of the justification condition, since the latter entails the former. In addition, we shall now have to admit that various examples which include the presence of belief but are otherwise akin to (E 78) and (E 79) indicate that justification is sometimes unnecessary for knowledge.[20]

2.1 *Unger on Nonaccidental Correctness*

Although Peter Unger presents one such example, concerning a crystal-ball-gazing gypsy (Unger 1967, pp. 165-167), he also provides an indirect criticism of the justification condition when he advances an analysis of knowledge which simply avoids including that condition. Unger suggests that "for any sentential value of p (at time t), a man knows that p if and only if (at t) it is not at all accidental that the man is right about its being the case that p" (Unger 1970, p. 48).

Georges Dicker interprets Unger's *analysans* as follows:

> S's being right that p is of a type, T, and occurs in certain circumstances, C, such that (1) for any proposition, h, and any person, P, whenever P is in C and P does something of type T

[20] D. W. Hamlyn (Hamlyn 1970, pp. 81-83) mentions D. H. Lawrence's rocking-horse winner, and an example due to A. Phillips Griffiths (Griffiths 1967; cf. Carrier 1971, p. 10; de Sousa 1970, p. 68; Goldman 1977, p. 114).

2. Attacks on the Justification Condition—193

which would count as being right that *h* provided *h* were true, then *P* is, indeed, right that *h*, and (2) it is not at all accidental that *S* is in *C*. (Dicker 1978, pp. 171-172)

But Dicker has confused what is not accidental within a situation with its not being accidental that one is in the situation. Unger allows that it may be accidental that *S* exists or is alive at *t* and thus that *S* comes to know *p* at *t*, even though, given *S*'s situation, it is not at all accidental that *S* is right that *p* at *t* (Unger 1968, pp. 159-160). In addition, clause (A) not only requires abnormally high standards for knowledge, but overlooks Unger's admission that a person may know a sum he has worked out even though his techniques of addition sometimes lead to mistakes (Unger 1967, p. 172).

A. J. Holland's interpretation of Unger's *analysans* avoids these misrepresentations:

S's belief[21] in *p* is such that (1) it occurs in 'favorable' circumstances, *C*, i.e., the belief is of a type, *T*, such that beliefs of type *T* are typically, commonly true in *C*, and (2) given *C*, both (a) what makes *S*'s belief true completely explains and causally suffices for *S*'s having the belief and (b) *S*'s having the belief causally suffices for what makes the belief true. (Holland 1977, pp. 560-561)[22]

John Barker interprets Unger as advancing only clause (2) (*sans* the phrase, "completely explains and") (Barker 1972, p. 314). George Pappas and Marshall Swain suggest that Unger may only mean to stress clause (2b) (Pappas and Swain 1978, pp. 19-20). But all three interpretations attribute to Unger a version of the conclusive reasons view criticized in Chapter 5.

Clause (1) in Holland's interpretation is compatible with Unger's remarks about fallible addition, and may allow the analysis to deal with the bumpkin example (E 46).[23] If clause (2b) is dropped because

---

[21] For simplicity, I henceforth restrict 'being right that *p*' to 'having true belief that *p*.'

[22] To allow for knowledge of the future, '*A* causally suffices for *B*' must be understood not to entail '*A* is a cause of *B*' or even, '*A* causally sustains *B*.'

[23] And Kenneth Collier's case of the hallucinating paranoid (Collier 1973).

of difficulties in the conclusive reasons view, Holland is still prepared to attack the resulting analysis for its inclusion of (2a). In Chapter 5, I mentioned Holland's argument that the character of even our observational beliefs will not "depend essentially on the way the world is. It will depend in part upon the character of our antecedent convictions" (Holland 1977, p. 568). In addition, it is not clear that examples analogous to the horserace prognosticator (E 78) can be encompassed by (2a).

Both these difficulties are avoided by J. L. Mackie's interpretation of Unger's *analysans*:

> S's believing p is related to the fact that p in some way such that if the fact had been different then the belief is at least likely to have been different. (Mackie 1969-1970, p. 249)

If Mackie's reference to likelihood is statistical, it overlooks the example of the retina-rotting drug (E 57), where the facts are never actually different while S has a relevant relation to them, and there is no basis for the statistical statement that Mackie would have us consider.

If Mackie's reference to likelihood is instead meant to deal with an objective propensity to form belief, given S's total situation, then the resulting analysis is too weak to exclude the case of the beloved speck (E 48) and too strong as well, because it rules out knowledge in the case of Eloise's phone call (E 49). It would also deny knowledge in any case where strong emotions or attitudes would have sustained belief in the absence of corresponding facts (Unger 1968, p. 158; Lehrer 1971).

Perhaps the latter cases can be dealt with by adding some type of relevancy requirement concerning the way in which S's belief may be sustained, but the resulting analysis will still improperly rule out knowledge in the following example:

(E 83)   *The Turned-Off Hologram*: As in (E 50), except that S has had no prior contact with the machine or Mr. Promoter, and now sees the vase in the box while the machine's alternating device is turned off. However, because Mr. Promoter wishes to remove the vase occasionally during the course of the exhibit, he has constructed the machine so that any time the vase is removed the hologram automatically is illuminated.

This example would not satisfy even an amended version of Mackie's condition, for there is no significant likelihood that had the vase been absent, S would not have believed it to be present. Indeed, in the example of noncompulsive belief (E 51), the likelihood is zero.

Most of the previous examples are compatible with Barker's interpretation of Unger's *analysans*:

> the occurrence of the belief in p is either an empirically necessary or an empirically sufficient condition for its being the case that p. (Barker 1972, p. 314)

Nonetheless, the resulting analysis improperly imputes knowledge in the case of the beloved speck (E 48).[24]

L. S. Carrier suggests that Unger's condition of knowledge is satisfied by the former's own most recent causal analysis (Carrier 1976, p. 242). But this interpretation leaves Unger open to the objections raised against Carrier in Chapter 5. In addition, Carrier's approach is unable to deal with examples such as the horserace prognosticator (E 78).

2.2 *Braine on Nonaccidentality*

David Braine attempts to avoid the justification condition and to develop a treatment of nonaccidentality similar to that found in clause (1) of Holland's interpretation of Unger. Braine analyzes S's knowing p as follows:

> S is in a state (1) which is acquired, (2) which has some actualization (exercise), (3) whose acquisition or actualization (exercise) involves rational thought or utterance, and (4) which is intellec-

---

[24] See also the case of the unloaded rifle (Barker 1972, p. 314).

tually desirable for a being of S's kind in regard to the fact that p. (Braine 1971-1972, pp. 54-55)

Braine then claims that the desirability-making characteristic involved in (4) is the following: either the state in question brings or its actualization (exercise) would bring S to the truth in regard to the question whether or not p by S's relying on grounds, reasons, or exercise of his faculties of a general type that would, relative to certain purposes, not accidentally but reliably or naturally result in S's coming to the truth, were S to rely on them (p. 61).

Inclusion of clause (1) arbitrarily rules out the possibility of innate knowledge, and clause (3) may be too restrictive to cover the knowledge of infants and dogs. Nonetheless, Braine's talk of the "natural" results of the processes that confer knowledge contains a useful insight if we relate the notion of what is nonaccidental in this context to what philosophers have called the 'normal' way in which causal contrast situations develop. (See Chapter 5, Section 5.) An account of knowledge as a representational ability will permit us to see this 'normal' development as an illustration of the way in which one may acquire and manifest such an ability or power. We may view situations in which one falls short of knowledge as involving differentiating factors that cause one to lack or fail to display knowledge.[25] To this extent, the upshot of recent work on the analysis of knowing tempts us to return to Aristotle's insight, of which Braine explicitly reminds us, that knowledge is an excellence or virtue. But only future discussion will decide whether a normative element enters in the straightforward way that Braine and Margolis have maintained, or enters indirectly through some type of reference to justification in the analysis of representation.

---

[25] Thus, it may be a 'matter of luck' that one is in a situation where one attains epistemic goals by acting rationally (since differentiating factors just happen to be absent), but not a matter of luck that, being in the situation one is in, one attains epistemic goals by acting rationally (since such a development is 'normal'). This distinction is overlooked in Coder 1974; Ravitch 1976.

3. ATTACKS ON THE TRUTH CONDITION

John Tienson has employed the following example in order to criticize the standard analysis for treating the truth condition as independent of the justification condition:

(E 84)   *The Two Suspects*: S is a detective who believes q: 'Black is innocent,' and also believes p: 'White is innocent,' and who has exactly the same excellent evidence for q as for p, evidence which is as good as you like, short of entailing either proposition. However, p is true and q false. (Tienson 1974, pp. 290-292)

According to Tienson, after S is told that one of the two is guilty, even he will admit that he had never known either to be innocent. Tienson defends this response by arguing that otherwise we are committed to r: 'S knew one of the two propositions to be true, but S is not now and has never been in a position to say which' (p. 291).

However, philosophers who accept cases such as the horserace prognosticator (E 78) are unlikely to find r counterintuitive. For such a prognosticator might pick the wrong horse occasionally if his ability is not completely foolproof. In addition, there is a distinction between the detective's knowing p and his preparedness to claim that he knows p (Alston 1976; White 1977). The normal expectation that a detective can name a culprit if he claims to know of one may make S reluctant to continue to claim knowledge in the above situation.

Robert Ackermann has been so bold as to propose outright rejection of the truth condition. He advances a "partial analysis" of knowledge in which the truth condition and justification conditions are replaced by the following condition: S can meet all current relevant nonmetaphysical objections to p. A current relevant objection is one (or equivalent to one) that has already been formulated, and a metaphysical objection is one which is of a type that does not depend on the details of S's situation but could be constructed for any other knowledge claim similar to p in certain respects (Ackermann 1972, pp. 65-67, 107).

Ackermann counts Mr. Nogot's awareness that q: 'Mr. Nogot does not own a Ford' as an objection to S's concluding p: 'Either someone in S's office owns a Ford or Brown is in Barcelona' (p. 115). Thus, we must construe Ackermann's concept of formulating an objection to be a technical one, covering merely someone's awareness of a proposition. For in Nogot cases S does not assert p aloud and Mr. Nogot need not realize that S believes p.[26]

Roger Gallie responds that q is "*no* objection to the proposition" p (Gallie 1975, p. 138). But Ackermann seems to be speaking of objections to S's accepting or asserting that proposition. Thus, if S were to be made to consider proposition q, S must be able to keep it from turning into a reason for him not to accept or assert p. In the Nogot examples, S must, according to Ackermann, "be able to demonstrate that q is false," and since S cannot, S does not know p (Ackermann 1972, p. 75). Gallie points out that once one has demonstrated something one knows it (Gallie 1975, p. 138). Thus, the specter of circularity is raised if we need to define "demonstrating" by speaking of knowledge.

My interpretation of Ackermann allows him to meet David Annis's objection that S may fail to know in a situation where no objections to p have been formulated, even though, given the available evidence, there are rather obvious objections to p (Annis 1974, p. 82). This criticism will be avoided provided that we technically define all propositions entailed by or supported by evidence of which someone is aware as themselves being propositions of which someone is aware.

The most glaring flaw in Ackermann's analysis, however, is its inability to prevent merely misleading defeaters of S's justification from denying S knowledge, as in the case of the demented Mrs. Grabit.

Ackermann defends his rejection of the truth condition by pointing to the fact that there are "contexts in which relevant objections show

---

[26] However, Ackermann himself speaks of objections to a claim as "reasons why it is doubted by others" (Ackermann 1972, p. 66).

a development over time'' (Ackermann 1972, p. 77). For example, Kit Carson knew p: 'Since the edges of the tracks were sharp, the Indians could be overtaken in two hours.' But Kit's modern counterpart needs to consider that the Indians may be heading for a rendezvous with a helicopter (p. 77). However, the shift in context here may be due to the logic of ''can'' and ''would'' statements and to the shifting reference of connected *ceteris paribus* considerations rather than to anything concerning the concept of knowledge (R. Clark 1973).

Philosophers have often noticed that common locutions such as the following initially appear to conflict with the truth condition: (1) The student's answers concerning ancient history show that she knew that the gods dwelt on Olympus; (2) The Greeks knew the gods dwelt on Olympus. Moreover, because certain philosophers regard a sentence such as, ''Hamlet was a prince of Denmark,'' as being false when its singular names fail to denote, Margolis has claimed that those philosophers must regard the truth condition as violated by the following statement: (3) Russell knew that Hamlet was a prince of Denmark (Margolis 1973b, p. 16).

Israel Scheffler suggests that such statements are elliptical for locutions which do not conflict with the truth condition: (1') The student's answers concerning ancient history show that she knew that it was believed that the gods dwelt on Olympus; (2') The Greeks believed they knew (or were sure) that the gods dwelt on Olympus; (3') Russell knew that Shakespeare's play asserts Hamlet to be a prince of Denmark (Scheffler 1965, p. 24).

D. W. Hamlyn, instead, maintains that we waive the truth condition in special cases, ones where ''before we start, all questions about the truth or falsity of the description in terms of which we express the subject of our knowledge claim'' (Hamlyn 1970, p. 96). He thereby treats ''knowing'' as what Robinson calls a dismantling word. However, Robinson denies that the truth condition is dropped in ''sober speech,'' and notes that (2) ''is shocking and gets a special effect thereby'' (Robinson 1971, p. 21).

But sentences (1) and (3) have little shock value. Moreover, it is undesirable to multiply elliptical uses beyond necessity. Future work may permit us to understand the above sentences as speaking of a person's ability or power to manifest or become involved in a representation of states of affairs which obtain in possible or fictional worlds related in certain ways to our own, where an analysis of the broadest category of knowing will characterize this relation in an univocal yet context-dependent fashion.

7.

Falsity and Rational Inquiry—a Solution to the Gettier Problem and a Perspective on Social Aspects of Knowing

In this concluding chapter, I shall mainly be concerned to explain the manner in which I proposed to deal with the Gettier problem and the social aspects of knowing near the end of the period with which the present survey is concerned (Shope 1979c; 1979d). What I believe to be the proper approach is partly suggested by the results of our discussion thus far, which may be summarized as follows.

1. Some Morals of the Preceding Discussion

The defeasibility analyses considered in Chapter 2 were to some extent successful in classifying instances of knowing because they often exposed the fact that awareness of a falsehood would reveal to S, or at least should reveal to S, a respect in which the justified status of S's actual belief was not that appropriate to having knowledge. But an undesirable side effect of such accounts often was to exclude knowing in cases where a falsehood did not pertain to any such inadequacy. The latter difficulty was avoided only in part by means of the strategy of gerrymandering the sources of justification. Analyses which we considered at the end of the chapter, beginning with those relying on condition (iv_8), attempted unsuccessfully to discount the harmless falsehoods, but at least the ones discussed in Section 1.46 managed to restrict their attention to falsehoods pertaining to the actual justification of S's belief and not merely hypothetical justifications. Nonetheless, they remained inadequate because they considered S's actual justification in terms of conditionals which concerned merely hypothetical effects upon the actual justification.

The approach explored in Chapter 3, which I shall develop more fully below, was to admit that what is crucial is not hypothetical effects upon S's justification and what they should reveal to S. Instead, what matters is the effect of falsehoods on our ascription of knowledge to S, or, better, what matters is whether falsehoods play certain roles in relation to S's actual justification. It appeared promising to describe the roles in question by relating them to epistemic explanations of the justified status of S's beliefs. But technical difficulties were encountered in generating a suitably detailed regress which would expose all the places at which falsehoods might interfere with knowing. Another significant discovery was that we need to force putative epistemic explanations to cover not merely what is in fact believed by S but to deal in some way with the justified status of various propositions beyond S's immediate ken. We noted that a concern with the latter propositions will be relevant to some of the social aspects of knowing, although we questioned whether these considerations should be articulated in terms of Ernest Sosa's concept of being in a position to know. A point which we acknowledged but did not at the time elaborate was Sosa's insight that attributions of knowing are in important ways relative to epistemic communities.

Chapter 4 provided some confirmation of the need to restrict consideration of the role of falsehoods to a sequence of explanations concerning justification that directly leads up to S's justified belief. Chisholm was seen to have opened his analysis to counterexamples because it allowed consideration of the role of falsehoods in side paths leading off from the type of sequence just mentioned. Sosa's attempt to cover all the social aspects of knowing by a consideration of what S is justified in believing inherited some strengths from its structural similarity to defeasibility accounts. But it also contained a fatal weakness that prevented it from rooting out all points where Gettierized links might occur, and did not contain a suitable replacement for the role played in Sosa's earlier account by the concept of being in a position to know. A comparison of Sosa's and Harman's views concerning available evidence revealed the need to acknowledge a complex background of social considerations concerning a mutually cooperative search for evidence and justifying grounds.

In Chapter 5, we explored the dangers of falling back upon a variety of conditionals in characterizing causal connections between S's belief and various preceding factors, and acknowledged the need to go beyond a strictly causal conception of the respects in which processes underlying belief are reliable. We also took note of the large role that methodological considerations may need to play in determining when a belief is justified and appropriately related to various respects in which S's situation is normal or abnormal. No satisfactory analysis of justified belief in terms of reliability proved to be presently available. Thus, it is advisable to provide a solution to the Gettier problem which refrains as much as possible from detailed commitments concerning the nature of justification.

The preceding chapter underscored the need for future research to consider a broad category of knowing, perhaps analyzable as some type of representational power or ability, which does not demand belief or justification on S's part as does a more narrow category of knowing for which the Gettier problem arises.

We shall now proceed to analyze this narrower category, which I have technically called justified factual knowledge. As Keith Lehrer has emphasized, it is a type of knowing with which philosophers have usually been concerned, for it involves contexts where propositional attitudes are at stake and we are concerned with questions and answers that form "the basis for critical discussion and confrontation in cognitive inquiry" in such a way that we require our interlocutors to have justified belief or acceptance of their answers (Lehrer 1974, p. 9).

2. Chains of Evidence and Justification-Making Chains; a Zenonian Difficulty

When attempting in Chapter 3 to extract a technique for forcing falsehoods into the open, we noticed that it is not adequate merely to insist, for example, that when e is a description of good evidence upon which the justified status of S's believing or accepting p depends, there be an explanation of why e describes good evidence for p and that the explanation have either the form, 'e describes good evidence for p because e describes good evidence for x and x entails p,' or the form, 'e describes good evidence for p because e describes good evidence for x and x describes good evidence for p.' In Gettier-type cases of certain sorts, x may be true, and the existence of the falsehood remain hidden, lurking somehow in the way e and x are related, or in the way x and p are related. We suggested at that point that a regress must be generated in order to flush out the falsehood.

It is important to notice the inadequacy of generating a chain of evidence leading up to proposition p by responding to each explanation of the above types with a demand that there be a similar explanation of each link that has been exposed between evidence and that for which it is evidence. For even then the chain may be insufficiently detailed to reveal relevant falsehoods. This may be illustrated by drawing inspiration from Zeno when we ponder a Gettier-type case such as the following:

(E 85)   *The Lying Physicist*: S applies to the motion of billiard ball b correct laws of motion, but learned them from a known authority who, unsuspected by S, wrote them down incorrectly but got S to believe the correct laws because of a fluke (e.g., alteration of the inscription in his letter by a drop of moisture). S correctly applies the laws to calculate the path of b from spatio-temporal location $(1,1)$ to its future location $(3,3)$, given S's knowledge of the values of other relevant variables, so that S justifiably believes p: 'b will be at $(3,3)$.'

Repeated imposition of the above requirement may generate a regress that never would hit upon any false statements, as the following beginning of a regress illustrates, where "v_i" states the value of relevant additional variables at time t_i:

Question: Why is e_1: 'b is at $(1,1)$ and v_1' good evidence for p?

Answer: Because e_1 is good evidence for e_2: 'b will be at $(2,2)$ and v_2' and e_2 is good evidence for p.

Questions: Why is e_1 good evidence for e_2; and why is e_2 good evidence for p?

Answers: Because e_1 is good evidence for $e_{1.5}$: 'b will be at $(1.5, 1.5)$ and $v_{1.5}$' and $e_{1.5}$ is good evidence for e_2: and because e_2 is good evidence for $e_{2.5}$: 'b will be at $(2.5, 2.5)$ and $v_{2.5}$' and $e_{2.5}$ is good evidence for p, respectively.

Questions: Why is e_1 good evidence for $e_{1.5}$; and . . . ?

Answers: Because e_1 is good evidence for $e_{1.25}$: 'b will be at $(1.25, 1.25)$ and $v_{1.25}$' and $e_{1.25}$ is good evidence for $e_{1.5}$; and

[We may continue to travel with Zeno beyond this point.]

A similar result emerges even if we acknowledge a need to shift from the more restrictive term, "evidence," to the broader term, "justified." Such a shift is appropriate insofar as it sounds more natural to speak of the authority's message as something that makes S justified in accepting the laws which S does, than to say the message itself is evidence that these laws hold. Moreover, in a Nogot example where S arrives at the disjunction, p: 'Either Mr. Nogot owns a Ford or Brown is in Barcelona,' which happens to be true only because of its second disjunct, the falsehood constituting its first disjunct cannot in any ordinary sense be called evidence for the disjunction. But we can say that S's being justified in believing that falsehood makes S justified in believing the disjunction. Such a shift would alter the above series of questions and answers by having each step consider what makes S justified in believing. The sequence would then begin by considering what makes S justified in believing p, and this might include not just e_1 but also S's justifiably believing the laws he has come to accept. But the sequence of questions and answers might never generate any more information about the source of his awareness of the laws of motion, at least if the sequence begins as follows:

> *Question*: Why does S's justifiably believing both these laws and e_1 make S justified in believing p?
>
> *Answer*: Because S's justifiably believing these laws and e_1 makes S justified in believing e_2, and S's justifiably believing these laws and e_2 makes S justified in believing p.

One might think that the reason the above question is faulty for our purposes is because it generates a sequence that is too 'forward-looking.' It tries to explain a path from something that justifies S's believing p to the latter. Perhaps the sequence should concern itself with the reverse direction, asking of each thing said to make S justified in believing something what makes S justified in believing it. This would generate what we may call a justification-making chain connected with S's believing p. In the above example, asking what makes S justified in believing these laws would at least start us in the direction of eventually uncovering a falsehood which S believes about why the exact inscriptions he received were in the letter.

But a wholly 'backward-looking' strategy for generating the sequence will fail if the very start of the sequence is not, to put it roughly, sufficiently 'close' to S's justifiably believing p. As we saw in Chapter 3, one might respond in a Nogot example to the question of why S is justified in believing that someone in the class owns a Ford by describing Mr. Nogot's behavior in front of S and Mr. Nogot's record of reliability in dealings with S. But going backward from *that* point will involve us in having already missed the relevant falsehood involved in the example.

Thus, we must somehow develop both a backward-looking and forward-looking strategy.

3. EPISTEMIC EXPLANATIONS AND JUSTIFICATION-EXPLAINING CHAINS

A bidirectional strategy was to some extent involved in Sosa's conception, discussed at the end of Chapter 3, of the way a 'tree of knowledge' relates to 'epistemic explanations.' For each node in the tree, each attribution of a degree of justification to some belief of S, the tree branches and provides a backing of propositions linked to the one in question in an epistemic explanation. And something of a forward-looking dimension was provided by the need for a given element, such as S's justifiably believing that Nogot behaved as he did and has been reliable, to be linked to the next closer element to the beginning of the tree, not by the mere statement that thanks to it the next closer element is true, but by forming part of an epistemic explanation of why the latter is true. Thus, Sosa believed that the tree will not just indicate that S's justifiably believing in Mr. Nogot's behavior and reliability is connected with S's justifiably believing p: 'Someone in the class owns a Ford,' but will indicate all portions of an epistemic explanation required to entail the justified (evident) status of p for S when added to premises expressing true epistemic principles. Sosa thought that this will force us to include in a putative tree for S and the proposition p the additional ascription of the false belief on S's part that it is Mr. Nogot who owns the Ford, since plausible epistemic principles would seem to lead us to interpolate this intervening stage in a forward-looking direction in order to provide the requisite epistemic explanations.

However, we saw that in the case of the clever reasoner (E 6), and perhaps in certain other cases, an epistemic explanation could be given of S's justifiably believing p without attributing a false belief to S. So we shall now need to rule out certain roles for false propositions even when they are not believed by S.

We demonstrated in Chapter 4 that Sosa's recent attempt to accomplish this by speaking of 'epistemic presuppositions' does not fully succeed. One of the difficulties is that he attempts only to consider whether there are false propositions S would be justified in believing on the basis of various propositions involved in the tree. Instead, we need in the present discussion to realize that what Sosa is attempting to deal with is not a dimension of S's own potential beliefs so much as another dimension of justification, a dimension which fundamentally concerns what propositions are justified. An analysis of knowing that can withstand Gettier-type examples yet be free of unwanted side effects needs to consider both justified beliefs and justified propositions. I pointed out in Chapter 3 that it is insufficient merely to require the *truth* of those propositions involved in epistemic explanations which the explanations do not require *S* to believe. Of course, if we were to require that someone or other *know* the propositions in question to be true, we would risk circularity in our analysis of knowing. So an attractive alternative to consider is that the propositions in question must be justified propositions (and later to acknowledge that this conception involves a type of relativity to an epistemic community which Sosa himself has emphasized).

The introduction of the idea of a justified proposition provides us as well with a new way of coping with the manner in which falsehoods are involved in Gettier-type situations. For the conception of an epistemic explanation may now be expanded to include explanations of why various propositions are justified, and Gettier-type cases will turn out to be ones where explanations of this type contain false propositions at certain points. But in contexts where we are concerned with the type of knowledge involving justified belief or acceptance, call it 'justified factual knowledge,'[1] one's belief or acceptance must be justified through its connection with a sequence of such explanations not involving falsehoods at those places.

I have proposed (Shope 1979c; 1979d) that we technically label the latter type of sequence a 'justification-explaining chain,' and that we make the following alteration in the standard justification condition when we analyze such knowledge:

(iii′)   *S*'s believing *p* is justified in relation to epistemic goals either through its connection with a justification-explaining chain related to the proposition that *p* or independently of anything making it justified, and the proposition that *p* is justified.[2]

---

[1] This label is intended broadly enough to include knowledge of mathematical truths and logical truths. However, I have included the term "factual" as a way of indicating that I am sidestepping the controversy as to whether knowledge that *p* is different when acceptance of *p* constitutes the making of a value judgment, or at least the making of certain sorts of value judgments.

[2] I shall not attempt here to decide whether there are beliefs that are justified without

The first member, m_1, of a justification-explaining chain related to the proposition that p is any true conjunction of the form,

'f_1 and that makes the proposition that p justified,'

where the first conjunct describes something sufficient to make the proposition that p justified. We may allow that such a conjunct might not be particularly 'close' to the proposition that p, in the sense that what it describes may only make the latter proposition justified thanks to making some other proposition justified. What we must do is to construct ensuent members of the justification-explaining chain so that all such connections are exposed. This will not happen if we merely ask what makes the proposition that f_1 justified. But we can guarantee that it eventually happens if we ask of the *entire* conjunction, m_1, what makes *it* a justified proposition, and do this for each successive answer to such a question. Thus, we shall not concentrate upon a justification-*making* chain related to the proposition that p, that is, a string of evidence leading up to the proposition that p or a succession of propositions each of which describes something that makes its successor justified and one of which makes the proposition that p justified. Instead, I have proposed the following definition:

A justification-explaining chain related to the proposition that p is an ordered set of propositions such that
    (a) the first member, m_1, is a true proposition of the form:

        'f_1 and that makes the proposition that p justified,'

---

anything making them justified, and have added the second disjunct in the first conjunct of (iii') for the sake of generality. Some philosophers would maintain that even in an example of 'basic' knowledge, e.g., where S knows p: 'I am thinking of the number 1,' something makes S's belief justified, e.g., p's being believed by the person whose mental contents are described by p. If a similar point can be made concerning all cases of basic knowledge, or if we are not to allow for the possibility of basic knowledge, then the second disjunct in the first conjunct of (iii') may be omitted. This would also permit us to drop the second conjunct since it would already be entailed by satisfaction of the remaining clause, thanks to the definition of a justification-explaining chain.

where the proposition that f_1 describes something sufficient to make the proposition that p justified;

(b) for any member, m_j, the successor of m_j is determined
as follows:

    (i) there is no successor of m_j if and only if m_j is
justified independently of anything making it justified;

    (ii) when m_j is justified only because something makes
it justified then the successor of m_j is a true proposition of the form:

$$\text{'}f_{j+1}\text{ and that makes }m_j\text{ justified,'}$$

where the proposition that f_{j+1} describes something sufficient to make m_j justified;

(c) each instantiation for f_j is a disjunction of conjunctions
of propositions which take any of the forms described
below (allowing disjunctions and conjunctions to contain
only one member):

    (1) 'h_2 describes evidence for h_1,'

    (2) 'h_2, and h_2 entails h_1,' where h_1 does not entail h_2,

    (3) 'h_i describes evidence for h_{i-1}, and h_{i-1} describes
evidence for h_{i-2}, and . . . , and h_3 describes
evidence for h_2,' where $n \geqslant i \geqslant 3$,

    (4) 'h_2 entails h_1,' where h_1 does not entail h_2,

    (5) a form described as in any of (1)-(4) but with
phrases of one or more of the following types substituting at one or more places in the description
for the phrase, "evidence for":

"good evidence for," "evidence of such-and-
such a strength for," "something that justifies,"
"something that justifies to such-and-such a degree,"[3]

---

[3] This list of substitute phrases is meant to cover all the ways in which propositions
become, in the usual philosophical terminology, 'reasonable,' 'acceptable,' or 'evi-

(6) any form other than one logically equivalent to a disjunction of conjunctions of propositions that take any of the above forms (allowing disjunctions and conjunctions to contain only one member); and

(d) for any one of h_1, h_2, . . . , h_n that is false, some member of the ordered set entails its falsity.

This definition contains clause (d) in order to allow for a case such as that of Mr. Spotter (E 28), where an account of S's justified belief might mention S's awareness that something described in a true proposition provides evidence for a falsehood. The need to allow for such cases also prompts inclusion of form (c4) in the definition, as distinct from form (c2).

Let us illustrate the utility of this definition, when combined with the modified justification condition (iii'), by returning to the original example of Mr. Nogot, and then to the variants involving the clever reasoner and Feldman's proposal.

In the original Nogot case (E 1), Mr. Nogot's belief is justified through its connection with a chain of epistemic explanations, but the latter is not a justification-explaining chain as defined above but a mere pseudo-justification-explaining chain. The chain of epistemic explanations could begin in various ways, depending on how 'close' we initially wish to come to the proposition that p. Of course, it cannot contain as its first member:

'Mr. Nogot owns a Ford and this entails that someone in the office owns a Ford and that makes the proposition, ''Someone in the office owns a Ford,'' justified.'

For the initial conjunct in this statement is false. So is its final conjunct, since even if Mr. Nogot's owning a Ford were a fact, this would not justify the proposition that someone in the office owns a Ford (although it would make it true).

---

dent.' If it does not, then further appropriate substitute phrases should be added to the list.

Suppose, instead, that we begin with

M_1: 'S has a justified belief that someone in the office owns a Ford and that makes the proposition, "Someone in the office owns a Ford," justified.'

We shall eventually see that even M_1 is false, for more is required for a proposition to be justified than that someone is justified in believing it. Letting that pass, and supposing that M_1 is true, the second member of the justification-explaining chain would have to cite not only something that makes the second conjunct of M_1 true, but also the first conjunct. But we cannot meet the latter requirement by continuing the chain with

M_2: 'S has a justified belief that Mr. Nogot owns a Ford; and the proposition that Mr. Nogot owns a Ford entails [describes evidence for] the proposition that someone in the office owns a Ford; and . . . ; and (all) that makes M_1 justified,'

where material that would surplant the ellipsis pertains only to either the second conjunct of M_1 or to justifying the ascription to S of a belief that someone in the office owns a Ford. But M_2 cannot be a member of a genuine justification-explaining chain as defined above, for it contains the false proposition, 'Mr. Nogot owns a Ford,' in a proscribed position, that is, in the position of h_2 in a conjunct of form (c4) [form (c1)].[4]

The same difficulty arises if we treat the original Nogot case by taking a cue from the variant concerning the clever reasoner, and offer as the second member of the putative chain

M_2': 'S has a justified belief that S would be justified in believing that Mr. Nogot owns a Ford; the proposition that Mr. Nogot

---

[4] At least it does so on the assumption that no later member of the chain asserts that the proposition in question is false. But I see no way of challenging this assumption. The case has no relevant similarity, for example, to that of Mr. Spotter (E 28). A similar point holds for all the putative chains that we shall consider in this section.

owns a Ford entails [describes evidence for] the proposition that someone in the office owns a Ford; and . . . ; and (all) that makes M_1 justified.'

I do not believe that we can temporarily forestall the difficulty which arises concerning M_2' by incorporating the entailment [evidential] claim into S's own belief:

M_2'': 'S has a justified belief that (a) S would be justified in believing that Mr. Nogot owns a Ford and (b) that the proposition that Mr. Nogot owns a Ford entails [describes evidence for] the proposition that someone in the office owns a Ford; and . . .; and (all) that makes M_1 justified.'

It seems to me that the above proposition is false, since S's mere justified belief in the entailment is insufficient if the entailment does not hold. So the entailment should, after all, be affirmed in a conjunct when describing what makes M_1 justified. However, suppose that I am wrong on this point. It would still be the case that in the next member of the putative chain an explanation must be given of why the materials mentioned in M_2'' do make M_1 justified, and I do not see how we can plausibly avoid at that point listing the conjunct of form (c4) [form (c1)] that was mentioned above, thereby reducing the whole putative chain to a mere pseudo-chain.

One might instead hope to draw inspiration for construction of a genuine chain from Richard Feldman's observations, and not mention at the start of the chain the proposition that Mr. Nogot owns a Ford. Suppose we let the second member of the chain be

M_2''': 'S has a justified belief [evidence that would justify a belief] that someone in the office has performed such-and-such deeds and has previously been generally reliable; and that makes M_1 justified,'

where the deeds in question are Nogot's behavior in front of S vis-à-vis the Ford.

But the ensuent member of the putative chain would have to indicate why the above member is justified. In order to prevent a return to contents already rejected above, one must give it the form

M_3: '. . . ; and the proposition that someone in the office has performed such-and-such deeds and has been previously reliable describes evidence for the proposition that the person in question in the office owns a Ford; and the latter proposition entails [describes evidence for] the proposition that someone in the office owns a Ford; and (all) this makes M_2''' justified.'

However, the penultimate conjunct in M_3 is of form (c4) [form (c1)] with the false proposition that the person in question in the office owns a Ford in a proscribed place. Moreover, the conjunct preceding that one is of form (c1) with the same false proposition in a prohibited location.[5]

These difficulties are forestalled only temporarily by substituting

M_3': '. . . ; and the proposition that someone in the office has performed such-and-such deeds and has been previously reliable describes evidence for the proposition that someone in the office owns a Ford; and (all) this makes M_2''' justified.'

One would still need in subsequent members of the chain to explain why M_3' is justified, and the problematic conjuncts which have temporarily been avoided will resurface.

We have been assuming that the attempt to construct for S a genuine justification-explaining chain to which S is relevantly related begins with M_1. But no significant difference is made if the chain begins more 'distantly' from the proposition that p, for example, by beginning with one of the following members:

---

[5] Similarly, if the term "evidence" is replaced by "good evidence" in this conjunct then the conjunct is of form (c5) with a false proposition in place of h_1. (This point was misstated in n. 11 to [Shope 1979c] as concerning instead a conjunct of form [c1].) A similar point may be made about an analogous change in the bracketed version of the preceding conjunct in M_3.

'S has a justified belief [evidence which would justify a belief] that Mr. Nogot owns a Ford, and that makes the proposition, "Someone in the office owns a Ford," justified.'

'S has a justified belief [evidence which would justify a belief] that Mr. Nogot has behaved in such-and-such a manner and has been generally reliable, and that makes the proposition, "Someone in the office owns a Ford," justified.'

'S has a justified belief [evidence which would justify a belief] that someone in the office has behaved in such-and-such a manner and has been generally reliable, and that makes the proposition, "Someone in the office owns a Ford," justified.'

No matter which of these three propositions were suggested as m_1, eventually one would either be led to abandon the attempt to construct the chain or find oneself appealing to putative links whose internal structure is in crucial respects the structure of links already found wanting in our previous discussion.

It is clear that the same types of difficulties will arise if we drop all mention of S's own beliefs at the start of the description of the first member of the chain and let it describe public evidence, for example:

M_1':   'Mr. Nogot has behaved in such-and-such a manner in the office and has been generally reliable; and that makes the proposition, "Someone in the office owns a Ford," justified.'

Of course, there is some public evidence available to Mr. Havit, which allows Mr. Havit to know that someone in the office (viz. himself) owns a Ford. But S's believing that someone in the office owns a Ford is not justified through its connection with that evidence, but only through its connection with evidence of the type mentioned in M_1' and other previously considered members of various pseudo-chains.

Given such a full discussion of the original case of Mr. Nogot, no further points need to be made about the way our solution to the Gettier problem copes with the case of the clever reasoner or Feldman's variant, since any initially plausible attempt to construct a justification-explaining chain in those examples would proceed through links whose contents would include conjuncts whose shortcomings have already been exposed above.

However, there are Nogot examples where the propositions, 'Mr. Nogot owns a Ford,' or 'The person in question in the office owns a Ford,' are not false, as in the case of the two Fords (E 18) or the case of lucky Mr. Nogot (E 22). In those examples, a falsehood would be exposed at a later point in any plausible attempt to construct a justification-explaining chain, namely, where we must attempt to explain what justifies a proposition to the effect that Nogot (the person in question) owns *a* Ford, and the explanation is not permitted to appeal to the false proposition that he owns the *particular* Ford which was involved in his deeds in front of *S*. In a variant where Mr. Nogot happens simultaneously to win in a lottery the particular Ford which he had borrowed in order to deceive *S*,[6] the relevant falsehood is that Mr. Nogot's behavior proceeds from an intention to convey true information or that the documents he displays record the legal act due to which Mr. Nogot owns the particular Ford that he does.[7]

4. A RATIONALE FOR THIS SOLUTION TO THE GETTIER PROBLEM

Rather than continue to illustrate the application of our solution to the Gettier problem, it will be more useful to indicate why it works, and then to use this understanding in order to articulate more precisely what may be called the fundamental structure of Gettier-type examples.

4.1 *Justification and Rationality: Epistemic Communities*

As a prelude, we need to take account of roughly what is involved in speaking of justification in the contexts with which we have been concerned.

---

[6] Such a case is reminiscent of a situation in Jean Paul Sartre's story, "The Wall."

[7] At some point, considerations about the 'normal' way for the evidence to relate to the truth of some propositions may become relevant. See the discussion of Castañeda in Chapter 5, Section 5.

When a speaker claims (in a context where S's 'justified factual knowledge' that p is at issue) that S's believing p is justified, she is claiming that believing is the justified propositional attitude for S. This is stronger than stating that believing is to some degree justified.[8] This distinction parallels one between saying that a person was justified in performing a certain action insofar as there were some good considerations in its favor and saying that the action was one that was justified. In speaking of S's action or propositional attitude as the one that was justified, a person is saying that by performing that action or holding that attitude instead of some alternative,[9] S manifested S's rationality more fully in relation to certain goals which the speaker has in mind. However, she may happen to have nonepistemic goals in mind, for example, moral goals, which are not relevant in this context to the type of justified belief involved in knowing. This accounts for the qualification concerning goals which I introduced above into the initial portion of justification condition (iii').

When speaking of a proposition as justified, as we do at the end of (iii'), we need to draw an analogous distinction between saying that a proposition is justified, and saying merely that it is to some extent justified. When we say that a proposition is justified or warranted in the former sense, we have some epistemic community in mind, and we are saying that the disposition or state which we call rationality that is possessed by members of that community would be more fully manifested in relation to epistemic goals by members accepting that proposition instead of competing propositions and instead of withholding acceptance of any of these propositions.

It is at this point that Ernest Sosa's insistence on the relativity of knowledge attributions to epistemic communities may be more fully

---

[8] It is also different from claiming that S's believing is, in the words of Robert Meyers and Kenneth Stern, "well-taken," i.e., likely to lead to greater attainment of S's (our) epistemic goals (Meyers and Stern 1973, p. 156).

[9] The alternative propositional attitudes when S is justified in believing h include at least the following: disbelieving h; what some philosophers call 'withholding' h, that is, neither believing nor disbelieving h; being prepared to bet that h is true while at the same time withholding h. In some cases, the alternatives also include offering h as a guess in answer to a question while at the same time withholding h.

acknowledged. Sosa reminds us, for example, that what counts as knowing a bear has passed by may be different in relation to a group of nature guides from what counts as knowing a bear has passed by in relation to other people, such as the tourists who frequent the area, and that even in ordinary conversations more than one point of view may be adopted in various knowledge-attributions: "The expert/layman distinction is replicable in many different contexts . . ." (Sosa 1974a, p. 118).

I have agreed (Shope 1979d) with the appropriateness of this relativism, again drawing a comparison between knowledge attributions and causal judgments. One prominent aspect of the philosophical view mentioned in Chapter 5 concerning the nature of singular causal judgments expressed by sentences of the form, "*c* was the cause of *e*," is to permit different speakers to have in mind different causal contrast situations and thus to make different statements when uttering a given sentence of that form. One speaker may make a true statement and the other a false one by uttering one and the same sentence, thanks to their referring to different contrast situations. Even when the sentence is used by each speaker to make a true statement, they may be referring to different causal contrast situations and be making different statements. As a result, speaker S_1 could even make the metalinguistic remark that when a given sentence of the above form was uttered by speaker S_2 it expressed a true statement but that the same sentence would not have done so if uttered by S_1. Sosa's insight is that analogous facts hold regarding our willingness to accept or to reject knowledge ascriptions depending on the group of inquirers we have in mind who are involved in more or less complex communicative links and possibly governed by different standards of inquiry.

4.2 *Truth, Explanation, and Epistemic Ideals*

Karl Popper has suggested that a consideration of the epistemology of science will illuminate the epistemology of everyday belief. But Popper himself expresses little interest in discussing knowledge as a state of a person, and prefers to emphasize a sense of the noun "knowledge" that refers to combinations of propositions organized into explanatory systems by groups of inquirers in a cooperative effort to achieve their epistemic goals.

I have maintained (Shope 1979d) that attention to such goals and systems will support my analysis of what it is to be a knowing subject. The reason false propositions are to be prohibited at certain places in a justification-explaining chain is because of their potential role in the type of explanatory structures of which Popper speaks, structures which extend beyond purely scientific knowledge and communities of scientists, yet which involve the potential cooperative interchange within an epistemic community referred to in speaking of a justified proposition.

We may grant that both within and outside scientific inquiry explanations are sometimes constructed and accepted that contain falsehoods which nonetheless are justified propositions. It is indeed our common fate to be situated so that, at the time, it would more manifest the rationality of the members of an epistemic community with which we are concerned to accept some unsuspected falsehoods. But Popper, and others, have stressed the aspirations of our efforts in epistemic communities. The resulting conception of an epistemically ideal situation, one in which we attained our epistemic goals, seems to me to provide an additional element that helps to give a point to our having a conception of the type of knowledge involved in 'justified factual knowledge.'

These aspirations include the goals of neither accepting false propositions in such explanatory structures as data to be explained nor utilizing falsehoods as part of an explanation unless the explanation treats them as falsehoods (as in the example concerning Mr. Spotter [E 28]). It is useful to have the conception of a type of knowing involving belief which is justified in relation to such epistemic goals. For it is a conception of a person's manifesting rationality (or manifesting it more fully) by participating in an actual portion of this ideal social situation. The person participates in it by grasping part of a justification-explaining chain, therein being connected with a set of explanations that do not present as justified any falsehood unless they also present it as being a falsehood.

A misunderstanding might arise at this point. For in the definition of a justification-explaining chain, allowance is made for the possibility of turning conjuncts of forms (c1) and (c3) into ones of form (c5) by substituting, e.g., the phrase, "something that justifies," for the phrase, "evidence for." So even if a proper use of the term "evidence" precludes putting a falsehood in the place of h_2 in propositions of form (c1) or (c3) without obtaining a false conjunct of one of those forms, the same may not be said regarding conjuncts obtained by the above transformations, e.g., 'h_2 describes something that justifies h_1.' For we have admitted that false but justified propositions may explain the justified status of some other proposition.

But the presence of such false, justified propositions would itself constitute a deviation from an epistemically ideal situation in the very chain which helps to generate the justified status of S's belief that p. For we have accounted for the justification of a proposition in terms of the rationality of its acceptance by members of an epistemic community, and have admitted that at least one epistemic ideal is to avoid accepting a false *explanandum* or *explanans*. The incorporation of such a falsehood into the chain would be adding a falsehood to the explanatory resources of the epistemic community in a nonideal fashion.[10] Our conception of justified factual knowledge accordingly excludes it.

4.3 *Explanatory Satisfactoriness versus the Search for Trustworthy Epistemic Steppingstones*

The above conception of 'justified factual knowledge' has been elucidated partly in terms of various items mentioned in a justification-

---

[10] I pointed to this fact rather obliquely in Shope 1979d by noting that in a Gettier-type example such as that of the clever reasoner (E 6), if the proposition, 'Someone in the class owns a Ferrari,' is to be "embedded in the type of explanatory system of which Popper speaks, its truth is not satisfactorily explained *via* the false proposition, 'Mr. Nogot owns a Ferrari,' and to believe the latter would partly be to fall short of our epistemic goals" (p. 26).

explaining chain which are satisfactory as a partial attainment of epistemic goals concerning truth and explanation. But our conception does not appraise the instrumental value of this attainment in furthering additional attainment of epistemic goals.

In this respect, the present conception of knowing is less demanding than the ones explored in Chapter 3 that were proposed by Chisholm and Sosa. Neither philosopher returned to the commonly rejected Cartesian view that knowledge requires a degree of trustworthiness involving infallibility. But they did require that the crucial items which explain the degree of justification involved in knowing *p* are steppingstones that would not by themselves tempt us to violate our epistemic goals by their grounding falsehoods outside the justification-explaining chain related to *p*.

I believe that the quest for epistemically trustworthy steppingstones in this sense involves arbitrary expectations concerning knowledge, as did the old quest for certainty. Moreover, we have seen that the newer quest does not contain the key to the Gettier problem. Any discomfort which we may feel in admitting that what gives us knowledge might also in some instances ground our acceptance of falsehoods may be eased by remembering a result that emerged in Chapter 2, Section 1.463. There we saw that there are ways of increasing *S*'s knowledge in some respects which crucially involve decreasing it in other respects.[11] Attaining what is good may have unwanted side effects, even in the area of epistemology. That is an aspect of our finitude, and one of the ways in which justification-explaining chains lack the degree of perfection of a Platonic 'tether' for true belief. When the elements in such a chain do not constitute a defect in explanatory structures, they may nonetheless invite one.

4.4 *The Fundamental Structure of Gettier-Type Examples*

One of the reasons that description G in Chapter 1 of the surface structure of Gettier-type examples was not especially informative was the vagueness of point (5), which only said that either the

---

[11] This possibility has been discussed by Carl Ginet (Ginet 1980).

justification condition holds regarding a falsehood q, or, at least, that S would be justified in believing q. The latter qualification was needed in order to deal with cases such as the clever reasoner, where S refrains from believing falsehood q. But no further attempt was made at that point to specify more exactly the relation of proposition q itself to the remainder of S's epistemic situation. Consequently, G provided only a necessary set of conditions for a Gettier-type example. For a non-Gettier-type example where S lacks knowledge because of the social aspects of knowing might happen to have form G if S simultaneously is (would be) justified in believing some quite irrelevant falsehood.

We may now provide a proper definition of Gettier-type examples, thanks to materials explained in our solution to the Gettier problem. This may be done by replacing (5) in G with the following condition:

(5′) q occupies a place in a pseudo-justification-explaining chain related to p through connection with which S's believing p and S's believing q is justified such that (a) q is not the final conjunct in any member of the chain and (b) up to and including the member in which q first occurs as a conjunct, the chain's differences from a (genuine) justification-explaining chain are only those entailed by the falsity of q, i.e., by the fact that q is false.

Thus, we have finally seen the sense in which 'all that goes wrong' in a Gettier-type case is that some proposition is false.

5. RATIONALITY, SCIENCE, AND SOCIAL ASPECTS OF KNOWING

Something different goes wrong when S fails to know simply because of a social aspect of knowing. (Of course, there is nothing to prevent us from constructing a complicated case where one set of considerations thwarts S's knowing because of Gettierized connections and a second set of considerations about social aspects thwarts S's knowing for a separate reason.)

In some cases where S fails to know because of a social aspect of knowing, 'all that goes wrong' is that some propositions (involved in some f_i in a putative justification-explaining chain) fail to be justified. As we indicated earlier, the analysis of a proposition's being justified already brings in a reference to an epistemic community by indicating that the disposition or state which we call rationality that is possessed by members of a given epistemic community would be more fully manifested in relation to epistemic goals by members' accepting the proposition instead of accepting competing propositions or withholding acceptance of any of these propositions.

Let us see how the analysis of knowing that I have proposed accords with our intuitions about various examples where social aspects of knowing figure prominently. It will again prove useful to advert to the practices of scientific communities, and to follow the common assumption that epistemic methods within such communities reflect what are presently our best (corrigible) judgments concerning the ways in which the disposition, state, or trait that we call rationality manifests itself in pursuit of epistemic goals. By treating everyday epistemic contexts analogously, we shall be able to account for our intuitions concerning an otherwise bewildering variety of everyday examples.

We may begin with the case of Tom Grabit's actual twin (E 10). One of the relevant factors determining the more rational epistemic attitudes for members of an epistemic community are the observational propositions that various members have actually accepted. For the community attempts to train its members to become generally reliable sources of information, and barring countervailing considerations, there is an initial rational presumption that a member's acceptance of his or her own observations is trustworthy, at least to some degree. But countervailing considerations may be present that affect the degree of trustworthiness, as in the case of Tom Grabit's actual twin. The crucial observational propositions which S accepts in that case do not become justified propositions because of any links in a justification-explaining chain of which S has hold. For S lacks the ability to detect the difference between Tom's stealing the book and his twin's doing so. If an observer reports that a particular entity was involved in a certain state of affairs but the observer lacks the ability to discriminate between the involvement of other entities contained within the observational situation or 'observational space' then it is not more rational for members of the epistemic community to accept the report merely on the observer's say-so.[12] Thus, S's being justified in accepting the observational propositions in question at most helps to justify S's own acceptance of p: 'Tom stole the book.' So in this example, there is no justification-explaining chain related to p of which S has hold.

The notion of being contained within one's observational situation or observational space is vague and dependent upon pragmatic considerations, including assessments of the risk of confusing various entities. This accounts for the corresponding lack of firmness in our intuitions as to whether S knows p in a variant of the above example constructed by John Barker:

(E 86)   *Tom Grabit's Twin's Accident*: As in the case of Tom Grabit's actual twin (E 10), except that the twin was merely on his way to the library on that day and never got there because of an automobile accident. (Barker 1976b, p. 307)

---

[12] By this last qualification, I mean to allow that the community might already independently know that the other entities were not in fact observed by S. In some such cases, to be sure, it is rational for members of the community to accept the observer's report. But they do not accept it merely on the observer's say-so.

My emphasis on how the rationality of other members of the epistemic community is displayed in trusting an observation report differs significantly from that of Douglas Odegard (Odegard 1978). He says that if you are concerned about my particular credentials for making a knowledge claim, and you are aware of additional evidence possessed by those surrounding me (even if it is misleading evidence) "then you can challenge me by introducing the . . . [additional] evidence on its own. When I fail to cope, you can conclude that I do not know" (p. 124). The evidence possessed by others is relevant to defeating a knowledge attribution, according to Odegard, because the putative *knower* would not fully manifest his rationality by continuing to believe if he had this evidence; whereas, I am stressing the way in which various members of the epistemic community would or would not manifest their rationality, or would more fully manifest it, given certain evidence. Odegard's view is based on the erroneous subjunctive conditional mentioned in n. 34 to Chapter 1 and criticized in n. 34 to Chapter 2.

As Barker has said when pointing out this lack of firmness, it is desirable for an analysis which purports to deal with our existing conception of knowing to retain the same degree of vagueness which is actually an aspect of our present conception (p. 306). Moreover, I agree with Barker's intuition that the closer the accident occurred to the library (and, perhaps, the closer it occurred to the time of Tom's theft), the less we are inclined to grant S knowledge (p. 307). For we take more seriously the possibility of including the twin within S's observational space and the risk of his being confused with Tom, especially if we presume that the twin was traveling with a firm larcenous intent.

It is important to understand why the case of Tom Grabit's actual twin is significantly similar to the following example, rather than to the case of Eloise's phone call (E 49):

(E 87)   *The Back-Up Generator*: S has a true belief that p: 'The electric company's generators are causing the lights to be on in my friend's house,' on the basis of S's familiarity with the setup and history of the company's equipment and supply lines and S's observations of the present illumination in the friend's house and in many surrounding homes. Unsuspected by S, the friend has a generator in the basement which would instantly illuminate the house automatically in case the company's power failed. (Pappas and Swain 1973, p. 75)

According to George Pappas and Marshall Swain, the case is a counterexample to any conclusive reasons analysis similar to Dretske's, since S does succeed in knowing p. But they do not discuss the fact that their example is similar, except for its temporal reference, to one which Dretske had explicitly treated as a failure to know:

(E 88)   *The Back-Up Volcano*: S has a true belief that p: 'Nearby mountain M erupted many years ago,' on the basis of S's geological training and the observations of present lava locations. This would be good enough for S to know p were

it not for the fact that, unsuspected by S, the geology of the area is such that another nearby mountain, N, would have erupted if M had not, because pressure had to be released, and N's erupting would have resulted in essentially the same type of lava distribution being here today. (Dretske 1971, p. 5)

Whether or not our intuitions are firm regarding (E 87) and (E 88), I believe that we should regard them as cases of ignorance. For they are similar to the case of Tom Grabit's actual twin because of the risk that is involved of S's conflating various alternatives.

In contrast, examples such as Eloise's phone call (E 49) include a further detail. In such cases, there is a state of affairs, r, which is present, and which S justifiably takes to be present,[13] and which does not entail p but does preclude (whether or not S realizes it) the participation of the alternative, e.g., the actress, in the situation in place of Eloise. In (E 49), state of affairs r is that S is speaking on the phone with the person S takes to be Eloise. We do admit that it is more rational for members of the epistemic community to trust the observational reports of someone who possesses such a nontrivial 'precluder,' that is, something thanks to which any (significant risk of) conflating relevant alternatives has been avoided. For application of rational methodological principles in the epistemic community will itself speak of S as possessing a precluder, thereby indicating that S's responses are appropriately guided by something rather than merely a matter of luck. No such precluding states of affairs are involved in cases such as (E 87) and (E 88).

However, in the case of the two volcanoes, even though both mountains are presently within S's observational space, their participation in the state of affairs that p took place, or would have taken

---

[13] Or at least S would be justified in taking it to be present, and does not take it to be absent. In order to avoid Gettier-type difficulties, we need further to specify that S's belief that it is present would be justified by its connection with a justification-explaining chain related to the proposition that r is present. (However, it may be necessary to waive this requirement about justified belief when S is an infant or young child.)

place, long ago. Moreover, the company's generator in (E 87) is spatially far away from S and we would not speak of S's affirming that p as itself an observational report. So the methodological point mentioned above concerning possession of a precluder needs to be worded without specifying whether the alternatives are within S's observational space. (Of course, these remarks presuppose some independent way of specifying relevant alternatives and the risk of S's conflating them, relative to the epistemic community in question; I make no attempt here to articulate such procedures.)

Barker and Klein have contrasted the case of the demented Mrs. Grabit (E 12) with the following cases:

(E 89) *Lying Mrs. Grabit*: As in (E 12), except that the twin does exist but was nowhere near the library, and Mrs. Grabit gives testimony to the effect that there was such a twin near the library and does so simply because she wishes to protect Tom. (Barker 1976b, p. 306; Klein 1976, p. 805)

(E 90) *Demented Mrs. Grabit and Company*: As in (E 12) and a number of Mrs. Grabit's relatives share her delusion about a fictitious twin. (Klein 1976, p. 810)

Seen from the perspective of the everyday epistemic community to which she and S belong, Mrs. Grabit's testimony might appear to constitute a critical challenge to S's opinion about the theft and to keep S's observations from generating relevant parts of any justification-explaining chain related to that opinion. But if Mrs. Grabit's views are demented, then even when they are shared by her relatives, they are no more relevant here than analogous challenges in a scientific community where, merely out of fear or mental illness, one or more scientists suggest, without further substantiation, that another scientist's observationally based report was due to a confusion of different entities within his observational situation (where those other entities are wholly fictitious). Members of a scientific community are regarded as being more rational in dismissing such flimsy challenges, and a similar point holds about the everyday epistemic community in relation to examples (E 12), (E 89), and (E 90).[14] A justification-explaining chain is not destroyed by such unsubstantiated challenges.

In Harman's newspaper example (E 9), the denials of the assassination can ultimately be traced to someone's intent to deceive, and the case has that much in common with (E 12). But the denials in the news reports purport to have originated from observations of eyewitnesses, and this is one important difference from all the Grabit cases. A second difference is that the newspapers or broadcasting stations issuing the denials are appropriately regarded as generally reliable sources of information, so that those around S who respond by not believing in the assassination are depending on background information about their sources of information that the everyday epistemic community does not possess concerning Mrs. Grabit. Even if mothers generally tell the truth about their children, those around S have not studied Mrs. Grabit's reliability.

Thus, we may compare the newspaper example to a situation where a putative experimental result is presented to a scientific community and appears to challenge the results of an earlier experiment. We regard it as more rational for the community to return to the basic issue and to investigate further, rather than simply to accept the original results and to base their appraisal of other hypotheses upon them. Even if the motivation of the scientists who presented the recent conflicting report was to lie and to deceive, the community needs to discredit their results before proceeding as before and trusting the earlier experiments. For the scientists who present the recent report are generally rationally regarded as having been trained with the aim of making them reliable sources and to have been duly accredited as such.[15] So the proposition S believes in the example fails to be a justified proposition.

---

[14] This is not to deny that if S were to know of the remarks of Mrs. Grabit and her relatives but not to know of their full setting, then S would no longer think herself justified in believing that Tom stole the book.

[15] Thus, I do not agree with Klein that one who shares Harman's intuition concerning case (E 9) should also grant that S lacks knowledge in case (E 90), assuming that Mrs. Grabit's deluded relatives are numerous (Klein 1976, p. 811).

Similar considerations apply to Klein's variation on Harman's example:

(E 91)   *The Lone Denial*: As in (E 9), except that only one news account has appeared that denies the assassination, and it achieves the same effects on those surrounding *S* as in (E 9). (Klein 1976, p. 810)

Since even one experimental investigation in science can call earlier results into question, this example differs in no important respect from Harman's example.

It is interesting to contrast the case of the lying Mrs. Grabit (E 89) with variations described by Barker:

(E 92)   *Lying Mrs. Grabit (Extended Version)*: As in (E 89), except that Mrs. Grabit includes in her testimony the statement that Tom was thousands of miles away that day. (Barker 1976b, p. 306)[16]

(E 93)   *Lying Mrs. Grabit (Indirect Version)*: As in (E 89), except that *S* was not present in the library and only read in a reliable newspaper that Tom stole the book. (Barker 1976b, p. 306)

(E 92) resembles the case of the demented Mrs. Grabit in that Tom's mother offers a reason for supposing not merely that *S*'s observations were open to error but that *S*'s conclusion was actually erroneous. In that respect, the case is closer to Harman's newspaper example than was (E 89). But even if Mrs. Grabit was raised to be truthful, there is no social structure closely monitored by the everyday epistemic community that exists to certify the nature of this training or her disposition as a result of having undergone it. Even our scrutiny of news media is greater, and the social context within which reporters are trained and monitored on generally reliable newspapers and broadcasting stations is at least somewhat more akin to that in a scientific community. Although one should not overemphasize this

---

[16] Barker does not mention Mrs. Grabit's claim that Tom was far away, but does cite sources for his example which include that detail. See Harman 1973, p. 142; Sosa 1970, p. 62.

comparison, it does explain why we are not so strongly inclined to say that S fails to know in (E 92) as in Harman's newspaper example. However, mothers' reports of their children's whereabouts are generally reliable regarding thousand-mile increments in those whereabouts, so I agree with Barker (p. 306) that we are less strongly inclined to say that S has knowledge in (E 93) than in (E 9) or (E 91). For it is less clear how to balance the general reliability of such mothers' reports against the existence of S's own observations.

I also agree with Barker (pp. 306-307) that we are less strongly inclined to say S knows in (E 93) than in (E 12), even though we do grant S knowledge in (E 93). This is because in the latter case any relevant justification-explaining chain connected with S does not contain the contribution made to the justified status of the proposition 'Tom stole the book' that S's observations did contribute in (E 12).

Klein suggests that we ponder the following, even more intricate examples:

(E 94) *The Lone Denial by a Habitual Liar*: As in (E 9), except that the denial is written by a reporter who happens to be a hitherto undetected pathological liar. (Klein 1976, p. 810)

(E 95) *The Lone, Demented Denial*: As in (E 9), but the reporter who advances the denial does so merely as a manifestation of a demented mental state, and there is no conspiracy of eyewitnesses.

In both these examples, the newspaper or broadcasting system in question remains a generally reliable source of information, and, once more in contrast to the Grabit cases, it putatively transmits information obtained from eyewitnesses. These examples may be compared to a situation in which a scientist offers an experimental report running counter to previous results but which is riddled with falsehoods motivated not by rational fear of the consequences of the earlier line of research or by a rational desire for status or fame, but instead by a deranged mental state and loss of touch with reality. Do members of the scientific community manifest their rationality less fully when they pay serious attention to that report (assuming that they have no way of telling that the investigator is ill)? I think that our intuitions are uncertain or wavering here because our concept of rationality and its attendant principles are to some extent vague. The community abides by its methodology in reopening the issue, yet at the same time is crucially influenced by the extreme irrationality of one of its members. We can account analogously for what I take to be our unclear intuitions about (E 95).

To the extent that (E 94) differs from (E 95) by assuming that the reporter's pathology does not affect this motivation for putting forth the report, it appears to me not significantly different from Harman's original newspaper example.[17]

The following case of Klein's is sufficiently similar to the original case of the demented Mrs. Grabit (E 12) to prompt a similar treatment:

(E 96) *Demented Mrs. Grabit Given Credence*: As in (E 12), except that those surrounding S believe Tom is innocent because they have read an account in a generally reliable newspaper of Mrs. Grabit's testimony. (Klein 1976, p. 810)

When those surrounding S accept Mrs. Grabit's remarks, they unwittingly deviate from their rational responsibility to follow up only genuine critical challenges to a proposition accepted by a qualified member of the group on observational grounds. So this does not prevent S from having hold of a significant part of a justification-explaining chain related to the proposition that p. Thus, I do not think we can say that when a sufficient number of hitherto reliable people around S accept a proposition that is in conflict with what S justifiably believes, this by itself is always sufficient to destroy the relevant justification-explaining chain and to deny S knowledge.

However, the next two examples may appear to conflict with such a view:

---

[17] This is not to deny that if those who surround S were to know that the reporter is a pathological liar, but not to know that his pathology failed to manifest itself when he wrote the report, then they would be less justified in taking that report seriously.

(E 97)   *Ignored Denials*: As in (E 9) or (E 91), except that the
         denials are reported only in newspaper editions of which
         nobody happens to buy copies, and they receive no general
         attention.

(E 98)   *Revoked Denials*: As in (E 9), except that the denials are
         reported only in newspaper editions read by few people
         before those editions are recalled. (Sosa 1974a, p. 117)

One might initially think that S retains knowledge in both these
cases and that this difference from some of the previous examples
can be explained by the mere fact that in the above cases fewer
people around S refrain from believing that Tom is the culprit. However, (E 97) is similar to an experimental report's being published
by a scientific journal yet lying unread by the scientific community
at large. Whereas, (E 98) is similar to a situation where the journal
retracts publication of that report. Once we realize this, I believe
that our intuitions are to grant S knowledge in (E 98) but not in (E
97). For only in the latter case would the epistemic community follow
the usual rational methods in assessing items in the news by rejecting
or withholding judgment on the claim that the assassination occurred.
It is regarded as a rational procedure, both within scientific and
everyday epistemic communities, to discount reports that have been
retracted by a generally reliable source.

Lack of knowledge because a proposition in a pseudo-chain fails
to be justified was anticipated during our discussion of Sosa's initial
treatment of 'trees of knowledge.' However, in the pertinent examples, it was not proposition p that failed to be justified in the
pseudo-chain. The case of the perceptual experiment (E 32) illustrates
the relevance of the social aspects of knowing because proposition
a': 'S's visual capacities are normal' failed to be a justified proposition. When we consider ascribing knowledge to S in that example,
the members of an epistemic community to which we refer are as
dependent as the scientists upon use of the given experimental instruments in order rationally to accept or reject a'. Such reliance

would unwittingly involve use of an instrument that is not in working order. So we do not regard the readings of the instrument as constituting appropriate evidence for use in guiding members of the epistemic community to accept or to reject the relevant propositions in the example. Thus, even if the scientists are justified in believing that a' is a justified proposition, that does not make it one in this case.

However, the ability of my analysis of justified factual knowledge to count (E 32) as an instance of S's failing to know does not depend upon this point. Suppose we allow a' to count as a justified proposition,[18] given the monitor's past history of working properly and its present lighting display. S still has no grasp of a genuine justification-explaining chain related to p: 'The tie is red.' For a putative chain of which S has any significant grasp would contain at some point a conjunct dealing with what justifies the proposition, 'The scientists are justified in believing that the machine is on the setting which allows S's visual capacities to remain normal' or else dealing with what justifies the proposition, 'The machine is on the setting which allows S's visual capacities to remain normal.' This would require inclusion in a later member of the chain some conjunct containing a false proposition at a proscribed place, for example, the conjunct

"the proposition that the monitor is working properly and indicates that the machine is on the setting which allows S's visual capacities to remain normal describes evidence for the proposition that the machine is on that setting, and the latter proposition describes evidence for a',"

where the italicized phrase labels a false proposition in the place of some h_i in a proposition of form (c3).[19]

---

[18] Obviously there are some examples where a' is not a justified proposition, such as the second version of the case of the red tie (E 30).

[19] I inappropriately telescoped the contents of the preceding two paragraphs into a single one when discussing this example in Shope 1979d.

On such an understanding of (E 32), the scientists are in a Gettierized situation regarding their true, justified belief in the proposition: 'Both a' and the machine is on the setting which allows S's visual capacities to remain normal.' Although my analysis of justified factual knowledge was initially developed in order to deal with a Gettierized situation faced by S concerning p, it proves to be strong enough to deal appropriately with a lack of knowledge on S's part due, in the above manner, to S's being thought of in relation to a group which is in a Gettierized situation regarding some proposition other than p. Since Gettier himself gave no hint of this possibility,[20] it seems to me best to avoid amending our definition of a Gettier-type example to include it, and instead to speak of such cases as ones where S fails to know because of one of the social aspects of knowing.

It is probably clear from my discussion of the above series of Grabit cases how my account deals with instances where S's failure to know is due to the fact that S has not considered evidence which, as Harman puts it, S "can" obtain, e.g., the case of the unopened letter (E 42). When considering Harman's views earlier, I noted that this point touches on a complex dimension of what Castañeda calls "methodological" considerations. The cases in question deserve to be regarded as another illustration of the social aspects of knowing. They are exactly those cases where members of the epistemic community more fully manifest their rationality by refraining from accepting p on the basis of the type of evidence S possesses when they do not also possess the additional evidence. So possession of S's evidence does not make proposition p justified, or make justified any proposition describing something sufficient to make proposition p justified. As a result, we cannot construct any genuine justification-explaining chain related to p of which S has a grasp in these cases. For it is only a pseudo-chain which can both speak of the evidence

---

[20] For the same reason, I think it best not to follow Harman in referring even to the newspaper example (E 9) as a Gettier-type case (Harman 1980, p. 164). Apparently he means to speak of any case where the standard conditions are insufficient for S's knowing p as a Gettier-type case.

that S possesses as sufficient to make some proposition justified and otherwise satisfy all the requirements for a genuine chain.[21]

In any complete theory of knowledge, one would flesh out the above account by articulating standards for the manifestations of rationality that could be systematically applied. One would also need to face the difficult question of how much of a justification-explaining chain S must grasp in order for S's hold on it to make S's believing p justified,[22] and whether the relevant requirements vary with the stage of mental, social, or historical development of S or of the relevant epistemic community. But that is difficult work for future inquiry into human rationality. I have only attempted to situate such issues in relation to an analysis of justified factual knowledge which is open to fewer objections than previous efforts, and to provide illustrations of the difficulties involved in developing this type of analysis with the aim of increasing a reader's sensitivity to a point where any limitations of the present account will be more rapidly exposed and any possible improvements in it will become more likely to be made.[23]

---

[21] William Lycan reports (Lycan 1977) divided intuitions within a group of people he has sampled concerning whether I have knowledge when situated as in the case of the unopened letter (E 42). Such a case is similar to (E 97). Since I do not receive the reports from Donald until the mail is delivered, the delivery may be treated as analogous to the publication of scientific results, and we may ignore Lycan's concern that a matter of degree slips into the situation because, prior to delivery, "the letters get closer and closer to my hall table" (p. 119). The mixed intuitions which Lycan reports may be accounted for by the fact that Harman's description of (E 42) leaves Donald's motivation for writing the misleading letters unspecified, and it is thus not clear whether to liken the example to (E 12), (E 89), or (E 92).

[22] See the example concerning Ms. Withit in Shope 1979c.

[23] I have frequently criticized philosophers who employ subjunctive conditionals for having committed the conditional fallacy. I believe that my own use of a conditional in order to characterize justified propositions is not open to similar objections.

A case that might appear to create a difficulty is one in which at time t, S knows p: 'S is the only member of the community who is thinking at t,' where this community is the epistemic community relevant to the knowledge ascription, and the rest of the community is asleep and thinking of nothing. My conditional analysis of justified propositions might appear to commit me to saying that if others in the community were presently accepting p rather than withholding it—as they actually do while asleep—then they would be more fully manifesting their rationality. (Compare my

6. FORECASTING THE FUTURE CONCERNING A BROADER CATEGORY OF KNOWING

Especially in the previous chapter, we have acknowledged that instances of justified factual knowledge may fall under an even broader category of knowing, a category that remains to be analyzed satisfactorily. Of course, quite a while ago, Gilbert Ryle characterized knowing by saying that "'know'" is a "capacity verb of that special sort that is used for signifying that the person described can bring things off, or get things right" (Ryle 1949, p. 133). But Ryle was largely concerned with the fact that we speak of *knowing how* as well as *knowing that*. We have seen that even within contexts where one speaks of S as knowing that p there are cases where justified belief or even belief is not required.

If this category of knowledge needs to be characterized as some

---

criticism of Roderick Chisholm in Shope 1978.) However, the antecedent of my conditional is to be understood as permitting at least a brief interval between the time at which the proposition may be spoken of as justified and the time at which members of the epistemic community who actually do not accept the proposition are imagined to accept it after consulting various other members. One obvious reason for permitting this is that observational propositions require time to be reported to other members of the epistemic community who are not making such observations. Time must therefore elapse before the latter members could be said to manifest rationality by accepting such a proposition on the observer's say-so.

Another case that might initially appear to constitute a counterexample is one where a scientist threatens to destroy the human race, e.g., by bacteriological contamination, if a scientific community does not accept his theory T in some area of research instead of the presently justified hypotheses in that area. If he has the power to carry out his threat then it will be in the community's interest to give the appearance of cooperation, should that be enough to satisfy him. But members of the community would not actually be able to regard themselves as sincerely testing or assessing the truth of other theories by means of T. For they would realize that the decisive factor in their behavior involves a disregard of the evidence bearing on T and on its competitors. So they would not be doing more than pretending to accept T in the relevant sense, i.e., as a basis for testing or critically appraising other theories.

Finally, because we do not regard rationality as a perfect guide in the search for our epistemic goals, it is no objection to my present explanation of justified propositions that the world might accidentally be destroyed as a result of our accepting and using in our research a particular justified proposition, thereby preventing human epistemic communities from attaining their epistemic goals.

type of capacity, ability, or power, then a suitable clarification of the nature of capacities, abilities, or powers and of the exact type involved will have to be provided. I have hinted that the type in question may concern either the occurrence in S's thought or behavior of something which represents states of affairs or at least the involvement of S with something that represents a state of affairs. A refinement of this viewpoint will require inspection of whatever metaphysical baggage is carried by speaking of states of affairs, since we need to consider the possibility of integrating epistemology with science. We shall also need to decide whether x's representing the state of affairs that p can in these contexts by analyzed in a scientifically unobjectionable fashion, for example, as a complex causal phenomenon. Quite possibly, the pertinent causal considerations concern ways in which the causal context helps to justify certain propositions about the state of affairs represented by x.[24] In those cases where S's knowledge counts as justified factual knowledge, it may be that the causal context of S's belief contributes to this justification. An additional question for investigation is whether this category of knowing may be seen to be broad enough even to encompass instances of *knowing how*, once reference to the relevant capacity, ability, or power is understood.[25]

[24] Notice that I do not say, "represented by S," but instead, "represented by x," letting "x" stand for either something which is an aspect of S's thought or behavior or merely something which S's thought or behavior involves S in. This approach spares us a difficulty which Norman Malcolm finds in the view that each manifestation of memory knowledge is one in which S represents something (Malcolm 1977, p. 120). Also see Stampe 1975 concerning causation and representing.

[25] When q is the proposition, 'S knows p,' there may be situations where the knowledge which S has that q falls only under the broader category of knowing as a representational ability but not under the narrower category of justified factual knowledge. However, my analysis of justified factual knowledge does not by itself entail this result. Even if S grasps only part of the justification-explaining chain related to p, it may be that S's belief that S knows p is justified by its own connection to a justification-explaining chain connected with q although S does not grasp each link in the chain connected with p. Indeed, perhaps S need not even conceive of a justification-explaining chain connected with p; for I have not claimed that the *analysans* in my analysis of justified factual knowledge is synonymous with 'S knows p' or that it provides the criteria to be used in coming to know that 'S knows p' is true. (See

We acknowledged at the beginning of our survey that in their attempts to construct analyses some philosophers restrict their interest to actual cases, rather than being concerned with quite hypothetical ones, such as those concerning the knowledge of a 'seer'—a type of person whose existence is obviously quite controversial. Thus it is important to recall that the present issues concerning a broad category of knowing also arose concerning actual cases of *idiots savants* and even more everyday situations involving unwitting remembrance and unpondered entailments. We thereby touch upon the concerns of cognitive psychology and not the presently questionable status of supposed psychics or seers.

I predict that an analysis of knowing which treats it as some type of representational power or capacity, and which has been prefigured in the preceding survey, will be one significant concern of epistemologists in the next decade of research. But I must also confess that I hope to make this a self-fulfilled prophecy.

Chapter 1, Section 7.) Thus, only further development of a theory of justification will allow us to decide when *S* knows that *S* knows.

There are numerous issues which I have not needed to deal with in the present work concerning the exact nature of grasping a portion of a justification-explaining chain. For example, they include issues as to whether those portions are believed or merely accepted in some other sense by *S*, whether they are consciously or unconsciously believed or accepted, and whether such beliefs or acceptances need to stand in particular causal relations to *S*'s believing or accepting *p*.

Bibliography

Aaron, Richard I. 1971. *Knowing and the Function of Reason*. London: Oxford University Press.

Ackerman, Terence F. 1974. Defeasibility Modified. *Philosophical Studies* 26:431-435.

Ackermann, Robert J. 1972. *Belief and Knowledge*. Garden City, N.Y.: Doubleday.

Almeder, Robert. 1973. Defeasibility and Scepticism. *Australasian Journal of Philosophy* 51:238-244.

———. 1974. Truth and Evidence. *Philosophical Quarterly* 24:365-368.

———. 1975. Defending Gettier Counter-Examples. *Australasian Journal of Philosophy* 53:58-60.

———. 1976. On Seeing the Truth: A Reply. *Philosophical Quarterly* 26:163-165.

Almeder, Robert and Arrington, Robert. 1977. Mannison on Inexplicable Knowledge and Belief. *Australasian Journal of Philosophy* 55:87-90.

Alston, William. 1976. Two Types of Foundationalism. *Journal of Philosophy* 73:165-185.

Annis, David B. 1973. Knowledge and Defeasibility. *Philosophical Studies* 24:199-203. Reprinted in Pappas and Swain 1978.

———. 1974. Review of Ackermann 1972. *Philosophical Quarterly* 24:81-82.

———. 1976. Review of Lehrer 1974. *Philosophia* 6:209-213.

———. 1977. Knowledge, Belief, and Rationality. *Journal of Philosophy* 74:217-225.

Armstrong, David M. 1969-1970. Does Knowledge Entail Belief? *Proceedings of the Aristotelian Society* 70:21-36.

———. 1973. *Belief, Truth, and Knowledge*. New York, London: Cambridge University Press.

Audi, Robert. 1980. Defeated Knowledge, Reliability, and Justification. In French, Uehling, and Wettstein 1980, pp. 75-95.

Aune, Bruce. 1975. Vendler on Knowledge and Belief. In Gunderson 1975, pp. 391-399.

Ayer, Alfred Jules. 1956. *The Problem of Knowledge*. Baltimore: Penguin Books.

Baier, Annette. 1976. Realizing What's What. *Philosophical Quarterly* 26:328-337.

Barker, John A. 1972. Knowledge and Causation. *Southern Journal of Philosophy* 10:313-324.

———. 1975. A Note on Knowledge and Belief. *Canadian Journal of Philosophy* 5:143-144.

———. 1976a. Audi on Epistemic Disavowals. *Personalist* 57:376-377.

———. 1976b. What You Don't Know Won't Hurt You? *American Philosophical Quarterly* 13:303-308.

Barnes, Gerald W. 1973. Unger's Defense of Scepticism. *Philosophical Studies* 24:119-124.

Bennett, Jonathan. 1974. Counterfactuals and Possible Worlds. *Canadian Journal of Philosophy* 4:381-402.

Binkley, Robert. 1977. Lehrer's *Knowledge*. *Canadian Journal of Philosophy* 7:841-851.

Black, Carolyn. 1952. Knowledge without Belief. *Analysis* 13:152-158.

Black, Max. 1974. An Immoderate Skepticism, Some Comments on Professor Unger's Paper. *Philosophic Exchange* 1:157-159.

Blose, B. L. 1977. What Never Happened to Jones: A Comment on the Analysis of Knowledge. *Philosophical Studies* 31:205-209.

———. 1980. The 'Really' of Emphasis and the 'Really' of Restriction. *Philosophical Studies* 38:183-187.

Bonjour, Lawrence. 1980. Externalist Theories of Empirical Knowledge. In French, Uehling, and Wettstein 1980, pp. 53-73.

Braine, David. 1971-1972. The Nature of Knowledge. *Proceedings of the Aristotelian Society* 72:41-63.

Cargile, James. 1971. On Near Knowledge. *Analysis* 31:145-152.

———. 1972. In Reply to a Defense of Skepticism. *Philosophical Review* 81:220-236. Reprinted in Roth and Galis 1970.

Carrier, L. S. 1971. An Analysis of Empirical Knowledge. *Southern Journal of Philosophy* 9:3-11.

———. 1976. The Causal Theory of Knowledge. *Philosophia* 6:237-257.

Carter, Randolph. 1977. Lehrer's Fourth Condition for Knowing. *Philosophical Studies* 31:327-335.

Castañeda, Hector-Neri. 1980. The Theory of Questions, Epistemic Powers, and the Indexical Theory of Knowledge. In French, Uehling, and Wettstein 1980, pp. 193-237.

Chisholm, Roderick M. 1957. *Perceiving: A Philosophical Study*. Ithaca: Cornell University Press.

———. 1964. The Ethics of Requirement. *American Philosophical Quarterly* 1:147-153.

———. 1966. *Theory of Knowledge*. 1st ed. Englewood Cliffs, N.J.: Prentice-Hall.

———. 1973. On the Nature of Empirical Evidence. In *Empirical Knowledge*, ed. Chisholm, Roderick M., and Swartz, Robert J., pp. 224-229. Englewood Cliffs, N.J.: Prentice-Hall.

———. 1977. *Theory of Knowledge.* 2nd ed. Englewood Cliffs, N.J.: Prentice-Hall.

———. 1978. Comments and Replies. *Philosophia* 7:597-636.

Clark, Michael. 1963. Knowledge and Grounds: A Comment on Mr. Gettier's Paper. *Analysis* 24:46-48.

———. 1977. Review of Lehrer 1974. *Mind* 86:142-144.

Clark, Romane. 1973. Prima Facie Generalizations. In *Conceptual Change*, ed. Pearce, G., and Maynard, P., pp. 42-54. Boston, Dordrecht: Reidel.

Coburn, Robert C. 1971. Knowing and Believing. *Philosophical Review* 80:236-243.

Coder, David. 1974. Naturalizing the Gettier Argument. *Philosophical Studies* 26:111-118.

Collier, Kenneth. 1973. Against the Causal Theory of Knowing. *Philosophical Studies* 24:350-351.

Danto, Arthur. 1968. *Analytical Theory of Knowledge.* London: Cambridge University Press.

de Sousa, Ronald. 1970. Knowing, Consistent Belief, and Self-Consciousness. *Journal of Philosophy* 67:66-73.

Dicker, Georges. 1974. Certainty without Dogmatism: a Reply to Unger's "An Argument for Skepticism." *Philosophic Exchange* 1:161-170.

———. 1978. Is There a Problem about Perception and Knowledge? *American Philosophical Quarterly* 15:165-176.

Donnellan, Keith. 1966. Reference and Definite Descriptions. *Philosophical Review* 75:281-304.

Dreher, John H. 1974. Evidence and Justified Belief. *Philosophical Studies* 25:435-439.

Dretske, Fred I. 1971. Conclusive Reasons. *Australasian Journal of Philosophy* 49:1-22. Reprinted in Pappas and Swain 1978.

———. 1972. Contrastive Statements. *Philosophical Review* 81:411-437.

———. 1975a. Review of Armstrong 1973. *Journal of Philosophy* 72:793-802.

———. 1975b. The Content of Knowledge. In Freed, Marras, and Maynard 1975, pp. 77-93.

———. 1979. Chisholm on Perceptual Knowledge. *Grazer Philosophische Studien* 7/8:253-269.

———. 1981. *Knowledge and the Flow of Information.* Cambridge, Mass.: Bradford Books.

Dunn, R., and Suter, G. 1977. Zeno Vendler and the Objects of Knowledge and Belief. *Canadian Journal of Philosophy* 7:103-114.

Feldman, Richard. 1974. An Alleged Defect in Gettier Counter-Examples. *Australasian Journal of Philosophy* 52:68-69.

————. 1979. Lehrer's Theory of Justification. *Australasian Journal of Philosophy* 57:266-273.

Freed, B.; Marras, A.; and Maynard, P., eds. 1975. *Forms of Representation*. Amsterdam, New York, Oxford: Elsevier.

French, Peter A.; Uehling, Theodore E., Jr.; and Wettstein, Howard K., eds. 1980. *Midwest Studies in Philosophy. Volume V: Studies in Epistemology*. Minneapolis: University of Minnesota Press.

Gallie, Roger. 1975. Review of Ackermann 1972. *Mind* 84:137-138.

Gettier, Edmund. 1963. Is Justified True Belief Knowledge? *Analysis* 23:121-123. Reprinted in Roth and Galis 1970.

Ginet, Carl. 1975. *Knowledge, Perception, and Memory*. Dordrecht: Reidel.

————. 1980. Knowing Less by Knowing More. In French, Uehling, and Wettstein 1980, pp. 151-161.

Goldman, Alvin. 1967. A Causal Theory of Knowing. *Journal of Philosophy* 64:357-372. Reprinted in Pappas and Swain 1978, and (with Revisions) in Roth and Galis 1970.

————. 1976. Discrimination and Perceptual Knowledge. *Journal of Philosophy* 73:771-791. Reprinted in Pappas and Swain 1978.

————. 1977. Innate Knowledge. In *Innate Ideas*, ed. Stich, Stephen P., pp. 111-120. Berkeley, Los Angeles, London: University of California Press.

————. 1979. What is Justified Belief? In Pappas 1979, pp. 1-23.

Goldstick, D. 1972. A Contribution towards the Development of the Causal Theory of Knowledge. *Australasian Journal of Philosophy* 50:238-248.

Goodman, Nelson, 1977. *The Structure of Appearance*. 3rd ed. Boston, Dordrecht: Reidel.

————. 1978. *Ways of Worldmaking*. Indianapolis, Cambridge, Mass.: Hackett.

Griffiths, A. Phillips, ed. 1967. *Knowledge and Belief*. London: Oxford University Press.

Gunderson, Keith, ed. 1975. *Language, Mind, and Knowledge*. Minnesota Studies in the Philosophy of Science, Volume VII. Minneapolis: University of Minnesota Press.

Hamlyn, D. W. 1970. *The Theory of Knowledge*. Garden City: Doubleday.

————. 1976. Review of Unger 1975. *Philosophical Books* 17:91-93.

Hanna, Joseph H. 1968. An Explication of 'Explication.' *Philosophy of Science* 35:28-44.

Harman, Gilbert. 1966. Lehrer on Knowledge. *Journal of Philosophy* 63:241-247.

———. 1968. Knowledge, Inference, and Explanation. *American Philosophical Quarterly* 5:164-173.

———. 1970. Knowledge, Reasons, and Causes. *Journal of Philosophy* 67:841-855.

———. 1973. *Thought.* Princeton: Princeton University Press.

———. 1976. Reply to Lisagor. *Philosophical Studies* 29:477.

———. 1980. Reasoning and Evidence One Does Not Possess. In French, Uehling, and Wettstein 1980, pp. 163-182.

Harrison, Jonathan. 1978-1979. If I Know, I Cannot Be Wrong. *Proceedings of the Aristotelian Society* 79:137-150.

Hart, H.L.A., and Honoré, A. M. 1959. *Causation in the Law.* London: Oxford University Press.

Hartnack, Justus. 1970. Some Logical Incongruities between the Concept of Knowledge and the Concept of Belief. In *Language, Belief, and Metaphysics*, ed. Kiefer, Howard E. and Munitz, Milton K., pp. 112-121. Albany: State University of New York Press.

Hilpinen, Risto. 1971. Knowledge and Justification. *Ajatus* 33:7-39.

Hoffman, William E. 1975. Almeder on Truth and Evidence. *Philosophical Quarterly* 25:59-61.

Holland, A. J. 1977. Skepticism and Causal Theories of Knowledge. *Mind* 86:555-573.

Hooker, Michael. 1978. Chisholm's Theory of Knowledge. *Philosophia* 7:489-500.

Johnsen, Bredo. 1974. Knowledge. *Philosophical Studies* 25:273-282.

Johnson, Oliver A. 1971. Is Knowledge Definable? *Southern Journal of Philosophy* 8:277-286.

———. 1979. Ignorance and Irrationality: A Study in Contemporary Scepticism. *Philosophy Research Archives* 5:368-417.

———. 1980. The Standard Definition. In French, Uehling, and Wettstein 1980, pp. 113-126.

Jones, O. R. 1971. Knowing and Guessing—by Examples. *Analysis* 32:19-23.

———. 1975. Can One Believe What One Knows? *Philosophical Review* 84:220-235.

Kant, Immanuel. 1963. *Critique of Pure Reason.* Translated by Smith, Norman Kemp. London, New York: Macmillan.

Kellenberger, J. 1971. On There Being No Necessary and Sufficient Conditions for Knowledge. *Mind* 80:599-602.

Klein, Peter D. 1971. A Proposed Definition of Propositional Knowledge. *Journal of Philosophy* 68:471-482.

————. 1976. Knowledge, Causality, and Defeasibility. *Journal of Philosophy* 73:792-812.

————. 1979. Misleading 'Misleading Defeaters.' *Journal of Philosophy* 76:382-386.

————. 1980. Misleading Evidence and the Restoration of Justification. *Philosophical Studies* 37:81-89.

Kress, J. R. 1971. Lehrer and Paxson on Non-Basic Knowledge. *Journal of Philosophy* 68:78-82.

Lehrer, Keith. 1965. Knowledge, Truth, and Evidence. *Analysis* 25:168-175. Reprinted in Roth and Galis 1970.

————. 1970a. Believing that One Knows. *Synthése* 21:133-140.

————. 1970b. The Fourth Condition for Knowledge: a Defense. *Review of Metaphysics* 24:122-128.

————. 1971. How Reasons Give Us Knowledge, or, the Case of the Gypsy Lawyer. *Journal of Philosophy* 68:311-313.

————. 1974. *Knowledge*. London: Oxford University Press.

————. 1975. Reply to Dr. Radford. *Philosophical Books* 16:6-8.

————. 1979. The Gettier Problem and the Analysis of Knowledge. In Pappas 1979b, pp. 65-78.

————. 1981. Self-Profile. In *Keith Lehrer*, ed. Bogdan, Radu, pp. 3-104. Boston, Dordrecht, London: Reidel.

Lehrer, Keith, and Paxson, Thomas, Jr. 1969. Knowledge: Undefeated Justified True Belief. *Journal of Philosophy* 66:225-237. Reprinted in Roth and Galis 1970.

Lemmon, E. J. 1967. If I Know, Do I Know that I Know? In *Epistemology: New Essays in the Theory of Knowledge*, ed. Stroll, A., pp. 54-83. New York: Harper & Row.

Levy, Steven R. 1977. Defeasibility Theories of Knowledge. *Canadian Journal of Philosophy* 7:115-123.

————. 1978. Misleading Defeaters. *Journal of Philosophy* 75:739-742.

Lewis, Clarence I. 1946. *An Analysis of Knowledge and Valuation*. La Salle: Open Court.

Lewis, David. 1973. *Counterfactuals*. Cambridge, Mass.: Harvard University Press.

Loeb, Louis E. 1976. On a Heady Attempt to Befriend Causal Theories of Knowledge. *Philosophical Studies* 29:331-336.

Lowy, Catherine. 1978. Gettier's Notion of Justification. *Mind* 87:105-108.

Lycan, William G. 1977. Evidence One Does Not Possess. *Australasian Journal of Philosophy* 55:114-126.

MacIntosh, J. J. 1979-1980. Knowing and Believing. *Proceedings of the Aristotelian Society* 80:169-185.

Mackie, J. L. 1969-1970. The Possibility of Innate Knowledge. *Proceedings of the Aristotelian Society* 70:245-257.

Malcolm, Norman. 1977. *Memory and Mind*. Ithaca: Cornell University Press.

Mannison, Don S. 1976a. 'Inexplicable Knowledge' Does Not Require Belief. *Philosophical Quarterly* 26:139-148.

————. 1976b. Why Margolis Hasn't Defeated the Entailment Thesis. *Canadian Journal of Philosophy* 6:553-559.

————. 1977. Knowing and Believing: A Reply. *Australasian Journal of Philosophy* 55:147-148.

Margolis, Joseph. 1972a. Knowledge, Belief, and Thought. *Ratio* 14:74-82.

————. 1972b. The Problem of Justified Belief. *Philosophical Studies* 23:405-409.

————. 1973a. Alternative Strategies for the Analysis of Knowledge. *Canadian Journal of Philosophy* 2:461-469.

————. 1973b. *Knowledge and Existence: An Introduction to Philosophical Problems*. New York: Oxford University Press.

————. 1976. Knowledge and Belief; Facts and Propositions. *Grazer Philosophische Studien* 2:41-54.

————. 1977a. Problems Regarding the Ascription of Knowledge. *Personalist* 58:5-17.

————. 1977b. Skepticism, Foundationalism, and Pragmatism. *American Philosophical Quarterly* 14:119-127.

Meyers, Robert G., and Stern, Kenneth. 1973. Knowledge without Paradox. *Journal of Philosophy* 70:147-160.

Miller, Richard W. 1978. Absolute Certainty. *Mind* 87:46-65.

Morawetz, Thomas. 1974. Causal Accounts of Knowledge. *Southern Journal of Philosophy* 12:365-369.

————. 1975. Skepticism, Induction and the Gettier Problem. *Journal of Critical Analysis* 6:9-13.

Morton, Adam. 1977. *A Guide Through the Theory of Knowledge*. Enrico and Belmont: Dickenson.

Munsat, Stanley. 1977. The Objects of Knowledge and Belief: Some Linguistic Considerations. *Dialogue* 16:575-590.

Nelson, Jack. 1978. In Defense of Not Knowing. *Philosophia* 8:317-339.

Odegard, Douglas. 1976. Can a Justified Belief Be False? *Canadian Journal of Philosophy* 6:561-568.

————. 1978. A Knower's Evidence. *American Philosophical Quarterly* 15:123-128.

Olen, Jeffrey. 1976. Is Undefeated Justified True Belief Knowledge? *Analysis* 36:150-152.

Olin, Doris. 1970. Knowledge and Defeasible Justification. *Philosophical Studies* 30:129-136.

Pappas, George S. 1979a. Basing Relations. In Pappas 1979b, pp. 51-63.

————, ed. 1979b. *Justification and Knowledge: New Studies in Epistemology*. Boston, Dordrecht, London: Reidel.

————. 1980. Lost Justification. In French, Uehling, and Wettstein 1980, pp. 127-134.

Pappas, George S., and Swain, Marshall. 1973. Some Conclusive Reasons Against Conclusive Reasons. *Australasian Journal of Philosophy* 51:72-76. Reprinted in Pappas and Swain 1978.

————, eds. 1978. *Essays on Knowledge and Justification*. Ithaca and London: Cornell University Press.

Pastin, Mark. 1977. Review of Lehrer 1974. *Noûs* 11:431-437.

Paxson, Thomas D., Jr. 1974. Prof. Swain's Account of Knowledge. *Philosophical Studies* 25:57-61. Reprinted in Pappas and Swain 1978.

Peterson, Philip L. 1977. How to Infer Belief from Knowledge. *Philosophical Studies* 32:203-209.

Plato. 1961. *Meno*. Translated by Guthrie, W.K.C. In *The Collected Dialogues of Plato*, ed. Hamilton, Edith, and Cairns, Huntington, pp. 353-384. New York: Bollingen Foundation.

————. 1973. *Theatetus*. Translated by McDowell, John. London: Oxford University Press.

Quine, W. V. 1970. *Philosophy of Logic*. Englewood Cliffs, N.J.: Prentice-Hall.

Radford, Colin. 1966. Knowledge—by Examples. *Analysis* 27:1-11. Reprinted in Roth and Galis 1970.

————. 1971. On Sticking to What I Don't Believe To Be the Case. *Analysis* 32:170-173.

————. 1975. Review of Lehrer 1974. *Philosophical Books* 16:1-6.

Ravitch, Harold. 1976. Knowledge and the Principle of Luck. *Philosophical Studies* 30:347-349.

Ring, Merrill. 1977. Knowledge: The Cessation of Belief. *American Philosophical Quarterly* 14:51-59.

Robinson, Richard. 1971. The Concept of Knowledge. *Mind* 80:17-28.

Rorty, Richard. 1965. Mind-Body Identity, Privacy, and Categories. *Review of Metaphysics* 19:24-54.

————. 1970. In Defense of Eliminative Materialism. *Review of Metaphysics* 23:112-121.

Rosenthal, David. 1976. Review of Vendler 1972. *Journal of Philosophy* 73:240-252.

Roth, Michael D., and Galis, Leon, eds. 1970. *Knowing: Essays in the Analysis of Knowledge*. New York: Random House.

Russell, Bertrand. 1948. *Human Knowledge: Its Scope and Limits*. New York: Allen and Unwin.

Ryle, Gilbert. 1949. *The Concept of Mind*. New York: Barnes & Noble.

Sanford, David. 1975. Intermediate Conclusions. *Australasian Journal of Philosophy* 53:61-64.

Saunders, John Turk. 1966. Does Knowledge Require Grounds? *Philosophical Studies* 17:7-13.

Saunders, John Turk, and Champawat, Narayan. 1964. Mr. Clark's Definition of 'Knowledge.' *Analysis* 25:8-9.

Scheffler, Israel. 1965. *Conditions of Knowledge*. Chicago: Scott, Foresman.

Schumacher, John A. 1975. Knowing Entails Believing. *Philosophy Research Archives* 1:246-272.

Scott, R. B. 1976. Swain on Knowledge. *Philosophical Studies* 29:419-424.

Shope, Robert K. 1967. Explanation in Terms of 'the Cause.' *Journal of Philosophy* 64:312-320.

———. 1973. Remembering, Knowledge, and Memory Traces. *Philosophy and Phenomenological Research* 33:303-322.

———. 1978. The Conditional Fallacy in Contemporary Philosophy. *Journal of Philosophy* 75:397-413. Reprinted in Boyer, David L.; Grim, Patrick; and Sanders, John T., eds. 1979. *The Philosopher's Annual*, 2:173-190. Totowa: Rowman & Littlefield.

———. 1979a. Eliminating Mistakes about Eliminative Materialism. *Philosophy of Science* 46:590-612.

———. 1979b. Knowing as a Representational Ability. Paper presented at the Sixty-Sixth Annual Eastern Division Meetings of the American Philosophical Association, New York City, December 28.

———. 1979c. Knowledge and Falsity. *Philosophical Studies* 36:389-405.

———. 1979d. Knowledge as Justified Belief in a True, Justified Proposition. *Philosophy Research Archives* 5:1-36.

———. 1983. The Significance of Freud for Modern Philosophy of Mind. To be published by L'Institut Internationale de Philosophie in *Chronicles of Philosophy 1966-1976. Volume IV: Philosophy of Mind*. Dordrecht: Reidel.

Skyrms, F. B. 1967. The Explication of 'X Knows that p.' *Journal of Philosophy* 64:373-389. Reprinted in Roth and Galis 1970.

Slaght, Ralph L. 1977. Is Justified True Belief Knowledge?: A Selective

Critical Survey of Recent Work. *Philosophy Research Archives* 3:1-135.

Slote, Michael A. 1966. The Theory of Important Criteria. *Journal of Philosophy* 63:211-224.

Sosa, Ernest. 1964. The Analysis of 'Knowledge that *p*.' *Analysis* 25:1-9.

———. 1969. Propositional Knowledge. *Philosophical Studies* 20:33-43.

———. 1970. Two Conceptions of Knowledge. *Journal of Philosophy* 67:59-66.

———. 1974a. How Do You Know? *American Philosophical Quarterly* 11:113-122. Reprinted in Pappas and Swain 1978.

———. 1974b. On Our Knowledge of Matters of Fact. *Mind* 83:338-405.

———. 1976. Review of Lehrer 1974. *Journal of Philosophy* 73:792-821.

———. 1977. Thought, Inference, and Knowledge: Gilbert Harman's *Thought*. *Noûs* 11:421-430.

———. 1979. Epistemic Presupposition. In Pappas 1979, pp. 79-92.

Stampe, Dennis W. 1975. Show and Tell. In Freed, Marras, and Maynard 1975, pp. 221-245.

Steiner, Mark. 1973. Platonism and the Causal Theory of Knowledge. *Journal of Philosophy* 70:57-66.

Stine, Gail C. 1976. Skepticism, Relevant Alternatives, and Deductive Closure. *Philosophical Studies* 29:249-261.

Suppe, Frederick. 1972. Misidentification, Truth, and Knowing That. *Philosophical Studies* 23:186-197.

Swain, Marshall. 1972a. An Alternative Analysis of Knowing. *Synthése* 23:423-442.

———. 1972b. Knowledge, Causality, and Justification. *Journal of Philosophy* 69:291-300. Reprinted in Pappas and Swain 1978.

———. 1974. Epistemic Defeasibility. *American Philosophical Quarterly* 11:15-25. Reprinted in Pappas and Swain 1978.

———. 1976. Defeasibility: A Reply to R. B. Scott. *Philosophical Studies* 29:425-428.

———. 1978. Reasons, Causes, and Knowledge. *Journal of Philosophy* 75:229-249.

———. 1979. Justification and the Basis of Belief. In Pappas 1979, pp. 25-49.

———. 1981. *Reasons and Knowledge*. Ithaca and London: Cornell University Press.

Thalberg, Irving. 1969. In Defense of Justified True Belief. *Journal of Philosophy* 66:794-803.

———. 1974. Is Justification Transmissible through Deduction? *Philosophical Studies* 25:347-356.

Tienson, John. 1974. On Analyzing Knowledge. *Philosophical Studies* 25:289-293.

Tolliver, Joseph T. 1978. On Swain's Causal Analysis of Knowledge. In Pappas and Swain 1978, pp. 109-119.

Unger, Peter. 1967. Experience and Factual Knowledge. *Journal of Philosophy* 64:152-173.

————. 1968. An Analysis of Factual Knowledge. *Journal of Philosophy* 65:157-170. Reprinted in Roth and Galis 1970.

————. 1970. Our Knowledge of the Material World. In *Studies in the Theory of Knowledge*. American Philosophical Quarterly Monograph Series, Number 4, ed. Rescher, Nicholas, pp. 40-61. Oxford: Basil Blackwell.

————. 1971. A Defense of Scepticism. *Philosophical Review* 80:198-219. Reprinted in Pappas and Swain 1978.

————. 1975. *Ignorance: a Case for Scepticism*. London: Oxford University Press.

Vendler, Zeno. 1967. *Linguistics in Philosophy*. Ithaca: Cornell University Press.

————. 1972. *Res Cogitans: an Essay in Rational Psychology*. Ithaca: Cornell University Press.

————. 1975a. On What We Know. In Gunderson 1975, pp. 370-390.

————. 1975b. Reply to Professor Aune. In Gunderson 1975, pp. 400-402.

————. 1978. Escaping from the Cave, a Reply to Dunn and Suter. *Canadian Journal of Philosophy* 8:79-87.

White, A. R. 1977. Knowledge without Conviction. *Mind* 86:224-236.

Williams, Michael. 1978. Inference, Justification, and the Analysis of Knowledge. *Journal of Philosophy* 75:249-263.

Index

Aaron, R. I., 17-18, 27, 44
ability, 113, 161-162, 178-180, 187,
 188-192, 196, 203, 236-238
abnormality, 112-113, 139-149, 154,
 196, 203, 232-234
accidentality, 192-196
Ackerman, T. F., 61
Ackermann, R. J., 121, 197-199
Almeder, R., 26-30, 33, 47-48, 178
Alston, W., 90, 197
alternatives, relevant or significant, 99,
 153, 158-164, 166, 223-227
analysis, 34-44; causal, 119-138, 149-
 170; conclusive reasons, 122-126,
 193-194, 225; defeasibility, 45-74,
 149-170; reliability, 123; standard, 3-
 21
Annis, D. B., 47, 57, 60, 164, 166,
 176, 182, 198
Aristotle, 196
Armstrong, D. M., 24, 119, 123, 125,
 127, 131, 132, 133, 184-186
Arrington, R., 178
Audi, R., 69, 73, 119, 132, 133, 162,
 163, 164
Aune, B., 177
Ayer, A. J., 7-9, 27, 171

Baier, A., 177
Barker, J. A., 67-69, 71, 72-73, 121,
 124-125, 181, 188, 189, 193, 195,
 224-225, 227, 229-230
Barnes, G. W., 183
belief: condition in standard analysis,
 3, 5-9, 10, 14, 18, 146, 171-192;
 reasons for, 78-80, 104, 122, 125,
 126-129, 143, 146, 147, 150-151,
 154, 156-158, 168-170, 176, 177,
 207
Bennett, J., 116
Binkley, R., 58

Black, M., 183
Blose, B. L., 49, 59, 183
Bonjour, L., 98, 123, 129, 144
Braine, D., 195-196

Cargile, J., 27, 183
Carrier, L. S., 121-131, 135-137, 192,
 195
Carter, R., 58-60, 74
Castañeda, H. N., 70, 116, 139 149,
 151, 154, 164, 216, 234
causal analysis of knowing, *see* analysis
certainty, 40, 41
ceteris paribus: clauses, 139-142; fallacy, 51
children, 113, 149, 153, 154, 169,
 196, 226
Chisholm, R. M., 6-8, 11, 20-21, 22,
 23, 27, 47, 59, 63-64, 96-103, 106,
 108, 173, 202, 221, 236
Clark, M., 24, 58
Clark, R., 98, 199
Coburn, R. C., 187
Coder, D., 51, 196
Collier, K., 128, 193
colorblindness, 21, 46, 88, 90-91, 94,
 232-234
conclusive reasons analysis, *see* analysis
conditional fallacy, 48-49, 51-52, 73-
 74, 111, 117-118, 125, 141, 170,
 235-236
counterexamples, technique of seeking,
 34-44

Danto, A., 187
defeasibility: analysis, *see* analysis; definition of, 45-47
defeater, 47-48, 49, 70-72, 75, 118
Descartes, R., 221

Library of Congress Cataloging in Publication Data

Shope, Robert K., 1939-
The analysis of knowing.
Bibliography: p.   Includes index.
1. Knowledge, Theory of. I. Title.
BD161.S49   1983   121   82-15099
ISBN 0-691-07275-2   ISBN 0-691-02025-6 (pbk.)

Robert K. Shope is Professor of Philosophy at
the University of Massachusetts Boston. He is a contributor
to many journals, including the *Journal of Philosophy,
Inquiry, Philosophy of Science, Philosophical Studies,*
and the *Canadian Journal of Philosophy.*